Reclaiming the Future of Christian Education

A Transforming Vision

Albert E. Greene

Purposeful Design Publications is the publishing division of the Association of Christian Schools International (ACSI) and is committed to the ministry of Christian school education, to enable Christian educators and schools worldwide to effectively prepare students for life. As the publisher of textbooks, trade books, and other educational resources within ACSI, Purposeful Design Publications strives to produce biblically sound materials that reflect Christian scholarship and stewardship and that address the identified needs of Christian schools around the world.

Unless otherwise identified, all Scripture quotations are taken from the New American Standard Bible (NASB), © 1960, 1962, 1963, 1968, 1971, 1972, 1973, 1975, 1977, 1995, 1997 by the Lockman Foundation.

Printed in the United States of America
16 15 14 13 12 11 10   5 6 7 8 9 10

Greene, Albert E.
   Reclaiming the future of Christian education: A transforming vision
   ISBN 978-1-58331-000-7   Catalog #6244

Design team: Michael Riester and D. A. Scott
Editor: Mary Endres

Purposeful Design Publications
A Division of ACSI
PO Box 65130 · Colorado Springs, CO 80962-5130
Customer Service: 800-367-0798 · www.acsi.org

CONTENTS

PREFACE

It would be unjust not to include a few words of explanation and appreciation for help received along the way in the preparation of this book. It is the result of more than forty years of effort in Christian schooling. It took me years to figure out what is distinctive about Christian schools (I'm sure I still have more to learn), and the ideas offered here are a summary of what I think these forty years have taught me. They are written out of a deepening concern for Christian parents who feel that a secular school is adequate for their children.

Two people, John Vanderhoek and Jon Andreas, read the entire manuscript and made useful comments. I am deeply indebted to them, and they are not to blame for any of the book's shortcomings. John Vanderhoek urged me to alter the early chapters to highlight modernity and postmodernity and their contrast to a Christian worldview and philosophy of education. That struck me as a particularly useful suggestion. I have used the chapters with a number of classes in Christian philosophy of education and am indebted to many students for perceptive comments and reactions. For Mary Endres' help as editor, and for DAScott's work in design and production, I am also deeply grateful.

Introduction

THE TASK OF PROPHETIC MINISTRY IS TO NURTURE, NOURISH, AND EVOKE A CONSCIOUSNESS AND PERCEPTION ALTERNATIVE TO THE CONSCIOUSNESS AND PERCEPTION OF THE DOMINANT CULTURE AROUND US.

WALTER BRUEGGEMANN, *THE PROPHETIC IMAGINATION*

Developing an alternative Christian consciousness among teachers and students in today's secularized society is not the work of one meeting, one memo, or one moment. Our thinking is thoroughly adulterated by Enlightenment concepts. It is as polluted as the most victimized parts of our physical environment. Genuine Christian thinking, the mental side of a Christian mind, is unintelligible to those who control the public media. Christian living, which is the other side of the Christian mind, is more a wistful goal than a practiced reality among the Lord's people.

Correcting this situation will be a long process. It will require patience and persistence in generous quantities. We must not be discouraged at the formidable size of the task, nor must we attempt to short-circuit the working of the Holy Spirit by pressing too hard for immediate results. In the long run, if we are faithful and obedient, we may expect the Lord to produce far-reaching changes through our educational efforts.

This book is about developing a new, transformed consciousness—a biblical consciousness—through teaching children in Christian homes, churches, and schools. It has grown out of this writer's more than forty years' work in and with Christian schools. In view of that, it must be to some extent autobiographical. Only what one has lived through is likely to be of real help to others on the pilgrimage. Frederick Buechner suggests that God speaks to us in every day of our lives and that it is possible to recover and treasure His speaking. If we do that, autobiography becomes a variety of prayer. Stories from one's life become a call to prayer, so it will be well if you can think of these pages as a call to prayer and a deeper understanding of what it means to teach Christianly. The chapters are certainly not a finished document on the philosophy of Christian education, nor on the content and practice of Christian schooling, though that is the direction in which they are headed.

I didn't intend to get into Christian school work at all. I wanted to teach Hebrew and Old Testament in a theological seminary. But the Lord had other plans. My wife and I responded to a call for help from the China Bible Seminary in Kiangwan, a suburb of Shanghai, China. This excellent girls' Bible school was experiencing increasing numbers of requests from young men who, because of the troubled travel conditions occasioned by the Sino-Japanese War, wanted to attend. So the school was looking for an American man to help with the men's side of the work. As a result, in late September 1940, we found ourselves disembarking in a typhoon rainstorm onto a dock in Shanghai.

This was only fourteen months before Pearl Harbor Day, and within a couple of weeks of our arrival, we received a letter from the American consulate advising us to return home, because the international situation was dangerous. Instead, after several weeks of prayer and probing, we were accepted as missionaries on loan at the men's language training home of the China Inland Mission in Chowkiakow, Honan province, free China. Thus began a five-year odyssey that lasted until the end of World War II.

Those five years were a lesson-packed training period for what we would encounter later on. During those years, no mission board was financially responsible for us. Nor did we have clear-cut guarantees of support from friends at home in the States. Yet support came in a quantity remarkably similar to that of the China Inland Mission friends we worked with. We had one baby and lost a second one. We experienced significant sickness and endured some bombing. The province went through a famine in which many villages lost up to ninety percent of their population as people died of starvation or moved away in search of food. After three-and-one-half years we were forced to evacuate to Chungking, the wartime capital of China, in the far west. After a year of teaching in a new seminary two hundred miles farther west in Szechwan, we left by way of India in the late spring of 1945 for a furlough at home. We arrived in New York a few days before the atom bombs were dropped.

After a year of furlough, during which I did graduate work in Old Testament in a theological seminary, we embarked once more for Shanghai in September 1946. We traveled from Portland on a Danish freighter, one of the last vessels to leave the West Coast until Christmas. A West Coast stevedores' strike effectively closed down the ports for those four months. We worked then for two years and three months in the rejuvenated compound of the China Bible Seminary in Kiangwan, joyfully ministering to a student body of more than two hundred young men and women. They were a sterling group, many of whom had experienced trials of faith in reaching the school and would undergo even more severe trials in the years to come. Then, in 1948, as the communist armies began to move south toward Shanghai, it became obvious that we would only burden our Chinese friends and co-workers if we stayed on. We left on a United States Navy transport on New Year's Eve.

What should we do next? After some months of inde-
cision, I accepted the pastorate of the small church in
north Seattle where we were members and where I had
been ordained. My older brother, Joe, was then living across
Lake Washington east of Seattle. He and his wife were send-
ing their four children twenty-five miles each way to a
Christian school in Seattle. They wanted a Christian school
on the east side, and I agreed to help by serving on the
school board. Then, two weeks before school was to open
in September 1950, the man who was to teach the upper
four grades notified us that he would not be coming. That
tipped the scales of my vocational uncertainty. I resigned
my pastorate and became the teacher of the upper three
grades—though we had no sixth graders that first year—
and principal of the school. It began in the basement of a
suburban community church with no telephone and two
outhouses in back. There were nine students to start with,
five of whom had the surname Greene. The student body
grew to seventeen in the first year, which ended in June
1951; and, by the time I left in 1979, it had grown to
around eight hundred. (In 1998 the school enrolled more
than fourteen hundred.)

During those twenty-nine years and since, I have studied to discover what it means to teach Christianly. How
should a Christian school differ, in twentieth-century America,
from a secular one? The answers came neither quickly nor
easily, and today they are still tentative and open to improvement. I cannot begin to name all those whose writing and
speaking and thinking have contributed to what follows, but
I hope you can accept it as a call to prayer and, in the process, find that your own perception of Christian education
is deriving some benefit.

CHILDREN AND THEIR NURTURE

Education and children are twinned ideas. However,
Jesus' thoughts on the subject are strangely different from

ours. He continually warned his disciples of their need to become like little children if they would enter the kingdom of heaven. Instead, we adults think of children as immature, pliable little persons that we are to develop into mature human beings, and of ourselves as the pattern to be followed in their shaping. We think of ourselves as having arrived, and we aim to make our students into our own likeness. To the extent we are able to hear Jesus' words on the subject, it is likely that our efforts at educating children will become more blessed and hence more successful. Hearing His words about children is a step in teacher training to which we ought to give much more attention.

There is no question about the importance of children in Jesus' scheme of things. When the disciples turned away the mothers who sought Jesus' blessing on their infants, He was angered and commanded that the little ones be given access to Him:

> BUT JESUS CALLED FOR THEM, SAYING, "PERMIT THE CHILDREN TO COME TO ME, AND DO NOT HINDER THEM, FOR THE KINGDOM OF GOD BELONGS TO SUCH AS THESE. TRULY I SAY TO YOU, WHOEVER DOES NOT RECEIVE THE KINGDOM OF GOD LIKE A CHILD SHALL NOT ENTER IT AT ALL" (LUKE 18:16-17).

His assertion that the kingdom of heaven belongs to them was repeated often. In His sermon on the fellowship of the kingdom in Matthew 18, He said that we should receive each child as if he or she were Jesus Himself. (Many commentators hold that this passage refers to young Christians rather than to literal children. I would include young Christians, but I find it difficult to limit the passage to them.) Jesus severely warned the disciples, who had just set an example of fierce competition for first place in the kingdom, not to cause the children to stumble. He climaxed His teaching in that sermon by adjuring them not to despise the little ones. He underscored the point by speaking of the concern for children on the part of His Father, the children's angels, and Himself as the good shepherd. Clearly, in Jesus' opinion, children rank right along with the poor, the oppressed, the widows, and the orphans as people we should be deeply concerned about. They are important. This is not to say that today's Christian parents are not concerned for their children. They are. It does suggest, however, that our concern may need to be reviewed in the light of a biblical worldview.

Traditionally, four agencies—three formal and one informal—have cultivated the minds and hearts of growing children. The home, the church, and the school have been the formal channels of child formation. Ideally, for Christians, the home was the place where children learned to love, the church where they learned about salvation from sin, and the school where they learned about the world around them. There have been times, never as frequent or powerful as they might have been, when the three exerted complementary and reinforcing formative influences on children. Since the Enlightenment, however, and especially in the last thirty years, the influence of the school has become increasingly at variance with that of the home and church. Today, the fact that most people even in evangelical churches seem to regard secular school education as acceptable for their children only deepens the public school's influence. That this view endorses the Enlightenment idea that ordinary things can be adequately understood without reference to God does not seem as yet to be a serious problem to the church and its members. It is most urgent, for the very preservation of the church, that parents become more concerned about the overall education of their children "in the discipline and instruction of the Lord" (Ephesians 6:4b).

Peer pressure and the impact of the culture are the fourth and informal agency that cultivates children's minds and hearts. Children have always learned from each other, for good and ill. Today, however, with the technological invasion of the home by television and the Internet, and with the exclusion of the gospel from public schools, cultural and peer pressures have gained hurricane force in the lives of children. Newspaper photos of hurricane damage will show roofs lifted off, shattered structures, and scattered wreckage of furniture and other possessions. Such images suggest tragic parallels to the impact that peer pressure and the culture make on today's youngsters. What is surprising is that the people who profess to belong to the Body of Christ seem so oblivious to the magnitude of the crisis. Christian schooling at home or in a Christian school, ceases to be a luxury and becomes an irreplaceable bastion for the communication of the faith to the next generation.

Biblical Wisdom

The study of philosophy has fallen into disrepute in this century. Professional philosophers have given up the attempt to explain the nature of the world and the purpose of human life. This situation led Francis Schaeffer to say, some years ago, that there was more philosophy to be found among poets and songwriters than among the philosophers.

It is well to remember that every Christian is called to be a philosopher in the true sense of that word, which means literally "a lover of wisdom." The Bible commands us to love wisdom.

Take my instruction, and not silver, and knowledge rather than choicest gold. For wisdom is better than jewels; and all desirable things cannot compare with her (Proverbs 8:10-11).

For this reason, since the day we heard . . . we have not ceased . . . to ask that you may be filled with the knowledge of His will in all spiritual wisdom and understanding, so that you may walk in a manner worthy of the Lord (Philippians 1:9-10).

Yet strangely, philosophy is still regarded by Christians with suspicion if not aversion. That isn't the import of Scripture at all:

SEE TO IT THAT NO ONE TAKES YOU CAPTIVE THROUGH PHILOSOPHY AND EMPTY DECEPTION, ACCORDING TO THE TRADITION OF MEN, ACCORDING TO THE ELEMENTARY PRINCIPLES OF THE WORLD, RATHER THAN ACCORDING TO CHRIST (COLOSSIANS 2:8).

The argument here isn't against philosophy as such, but against Greek and pagan philosophy, which lacked the benefit of divine revelation. There is a love of wisdom that is "according to Christ." The following chapters represent an effort to present in brief outline the shape of a Christian philosophy that expresses itself as a transforming vision. Without such a vision, or biblical consciousness, it is naive to expect to explain the creation in such a way that children will learn to know, love, and serve the Lord through a curriculum built exclusively from that creation.

We will consider, in Part One, some aspects of modern Western culture and some biblical revelations that press us to provide a distinctively Christian schooling for our children. Part Two will sketch briefly the main points in a Christian philosophy. Part Three will deal with the content of Christian schooling, recognizing that the curriculum consists entirely of created things. Part Four will deal with methods in Christian schooling under the rubric of the "being" side of a Christian mind. The Conclusion will try to draw these ideas together.

PART 1

UNDERSTANDING THE TIMES

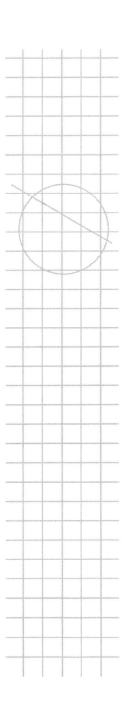

THE ENLIGHTENMENT   1

In the Old Testament world the people of Issachar were known as "men who understood the times, with knowledge of what Israel should do" (1 Chronicles 12:32). It would be foolish to discuss Christian schooling at the close of the twentieth century without first inquiring into the times and, on that basis, discussing what we ought to do. To neglect this step would be to assume that anyone with common sense knows what school is about and that the important questions deal with the *how* of teaching rather than the *why*. The description of the people of Issachar in 1 Chronicles may refer to their understanding that the time had come for the entire people of Israel to anoint David as king and so to come together under one rule. Here, our question is, What is the nature of education, and how ought Christians to provide for the upbringing of their children? To discover the answer, we have to know something about the times in which we live. The New Testament notes the urgency of this sort of wisdom:

> THEREFORE BE CAREFUL HOW YOU WALK, NOT AS UNWISE MEN, BUT AS WISE, MAKING THE MOST OF YOUR TIME, BECAUSE THE DAYS ARE EVIL. SO THEN DO NOT BE FOOLISH, BUT UNDERSTAND WHAT THE WILL OF THE LORD IS (EPHESIANS 5:15-17).

After outlining the duties of husbands, wives, children, slaves, and masters, the following passage culminates in an appeal to put on the full armor of God. It adds that our struggle is not against particular people but against "the world rulers of this darkness, against the spiritual forces of wickedness in the heavenly places." That is quite a distance from our commonsense understanding of what schools are really all about.

The problem with the commonsense approach is just that—it is common. It is shaped fundamentally by the consciousness of our society. Sociologists have come to believe that it is extremely difficult to hold something as true when the society at large sees it as false. To differ from the going social view involves what Peter Berger calls "cognitive deviance," and he insists that there are very strong social and social-psychological pressures to prevent it. He goes on to say:

> UNLESS OUR THEOLOGIAN HAS THE INNER FORTITUDE OF A DESERT SAINT, HE HAS ONLY ONE EFFECTIVE REMEDY AGAINST THE THREAT OF COGNITIVE COLLAPSE IN THE FACE OF THESE PRESSURES: HE MUST HUDDLE TOGETHER WITH LIKE-MINDED DEVIANTS—AND HUDDLE VERY CLOSELY INDEED. ONLY IN A COUNTER-COMMUNITY OF CONSIDERABLE STRENGTH DOES COGNITIVE DEVIANCE HAVE A CHANCE TO MAINTAIN ITSELF (A RUMOR OF ANGELS, P. 17).

Berger is discussing the denial of the supernatural in a secular society, but the principle extends equally to commonsense ideas about schooling.

If we are to understand the way today's Christians think about their children's education, it is important that we think back a few centuries and compare the way people in the West view life and the world today with the way people once saw them. To do so, we need to give attention first to a major development in recent history commonly known as the Enlightenment.

THE HISTORY OF THE ENLIGHTENMENT

To talk about the Enlightenment, we first need to distinguish it from several other movements associated with the beginning of modern history. The Renaissance, for example, has been defined as "the transitional movement in Europe between medieval and modern times beginning in the fourteenth century in Italy and lasting into the seventeenth century, and marked by a humanistic revival of classical influence expressed in a flowering of the arts and literature and by the beginnings of modern science." This movement is often, but erroneously, thought of as antagonistic to Christianity. While it was antagonistic to the church in southern Europe, particularly in Italy, in northern Europe it included the publication by Erasmus of a new and improved translation of the New Testament. He did this between 1516 and 1536, right at the time Martin Luther was entering into his contest with the Roman Catholic Church. So the Renaissance had both positive and negative sides in its relation to the church and the Bible.

The Reformation, whose two most important leaders were Martin Luther and John Calvin, began in 1517 with Luther's posting of his ninety-five theses on the door of the Wittenburg church. In a generation the Reformation was continued by John Calvin of Geneva. Under the watchwords "by faith alone" and "by Scripture alone," the movement seemed to promise a radical break with the established philosophy of scholasticism, which had been given its enduring form by Thomas Aquinas of the University of Paris in the thirteenth century. But Luther and Calvin were theologians, not philosophers, and since the men who founded schools for them did so in terms of Catholic scholastic philosophy, the promise did not materialize.

The beginning of the scientific revolution belongs to this same period. Nicholas Copernicus (1473–1543) is commonly regarded as the first modern scientist. His work *On the Revolution of the Heavenly Bodies* proposed that the sun, not the earth, is the center of our universe. It contradicted the view of Ptolemy, which scientists had held since the middle of the second century. More importantly, based as it was on mathematics, Copernicus' work introduced the idea that we can learn about our environment empirically by the use of mathematical formulae. *The Discourse on Method* by René Descartes (1596–1650) gave a significant push to the development of science, but it was

Isaac Newton (1642–1747) and John Locke (1632–1704) who really introduced the concepts of human reason and mathematics as the keys to discovering the truth about the world and reality. Craine Brinton says of them, "Together, Newton and Locke set up those great clusters of ideas, Nature and Reason, that were to the Enlightenment what such clusters as grace, salvation, and predestination were to traditional Christianity."

What might easily escape our observation here is that the scientific revolution, which began strictly as a reasonable investigation of the world around us, passed over quickly into a worldview that was philosophical rather than scientific. This worldview was rationalism. The early scientists did not think of their work as threatening to Christianity at all. In fact, it was their confidence in the regularity of laws and processes in a creation controlled by a sovereign God that led them to their investigations. Science began in the West rather than the East for this reason. But a worldview is different from a scientific study. When Carl Sagan said on television that "the cosmos is all there is, all there ever was, and all there ever will be," he was talking philosophy rather than science, a shift that often takes place without notification. This kind of thinking has led to the common conception that science is opposed to Christianity, which is not necessarily true at all.

The transition from science to philosophical worldview was, to a large extent, the work of a group called the *philosophes*. Prominent among them were men like Voltaire, Diderot, and d'Alembert, editors of *The Encyclopedia;* and Montesquieu and Rousseau. Working together, they developed the worldview of rationalism in such a way as to neutralize and sidetrack the confidence in biblical revelation that was widespread until then. Thus it came about that by the middle of the eighteenth century, Enlightenment ideas had taken a firm hold on the general consciousness. People had begun to feel that what their forefathers had believed in the late Middle Ages was largely superstition and what was now understood through reason was dependable fact.

Lesslie Newbigin makes the point that the word *enlightenment* is heavily charged with religious significance. Buddha's climactic experience was known as enlightenment. Christ claimed to be the light of the world. Thus the Enlightenment was not irreligious; it was a new religion. Ronald A. Wells insists that Christians "must not be on the defensive on behalf of religion against irreligion. The Enlightenment faith *is* a religion—a counter-religion to be sure, but a religion nevertheless" (*History Through the Eyes of Faith*, p. 137). The playing field would be much more level if this were recognized today. In the early days of the Enlightenment, the result was that Christianity, whether Catholic or Protestant, was increasingly pushed aside in the interest of what was thought to be the solid truth of rationalism.

So it came about that by the middle of the eighteenth century there was a widespread public sense that something new had happened in human understanding of the universe and life within it. This new vision came to be known as the Enlightenment. It was a new understanding of reality, thought to be much more reliable than the ancient ideas of Middle Eastern religions and likewise superior to the biblical explanation. Both of these were now thought to be superstitious and undependable.

It is worth noting that a change in the explanation of reality does not take place unless it is founded on a consciousness that does not need to be proved. In the Enlightenment this underlying foundation was found in the reliability of human reason as expressed in the scientific method. This approach had been so successful in unlocking a new understanding of astronomy, physics, chemistry, and the other natural sciences that it was easy for people to believe that human reason must be capable of unlocking all the secrets of human life and relationships.

THE ENLIGHTENMENT CONSCIOUSNESS

It may be worthwhile to summarize the new form of human consciousness that developed with the Enlightenment, encouraged and supported by the amazing improvements in living standards that the scientific revolution continued to secure. To begin with, reality was now considered to be what is physically "out there" as discovered and described by the scientific method. Since science can deal only with what can be measured empirically, the existence of a spiritual realm became increasingly dubious.

One of the most important, and catastrophic, elements in the Enlightenment consciousness is the concept that facts are neutral or value free. Up until the Enlightenment everyone had thought of what we now call facts as carrying within them implications of purpose or meaning. Francis Bacon, the father of the scientific revolution, urged his followers to forget purpose and simply seek for the causes of things. This, he said, would provide them with power to control the cosmos.

The idea that facts are neutral and provide us with the truth is now so deeply settled in the common mind that to question it is to seem mentally unbalanced. Yet in reality it is a thoroughly idolatrous position. Jacques Ellul calls it "the great modern Moloch," the source of a wide variety of other modern idolatries. He comments that if God does not seem to be real any more, it is because He does not seem to be a fact (*The Presence of the Kingdom*, p. 37).

Truth, since it is attached in the Enlightenment consciousness to scientific fact, is now no longer an absolute. Science undergoes radical changes, as astronomy did between Ptolemy and Copernicus, or physics between Newton and Einstein. If all we can know of truth depends on science, truth itself is now relative. What is true today may not be true any more tomorrow.

Knowledge is now limited to empirical facts, and rationalism has taken the place of revelation. The human world is divided into the public area, which can be dealt with scientifically, and the private area of purpose, value, morality, and ethics, which is subject to no control except the individual's own. It is this consciousness that has elbowed religion out of any determinative place in public thinking and left it confined to the private area of individual perspective.

One of the most powerful items in Enlightenment consciousness has been the conviction that the dogma of original sin is one of the worst things that ever happened to the human race. Humans are now assumed to be basically good. Their capacity to improve the world flows out of their rationalism. The problems that afflict the world are supposed to flow out of the corrupt institutions of society rather than the wayward hearts of individuals.

As the Enlightenment progressed, a subtle change took place in connection with the idea of progress. In the ancient world of the Near East, the only group that possessed any solid concept of progress in history was the Hebrews. Everyone else thought of history as an unceasing round of repetitive events that were not going anywhere in the long run. The Hebrews, believing in a sovereign Creator, held that the original creation had been corrupted by human sin, but that God was at work in the world to bring it back, ultimately, to His original intent for it. Thus there was progress in history and a final objective. As the rationalist worldview permeated the Western world, confidence in the capacity of human reason to improve conditions and bring in a utopian situation for humans preempted the concept of progress and insisted that science would continue to lead to better and better living. Hope for heaven in the world to come was replaced by confidence in Enlightenment thought to improve life down here. Inevitable human progress thus established itself as a basic tenet of the Enlightenment. The theory of evolution, effectively introduced by Darwin in the mid-nineteenth century, fitted perfectly with this concept and has become established in modern life as a primary "fact." With this shift from pessimism to optimism about the capacity of humans to improve life in the world without the influence of God came a deepening emphasis on human rights and a growing confidence in free human democracy as the form of government that could be trusted to renew the world.

These are some of the most important aspects of modern consciousness as developed through the Enlightenment. There have recently been radical changes in the prevailing public consciousness. We will discuss them in the next chapter under the heading of postmodernism. First, though, we need to look at the impact of the Enlightenment on education.

THE EDUCATIONAL IMPACT OF THE ENLIGHTENMENT

Our interest here is in what Enlightenment thinking did to education at the elementary and secondary levels. The development of an Enlightenment consciousness took place largely in the universities. However, schoolteachers are trained at the universities, and it is not surprising that changes in thought patterns at that level should produce changes all the way down the school ladder.

Schools in the United States were originally connected principally with churches or were conducted for the purpose of promoting literacy so that people could read and understand the Bible. Colleges were begun to provide ministers for the churches as well as lawyers and doctors for the general population. It was not until the latter half of the nineteenth century that ministers became less and less prominent in American colleges. This was due in large part to the influence of the German universities and the "higher criticism" of the Bible that began in them.

Changes in the lower schools took place slowly, and it was not until the early part of the twentieth century that the prominent aspects of Enlightenment thinking could be seen to have triumphed in elementary and secondary education. Some of its most important influences are the following.

The goal of education shifted from biblical understanding to success in life, particularly economic success. As interest in the life to come faded because of the growing promise that human progress could provide a virtual heaven on earth, the point of schooling shifted from a concern with the Bible to a concern with the desire for earthly success.

The concept of the nature of the child as learner also underwent radical alteration. The student was now thought of either as a highly developed animal to be conditioned by the methods of behaviorist psychology or as an independent operator capable of making life meaningful through human reason. The idea of inborn sinfulness was eliminated, and blame for misbehavior was placed either on some form of illness or on the imperfections of society's institutions. Individual rights achieved increasing importance; individual responsibility faded out of the picture. Competition took an increasing place in the school program with the growing importance of equipping students to control and dominate the environment and even the people within the environment.

Truth came to be seen more and more as the outcome of scientific or rational investigation. Since science cannot deal with those elements in life that resist measurement and quantification, truth was increasingly seen as neutral facts. The acquisition of facts and the skills needed for using them assumed growing importance without any agreed understanding of the moral or ethical use of one's knowledge and skills.

The separation of life into the public and the private spheres had a profound impact on elementary and secondary schools. As education became increasingly a function of government, the separation of church and state meant that any reference to religion in the public school became suspect. The first clause of the first amendment to the Constitution, forbidding the establishment of a national church, was grievously misinterpreted to rule religion out of any influence in schooling. The second clause, forbidding the state from hindering the free exercise of religion, suffered equally serious misinterpretation. The result was that reference to religion, particularly to Christianity, was increasingly restricted in the schools. While there has been some recent effort to reintroduce a secular study of religion, and include the role of religion in historical studies, the damage has not been effectively undone.

Perhaps the most damaging result of Enlightenment thought in the schools has been the neglect of instruction in morals and ethics. This outcome is understandable but not excusable. If truth is only what science can substantiate, then ethics cannot be taught because it belongs to the private rather than the public side of life. It is not excusable because the split of human life into this sort of dualism is totally unjustifiable. There is much in life that cannot be quantitatively measured. In fact, the most important things in life belong in that category. Because schools are unable to deal with those things, it is impossible for them to meet the needs of young students effectively. What this really comes down to is that the government, whose real biblical responsibility is to see that public justice is done, has no prerogative to control education. It is impossible to educate properly without dealing with ethics and religion, but the government has no right to dictate to its people what their morality or religion should be. That is a religious activity and is therefore outside the proper bounds of a democratic form of government, or any other.

These are some of the most important consequences of Enlightenment consciousness in today's public schools. However, the Enlightenment is virtually a thing of the past, and before we can sketch a comparison between a Christian form of schooling and the present public form, particularly in the United States, it is important to know what is happening in the public consciousness. The changes are in some ways helpful to a Christian response to the positions of the Enlightenment. In other ways they make the task of Christian schooling all the more difficult. These are issues we will deal with in the next chapter as we discuss what is known as postmodernism.

NOTES

POSTMODERNISM

2

The Enlightenment began with considerable enthusiasm and promise. By the mid-eighteenth century, people were convinced that the world stood at the verge of a new age when science would bring them to a new level of peace, prosperity, and happiness. Two hundred years later that promise had faded. The twentieth century had become what Wells calls "the age of anxiety." How could it happen that a period which seemed to offer such promise could so quickly seem in the eyes of most people, whether scholars or not, to be a failure?

As the century began, optimism was widespread that the world was on the verge of a new era of peace and progress. However, several twentieth-century developments pricked the bubble of hope that had grown up around the Enlightenment and led to a far-reaching loss of confidence. The first was World War I (1914–1917). Technological advances made the fighting far more deadly than ever before, but it was hard to see what societal gains had been purchased by the phenomenal suffering and loss of life in the protracted trench warfare. Then came the Great Depression of 1929 and, soon after, the advent of Hitler's Third Reich in Germany and Mussolini's fascism in Italy. These events led inescapably to World War II and the involvement of the entire globe in a conflict of unprecedented proportions. Before it was over, the holocaust had taken place, and at the war's end the atomic bomb had been dropped on Hiroshima and Nagasaki. The result was a general loss of confidence in the Enlightenment promise of unceasing progress. This whole development has been starkly described by Zbigniew Brzezinski in *Out of Control: Global Turmoil on the Eve of the Twenty-First Century* (1993).

In terms of prevailing worldviews, the change can be traced back into the nineteenth century. The mechanistic emphasis of rationalism, the worldview of the Enlightenment, proved uncomfortable to a good many thinkers. The result was the development of romanticism with its emphasis on human feelings and the beauties of nature. Walt Whitman and Ralph Waldo Emerson are American examples. Furthermore, by the end of the nineteenth century, philosophers had despaired of the possibility of constructing a trustworthy description of reality. Metaphysics, the division of scholarly philosophy that deals with what lies behind physical reality, fell by the wayside. Philosophical emphasis in the twentieth century turned to pragmatism in epistemology and existentialism in axiology. John Dewey is the best American representative of the former. His position, variously known as pragmatism, instrumentalism, and experimentalism, was that humans do not discover truth; they make it by the use of the scientific method. Whether there is any such thing as objective truth "out there" we have no way of knowing, Dewey said. Axiology is the branch of philosophy that deals with ethics or values and beauty. Existentialism, which centers its attention in this area, has been better represented in Europe than in America. French dramatists Jean-Paul Sartre and Albert Camus are two of the best-known names. Existentialism is disinclined even to be called a philosophy. Its contention is that we as humans have no underlying nature to determine who we will be; rather, we make ourselves what we are by our choices. It is not a happy or encouraging definition of humanity. As we shall see, both pragmatism and existentialism are obviously roots of the perspective that has replaced Enlightenment modernity, an outlook that has come to be known as postmodernism.

THE POSTMODERN CONSCIOUSNESS

It is not easy to pinpoint just when postmodernism began. One scholar puts it in 1972 with the dynamiting of

the Pruitt-Igoe housing project in St. Louis. This architec-
turally modern and technologically advanced effort to
provide housing for the poor had become so crime-ridden
that life there was impossible. Another scholar puts the
beginning at the fall of the Berlin Wall. Probably most
scholars would agree with a date falling in the 1960s with
the decade's youth rebellion.

There is not even scholarly agreement that
postmodernism is anything but the logical outgrowth of
Enlightenment modernism and its weaknesses. However,
it is possible to identify enough elements of the postmodern
consciousness to assure us that, however and whenever it
originated, it is clearly distinguishable from modernism.
In some ways the change is helpful to a Christian
worldview. In others, as we shall see, it is not. The clearest
evidence for postmodernism as a new perspective is found
in the areas where it differs sharply from modernism.

To begin with, postmodernism questions the existence
of any final truth. The Enlightenment condemned the Christian dependence on revealed truth but still held to the idea
that human reason could identify something called truth
even if that something might be subject to change because
it was dependent on the scientific method. Postmodernists
question the very existence of truth. Gene E. Veith Jr. puts
it in this way: postmodern views "respond to the failure of
the Enlightenment by jettisoning truth altogether. The in-
tellect is replaced by the will. Reason is replaced by emotion.
Morality is replaced by relativism. Reality itself becomes a
social construct" (*Postmodern Times*, p. 29). The move from
pragmatism, which makes truth dependent on human for-
mulation, to something like existentialism, which doesn't
recognize any truth at all, is clearly evident.

Postmodernism is dubious about any attempt to explain the whole of reality. Warren A. Nord traces one of
the roots of postmodernism back to Nietzsche at the end
of the nineteenth century. Then he quotes Jean-Francois

Lyotard, a French postmodernist scholar of the 1960s and 1970s, who says that postmodernists are incredulous "toward overarching accounts of reality" (*Religion and American Education*, p. 59). Modernism thought that the scientific worldview had superseded all those that preceded it, including the Christian one. Postmodernism denies this claim and says that all philosophic attempts to define reality are just stories that may or may not have any objective value at all. They must be deconstructed, or shown to be of no definite objective value. In fact, the very definition of objective reality is regarded as impossible. There may not be any such thing as reality after all. (Here is an instance of postmodernism's glorying in contradictions!)

Postmodernism is obviously a very negative perspective, but we haven't reached the bottom yet. Postmodernism is even dubious about the rational, independent self. It claims that humans are shaped by their language and their society. There is nothing autonomous or independent about them in the final analysis. The nonphysical, enduring self is a complete illusion. This radical devaluation of the human being is summed up by Veith as follows:

> IF THERE ARE NO ABSOLUTES, IF TRUTH IS RELATIVE, THEN THERE CAN BE NO STABILITY, NO MEANING IN LIFE. IF REALITY IS SOCIALLY CONSTRUCTED, THEN MORAL GUIDELINES ARE ONLY MASKS FOR OPPRESSIVE POWER AND INDIVIDUAL IDENTITY IS AN ILLUSION (*POSTMODERN TIMES*, P. 72).

The attack on the human person occurs in connection with postmodernism's controversy with humanism. Veith again says:

> THE POSTMODERNISTS ATTACK HUMANISM ON TWO FRONTS. NOT ONLY DO THEY SEEK TO DECONSTRUCT THE CONCEPT OF INDIVIDUAL LIBERTY; THEY ALSO DECONSTRUCT THE CONCEPT OF UNIVERSAL HUMANITY. THUS, ONE DECONSRUCTIONIST ARGUES THAT THE WORD *WE* IS A "FORM OF GRAMMATICAL VIOLENCE" (IBID., P. 77).

The philosophical roots of postmodernism seem to lie mainly in the philosophy of Martin Heidegger. His views have been described as antihumanist. He denied the idea of a common humanity and said that "Human beings . . . are no longer at the center. There is no center" (Ibid., p. 74). Out of this deconstructionist position have grown two important postmodern ideologies, "environmentalism and political radicalism." Both of these severely diminish the importance of the human and the human race.

Language fares little better with postmodernism than the human self. It is not something which expresses facts; it makes them. And there is no way of telling whether the facts of one language are more valid than those of another. In fact, postmodernists generally agree that language not only binds us; it also regularly hides a pursuit of power. There is no such thing as writing that simply tells a true story. Writing always contains a hidden effort to justify the power of a dominant elite and to make legitimate their control over an oppressed group. It is in the study of literature and poetry that deconstructionism comes most powerfully into its own. Since words have no fixed meaning, the interpretation of a poem or a piece of literature becomes simply an exercise in making the words say what the interpreter wants them to say. This will regularly result in the justification of a group that holds power in a situation.

Given the above aspects of postmodern consciousness, it is not hard to see that the concept of progress, so important to the Enlightenment, ceases to be either valid or important. We are perceived to be, in effect, caught in a new Dark Ages, when the trusted foundations of individual and social life have been washed away and there is no telling what may lie ahead.

It is worthy of note that Nietzsche, who proclaimed the death of God, is regarded as almost the father of postmodernism. This gains significance when it is recalled that Hitler's Third Reich was an expression of the philosophy of Nietzsche. Hitler is dead, and Nazism has been, for the time being, exposed and repudiated. But Nietzsche's philosophy has not been contradicted, and, given the perspective of postmodernism, there is no reason to suppose we are not in danger of a recurrence of the kind of political development represented in Nazism.

One further aspect of a postmodern consciousness is the resurgence of tribalism. With the postmodern view of governments as fundamentally power hungry and untrustworthy, human allegiance tends to gravitate to smaller groups with a common identity within the larger public. This new tribalism shows up in the revival of petty nationalisms in areas recently relieved of the oppression of communism, as in central Europe. It reveals itself in the fragmentation of college and university student bodies into peer groups with common identities, such as African Americans, gays and lesbians, and feminists. These groups tend to see themselves as having been exploited and to demand special treatment because of that.

Altogether, then, the postmodern consciousness is essentially hopeless. When, in 1974, Lesslie Newbigin and his wife returned to England after thirty-eight years of missionary work in India, he was frequently asked what was the greatest difficulty they faced when they returned from India to England. His answer was always "the disappearance of hope"(*The Other Side of 1984*, p. 1). In India, he said, no matter how bad things got, there was always something to be done, some hopeful plan. But in England Newbigin encountered a hopelessness he had not known before. England was already deeply influenced by postmodernist thinking. Human beings cannot live without hope, and it is of primary importance that American Christians should become aware of the implications of postmodernism, especially for the schools in which most children of Christians are trained.

THE EDUCATIONAL IMPACT OF POSTMODERNISM

Does postmodernism really make any difference to education in the schools today? Most Americans are not even familiar with the postmodern consciousness described above. They would deny most of what postmodernism asserts to be true, for public awareness always lags well behind the most recent scholarly thinking. But all Americans and other citizens of the world are already involved in cultural and societal developments that can be traced directly to postmodernism. The troubles that have devastated Rwanda in Africa and the former Czechoslovakia in central Europe illustrate the return to tribalism characteristic of postmodernism. But even ordinary American life is more intimately influenced than most of us suspect. "Postmodern worldviews and postmodern culture surround us. Ordinary Americans cannot avoid these. Postmodernism shapes our lifestyles, the way we make a living, how we educate our children, and how we approach our personal problems and those of society." (Veith, *Postmodern Times*, p. 175). Television, for instance, pervades and influences American life. It replaces reading for many people. It does not promote thinking. The advertisers want us not to think but to feel, and to buy. The culture works to change us from producers into consumers.

Postmodernism does influence public education, and often, tragically, Christian school education as well. The cutting edge of postmodernism is located in the universities. But the universities train teachers. They also influence deeply the bureaucrats who dominate the school boards and the people who make proposals for reform in education. Let us look, then, at some of the ways in which postmodernist consciousness appears in the curriculum and teaching methods of today's public schools.

To approach this topic first in the most general way, there can be no real question that modernism, following the lead of the Enlightenment, has succeeded in causing public schools to indoctrinate students against religion and, particularly, against Christianity. Under the specious umbrella of separation of church and state, reference to Christianity is now almost totally absent from the public school curriculum. The claim is that this position is religiously neutral; the reality is that secularism, while it purports to be neutral, functions as a religion. Textbooks have been similarly drained of significant religious or Christian content. If it were not so sad, the public school effort to exclude God from the classroom would be humorous.

The question now is, What will postmodernism do to the pattern of excluding Christianity from classrooms and texts that was established by the Enlightenment? In some ways, the perspective of postmodernism might seem to offer hope for a change. Postmodernism does not support the rationalist claim that science has made religion irrelevant. Postmodernism rejects all worldviews, including science, that claim to explain reality. In some ways this might seem a helpful change for Christians, since it undercuts the present public reliance on science as the sole source of truth. But in other ways the prospect is not good. While postmodernism regards the rationalist worldview as unreliable, at the same time it objects violently to the Christian claim to have the only true worldview. Postmodernists claim that there is no one true worldview because there is no such thing as absolute truth. The prospect for a change in public education that will allow the inclusion of a Christian worldview is not good.

Turning to particulars in the impact of postmodernism on schooling, we are likely to see increasing changes in the goals of schooling. Veith speaks of this as follows:

WHEREAS CLASSICAL SCHOLARSHIP SOUGHT THE TRUE, THE BEAUTIFUL, AND THE GOOD, THE POSTMODERNIST ACADEMY SEEKS "WHAT WORKS." THE TRADITIONAL ACADEMIC WORLD IS OPERATED BY REASON, STUDY, AND RESEARCH; POSTMODERNIST ACADEMIA IS GOVERNED BY IDEOLOGICAL AGENDAS, POLITICAL CORRECTNESS, AND POWER STRUGGLES (IBID., P. 58).

The current interest of the educational establishment in so-called "outcome-based education" may be a sign of a move in the latter direction.

As to the nature of the student, postmodernism is even less compatible with a biblical perspective than was modernism. Modernism saw the human child simply as the peak of evolutionary change; postmodernism denies the very existence of an autonomous and independent self. We are formed, it says, by our culture, our language, and our society. There is therefore no place for individual identity or for a sense of selfhood or a discrete and integrated human soul. "Modernism," says Veith, "was activist, optimistic, and self-confident. Postmodernism is passive, cynical, and insecure" (Ibid., p. 83). The conflict with the biblical picture of humanness was clear enough in comparison with the modernist concept of evolution; it is even clearer when looked at beside the postmodern denial of any distinct self at all.

Postmodernism rejects truth in the sense of a valid account of the way things have been historically or are today. The implications for the teaching of science, history, and sociology in the elementary and high schools are devastating. All religious and philosophical accounts of the past are held to be simply cover-ups for the justification of power held by elites and of the oppression of minorities. The consequences for studies of the history of the United States, for example, are drastic. Gone are pledging allegiance and saluting the flag. Children no longer learn about George Washington and the cherry tree, nor is the American economic system given preferential treatment. Emphasis is placed on the evils of Western invasion and colonization of the New World, from Christopher Columbus to the mistreatment of Native Americans.

This direction in education is an expression of the postmodern stress on multi-culturalism. It grows out of the "hermeneutic of suspicion" that characterizes postmodernism and sees little but domination of minorities and seizure of power in the history of Western culture. However, the insistence on teaching about other cultures is poisoned by the post-Marxist inclination to see only power-grabbing in any culture. Thus cultures are studied superficially. Their underlying commonality is denied because postmodernism's anti-humanism does not recognize anything common in the race as a whole. The result is a new tribalism that pits ethnic group against ethnic group and divides universities into pockets of minorities that are increasingly dissociated from each other.

With the disappearance of truth goes the disappearance of moral principles. If reality is simply a social construct, then one morality is as good as another. (It is ironic that postmodernism can even talk about what is "good" since it denies the existence of all absolutes.) Enlightenment modernism separated facts from meaning or value and thus abandoned any objective basis for teaching morals. Hence the advent of "values clarification" as a substitute. This meant that children were encouraged to evaluate moral questions on their own and develop their own morality. Postmodernism will only deepen this sort of approach to ethics. Veith puts it this way:

> TEACHERS, CONVINCED THAT THERE ARE NO OBJECTIVE TRUTHS TO LEARN, TEACH "PROCESSES" INSTEAD, OFFERING "EXPERIENCES" INSTEAD OF KNOWLEDGE AND ENCOURAGING THEIR STUDENTS TO QUESTION EXISTING VALUES AND TO CREATE THEIR OWN (IBID., P. 59).

Significantly, freedom of speech, which is so vigorously asserted in many instances today, is already suffering in schools. Political correctness dictates what can and cannot be said in the university. In the lower schools, since tolerance for everything is so important to postmodernism, students are not allowed to say anything that might be questionable or objectionable to any other students in the school.

We live in the information age, and Veith points out that we now have a new class of people who deal in information. This includes teachers at all levels, people in the media, planners, and members of the helping professions (psychologists, therapists, and even clergymen). They are highly influential because information has become so important. This class tends to be liberal and morally permissive. It values change and sees no problem in the far-reaching alteration of sexual and other traditional moralities. Its influence in the lower schools is captured by Veith's comment: "Since the educators run the universities and the public schools, they expose every student to their principles" (p. 181).

CONCLUSION

Postmodernism as a way of thinking has not yet reached the popular level. However, social attitudes and processes that stem from the postmodern consciousness are widespread. Many people who hold to traditional ideas of God and of theology are involved daily in ways of thinking and living that grow directly from postmodernist ideas. The influence of these ways on the education of the vast majority of American children is easy to demonstrate.

The question is, what should Christian parents be doing to avoid having the next generation of Christians swept down the tube with the rapidly changing American and Western ways of thinking and living? This will be the theme of the next chapter.

NOTES

An Alternative Consciousness

3

The preceding chapters have provided a brief overview of where American society is today in its consciousness of modern life. The problem is that the American Christian church is deeply involved in society, creating a dangerous problem for that church. While many of its members, particularly evangelicals, continue to cherish their belief in God and even in orthodox theological doctrines, they feel no strain in participating in views and practices that have been shaped by modernism and postmodernism. Nord highlights the problem:

No doubt the great majority of Americans continue to believe in God. But the great majority of Americans also lead largely secular lives and think about the world in largely secular terms. An intellectual wall of separation divides religion from our public culture; it is no longer obvious to most of us what difference our religious beliefs and traditions should make. We have privatized our religion as we have secularized our culture (*Religion and American Education*, p. 61).

Thus the Christian church is heavily involved in dualism. The impossibility of living life on two different planes and the idolatry involved in that practice will concern us in the next section. For the moment let us simply recognize that it is happening to us on a wide scale. Nord continues:

No doubt most conservatives, indeed most fundamentalists, have come to terms with large segments of secular modernity in their everyday lives, but they hold fast to the premodern truths of Scripture and tradition—at least concerning what they take to be theological essentials (*Ibid.*).

The seriousness of this problem surfaces when we remember that the church is the Body of Christ on earth. It is the appointed community responsible to declare the truth of God to an unbelieving world. If, however, it has already capitulated to the world's way of thinking, it is in no shape to fulfill the Great Commission. Lesslie Newbigin comments:

THE CHURCH HAS LIVED SO LONG AS A PERMITTED AND EVEN PRIVILEGED MINORITY, ACCEPTING RELEGATION TO THE PRIVATE SPHERE IN A CULTURE WHOSE PUBLIC LIFE IS CONTROLLED BY A TOTALLY DIFFERENT VISION OF REALITY, THAT IT HAS ALMOST LOST THE POWER TO ADDRESS A RADICAL CHALLENGE TO THAT VISION AND THEREFORE TO "MODERN WESTERN CIVILIZATION" AS A WHOLE. LOOKING AT THE WORLD MISSIONARY SITUATION AS A WHOLE, THIS FAILURE IS THE MOST IMPORTANT AND THE MOST SERIOUS FACTOR IN THE WHOLE WORLD SITUATION, BECAUSE THIS WESTERN CULTURE HAS PENETRATED INTO EVERY OTHER CULTURE IN THE WORLD AND THREATENS TO DESTABILIZE THEM ALL (*THE OTHER SIDE OF 1984*, P. 23).

Brueggemann approaches the same topic from a slightly different perspective:

THE CONTEMPORARY AMERICAN CHURCH IS SO LARGELY ENCULTURATED TO THE AMERICAN ETHOS OF CONSUMERISM THAT IT HAS LITTLE POWER TO BELIEVE OR TO ACT.... OUR CONSCIOUSNESS HAS BEEN CLAIMED BY FALSE FIELDS OF PERCEPTION AND IDOLATROUS SYSTEMS OF LANGUAGE AND RHETORIC.... THE HYPOTHESIS I WILL EXPLORE HERE IS THIS: *THE TASK OF PROPHETIC MINISTRY IS TO NURTURE, NOURISH, AND EVOKE A CONSCIOUSNESS AND PERCEPTION ALTERNATIVE TO THE CONSCIOUSNESS AND PERCEPTION OF THE DOMINANT CULTURE AROUND US.* THUS I SUGGEST THAT PROPHETIC MINISTRY HAS TO DO . . . WITH ADDRESSING . . . THE DOMINANT CRISIS THAT IS ENDURING AND RESILIENT, OF HAVING OUR ALTERNATIVE VOCATION CO-OPTED AND DOMESTICATED (*THE PROPHETIC IMAGINATION*, PP. 11-13).

It will now be apparent why this chapter is entitled "An Alternative Consciousness." If I understand the biblical version of where we are as a people today, nothing is more important for the church than that it should cultivate a transformed consciousness.

Where should this take place? Certainly it should happen in local congregations and in the theological seminaries where pastors and preachers are trained. It should be happening in Christian families. But this is not a project of one Sunday or one month or one year. It will take years, and radical reawakenings, for it to begin to produce the impact on society that the witness of the church should be producing. As we consider the decades- or generations-long process that is needed, the educating of our children bulks large. Can we afford to leave them for twelve and more years under the daily influence of a postmodernist consciousness? The plea of this book is that, if we seriously intend to reawaken as a church to the biblical view of life and reality, we dare not fail to train our children, whether in Christian schools or in Christian home schools, in a transformed, biblical consciousness.

This contention will undoubtedly meet the objection that we will further divide society if we do this. The simplest way to answer that is to ask whether it occurred to the first-century Christians to ask whether they were risking the development of splits in the society of the Roman Empire. Clearly, the answer is no. At the cost of severe persecution and often martyrdom, they bore witness to the transformed consciousness into which the gospel had brought them. Dare we do less today?

It may be well to review briefly the biblical mandate for this endeavor. Romans 12:1–2 expresses it well: "And do not be conformed to this world, but be transformed by the renewing of your mind, that you may prove what the will of God is, that which is good and acceptable and perfect." 2 Corinthians 10:5 puts it this way: "We are destroying speculations and every lofty thing raised up against the knowledge of God, and we are taking every thought captive to the obedience of Christ." 1 Corinthians 2:16 goes so far as to say, "But we have the mind of Christ." The urgency of an alternative consciousness could hardly be more powerfully mandated.

The mandate is reinforced by biblical and church history. Moses was educated in the best university Egypt afforded, and he was a leading student there. But he had an entirely different perspective from the one the university attempted to impose on him. Daniel and his friends exhibited the same distinctiveness in the university of Babylon. Paul was highly trained in the rabbinical schools of first-century Judaism, but he emerged from his contact with God on the road to Damascus with a totally changed understanding of Christ and the world. In the early fifth century A.D., Augustine, Bishop of Hippo, enunciated a Christian worldview that shaped academic thinking for a thousand years. The ancient Graeco-Roman culture and consciousness were breaking down, and Augustine provided a Christian alternative. In the Reformation of the sixteenth century, something similar took place. Luther and Calvin provided a new insight into the way things should be looked at. While this did not produce as radical a change as it should have, it nevertheless provides an instance of Christian thinking as an alternative consciousness.

Consciousness as we are discussing it represents an expression of a worldview, and worldview is the foundation for philosophy. Worldviews are generally held below the level of consciousness. Everyone has one, but we are seldom aware of what ours is. In *The Transforming Vision* Walsh and Middleton illustrate this point by a comparison between the way babies are bathed in Japan and in Canada. In Japan the grandmother takes the baby in her arms into the big bathtub where there are lemons floating to keep the evil spirits away. It is a warm, comfortable experience for the child. In Canada the bathroom is prepared like an operating theater. The child is placed on the table, and washcloths and cotton-tipped toothpicks become the instruments of bathing. It is a much colder and potentially frightening process. The difference lies in worldviews. The Japanese worldview stresses community and group identification; the Canadian stresses rugged individualism.

When a worldview is brought to the conscious level and logically worked out into what we are calling a consciousness, or perspective, we have a philosophy. Many people, including many Christian school teachers, are leery of philosophy. As we will see in the next section, this may be an unjustifiable attitude, but it is there nonetheless. Many Christians, if pressed on the subject, would say that theology stands in for philosophy, and we do not need anything more.

The problem with this position is that theology is a reasoned exposition of what the Bible teaches about the history of salvation. It tells the story of creation, the fall, and God's program of restoration culminating in the death and resurrection of Christ and in His ultimate return. Systematic theology is a discipline like ethics, history, natural science, or mathematics. Its responsibility is not to describe the relationships among the sciences or the overall situation within which they exist. That is the domain of philosophy. While the two disciplines overlap in many ways, theology is not an adequate substitute for philosophy.

A Brief Outline of a Biblical Consciousness

If the goal of Christian schooling is the inculcation, by the gracious work of the Holy Spirit, of a biblical consciousness in the minds and hearts of the children of Christian parents, then it will be worthwhile to sketch very briefly here the major elements in such a consciousness. These will be developed in more detail in the next section, but a brief description here will help us to contrast it with both the modern and the postmodern consciousness.

The Christian mind begins with the recognition of the living God whose sovereignty extends over the entire reach of human consciousness and of reality itself. It believes in creation out of nothing as the true account of the origin of all things. It holds that the completed creation was good until it was marred by the deliberate sin of our first parents. It sees history as the story of fallible human efforts to manage God's creation, usually without any dependence on God. It perpetuates the early Hebrew idea that there is progress in history, reaching a climax in the incarnation of Christ and a conclusion in His ultimate personal return and the outward establishment of God's redeemed kingdom.

The Christian mind conceives of humans as creatures made in the likeness of God and capable of social relations with Him and each other, though such relations are now possible only through Christ's redemption. People are more than high-class animals; they are a mysterious combination of physical and nonphysical being that will continue to exist even after death stills the physical side.

Truth, from the biblical perspective, is not something forced out of reality by the scientific method, though science is recognized as a valid human responsibility that is one way of fulfilling God's commission of the first humans to develop the creation in which He had placed them. Neither is truth something that humans make. Truth actually a Person, Jesus Christ, who is pleased to reveal God to us through the various sides of the creation. There are not two kinds of truth, secular and spiritual, the former being accessible to any rational human and the latter being dependent on God's revelation in the Bible as opened up to people by the Holy Spirit. Thus the Christian mind denies the possibility of a distinction between secular and spiritual truth because it realizes that every created thing reveals God and thus cannot be isolated from "the facts."

Knowledge is not limited to what can be proven scientifically. Knowledge involves a willingness on the part of God to be known in and through the creation He upholds. There is more to knowledge than reason. God gives people an intuitive insight that is an essential element in every growth to new human knowledge. It is not only people who cannot be known unless they are willing to reveal themselves to the knower. The entire creation is genuinely knowable to us only as God shows Himself in it. What passes for knowledge in both modern and postmodern perspectives is really a hollow substitute for genuine knowledge.

Community, which is denied by postmodernism as an unreality, is found in its true form in the church of Jesus Christ, where His disciples are joined to Him and to one another by the indwelling of the Holy Spirit. The multicultural perspective of postmodernism results only in tribalism and in the contradiction of any commonality among the various peoples of the race. Christianity, on the other hand, celebrates the union of people from every tribe and tongue and nation, a union created by the common indwelling of the Holy Spirit and the infusion of Christ's love.

THE EDUCATIONAL IMPLICATIONS OF AN ALTERNATIVE CONSCIOUSNESS

The schooling that should take place in the light of an alternative Christian consciousness involves the same physical and nonphysical realities than are common to the secular school. What such schooling does is uncover a whole new set of meanings to the so-called "facts" of, for example, science. If there is a true and living God who is pleased, once we have returned to Him through Christ's redemption, to make Himself known to us through His ongoing upholding of the creation, then the facts are not neutral but motivational. They lead to deepening awe for the Creator, to thanks and love and service to Him. And so we begin to see the ordinary school subjects as a means by which our students can develop a friendship with God.

The contrast between the two kinds of schooling could hardly be greater. The irony of supposing that schooling which denies the reality of God and creation can satisfactorily meet the needs of the children of Christians is suddenly starkly evident.

In schooling from a biblical consciousness, the nature of the student is fundamentally different from what is assumed in either modern or postmodern consciousness. The child is a self-conscious individual capable of change that will lead to fellowship with God as well as with others. The child who is hampered by an innate and sinful insistence on independence from God can be transformed by the grace of God into a person who delights in knowing God and wills to please Him. Bearing God's image means being capable of responding to Him and responsible to do so. The work of the Christian school is to help the child realize that even ordinary studies, since they reveal God, are occasions for response to Him. As this reality is gently but repeatedly emphasized, the child begins to develop an alternative perspective, a biblical consciousness.

In a school of this sort, the separation of church and state in education is seen for the falsehood it is. No part of life is isolated from God. Life simply cannot be lived on two different levels. While it is true that our nation ought not to adopt a national church, the separation of religion from any aspect of life is simply impossible. What happens is that some aspect of the creation becomes supreme in education and life instead of the living God. This is idolatry, and idols make very poor masters. They promise freedom and deliver bondage.

The treatment of technology is another point at which the distinctiveness of a Christian school approach can be seen. The Christian school will instruct students in modern technology as fully as they are gifted to receive such instruction, but it will do so with a great deal of care to avoid idolatry. Veith insists that technology has a powerful place in the development of the postmodern mind. He cites Neil Postman, who says that today's information media deeply influence the way people think. Television is not interested in encouraging people to think. What is important is that they be entertained, have pleasant feelings, and in consequence purchase the items offered in the commercials. Veith comments:

> An individual television drama will usually have the coherence of a traditional plot line, though the story will be constantly interrupted by commercials. . . . But the way television presents *facts* in the news, talk shows, or docudramas exemplifies the tenets of postmodernism. Television blurs the line between truth and entertainment (*Postmodern Times,* p. 81).

That technology can assume a religious quality and hence be offensive to the Christian school perspective is evident in Postman's words:

> Important distinctions are made among the different meanings of "belief," but at some point it becomes far from asinine to speak of the god of technology—in the sense that people believe technology works, that they rely on it, that it makes promises, that they are bereft when denied access to it, that they are delighted when they are in its presence, that for most people it works in mysterious ways, that they condemn people who speak against it, that they stand in awe of it, and that, in the born-again mode, they will alter their lifestyles, their schedules, their habits and their relationships to accommodate it. If this be not a form of religious belief, what is? (*The End of Education,* p. 38)

Morality is another important area in which Christian schooling is different and demanding. When the rationalist worldview used science to strip facts of their meaning and make them strictly neutral, it removed the basis for teaching ethics or morality in the public school. The claim that it is impossible to get an "ought" from an "is" left both modernism and postmodernism without any adequate basis for teaching values or morality. The Christian school claim ought to be that since all "facts" are created and since the living God would not make something that is meaningless, then there is no area in the curriculum that does not call on students for a response. This means that so-called neutral facts lay obligations on us as we deal with them. Since our response is to the God who speaks in and through the "facts" of His creation, there is no basis for separating facts from values. Ethics runs all through the curriculum.

Before leaving this topic, it may be well to look for a moment at what Veith calls "evangelical postmodernism." He mentions Christian schools and colleges, Christian bookstores, and Christian music, and notes that the development of these is one way in which evangelicals reflect postmodern ideas. Postmodernism denies the possibility of a common humanity and advocates, instead, a new kind of tribalism. Today's distinct evangelical subculture illustrates this trend.

Veith goes on to comment that it is dangerous to object to this sort of evangelical subculture because without it we could very well see the disappearance of Christian culture altogether. "As postmodernist pressures intensify, having counter institutions already in place may prove invaluable for Christians to stage an effective resistance" (*Postmodern Times*, p. 210). His further comment is that the difficulty is not that Christians have their own cultural institutions but that they are so very similar to the cultural institutions of the surrounding world. "The mindset cultivated by the evangelical subculture often startlingly resembles that of secular postmodernism" (Ibid., pp. 210–211).

CONCLUSION

In response to the challenge of both modernism and postmodernism, our goal must be to inculcate another kind of consciousness among Christian school students in ways that will lead to a renewed Christian culture. The creation belongs to God. The goal of Christian schooling is an exploration of the creation that deepens a student's knowledge of God and his or her response in service to God. Children come to school with differing gifts, all of which are meant to contribute to the life of the Christian community. Children need to be helped to explore God's creation along the avenues for which their gifts qualify them. Those with academic gifts need to be challenged to unfold those gifts as fully as possible. But we must avoid the impression that academics represent the fullness of what school is all about. Knowing God in and through the creation is what is important, and students must be helped to explore the creation along the lines of their own gifts. Then the whole school community will enjoy the unfolding of all the gifts in a way that recognizes the value of each and begins to promotes the growth of Christian love to God and neighbor.

The remainder of the book will attempt to sketch, in abbreviated form, a description of a Christian worldview and philosophy as well as its implications for curriculum and for teaching methods. Before beginning that portion, however, there are two introductory aspects of Christian teaching and learning that will fit here better than anywhere else. When these are completed, the second main portion of the book will deal with a Christian philosophy. The third will address the content of a Christian curriculum, and the fourth, some specifically Christian methods in education.

NOTES

TEACHING AND LEARNING AND GOD

4

Teaching from the perspective of a Christian consciousness is like a diamond. If we turn it slightly, we can expose a facet that will repay our scrutiny. How are teaching and learning related to the active presence of God in our human minds and hearts? What alternative consciousness is possible for us? What renewal of the mind is needed?

The usual assumption is that ability to learn is a matter of one's genes, gifts, and childhood background. Some students learn easily; others don't. Some students have learning disabilities or are so traumatized by poor home conditions that learning is virtually impossible for them. Whatever the case, we unconsciously define learning in terms of book learning in school. But there are many other kinds of learning. Students who do poorly in academic studies often turn out to be exceptional business or sales people. Success in the arts is not tied to logical-linguistic learning, and artists and musicians are not necessarily outstanding in academics. Neither Albert Einstein nor Thomas Edison did well in school. Howard Gardner has identified at least seven kinds of intelligence, and he insists that they tell us children learn in different ways (*The Unschooled Mind*, Ch. 1). So we need to look closely at what we mean by learning, for learning takes many forms and is more than the acquisition of facts and skills.

Teaching isn't clear-cut either. It is treated today as a profession, and preparation for it is heavily laced with techniques, many of which are highly useful. But is teaching simply a professional skill? Parents, especially mothers, are said to teach children half of all they will ever know before the children are five years old. Craftsmen teach apprentices, and business people teach employees. So there are questions about how to define both teaching and learning. And we still haven't touched the question of whether and how God is involved.

When Paul says that "we live and move and have our being" in God (Acts 17:28), he implies that God is active in both teaching and learning. These activities do not happen simply because of "natural law" and human ingenuity. Teaching is something God does, either directly or through an agent. Learning is something enabled by God. Neither is solely secular in the modern sense of human experience that takes place without any touch with Him. Teaching should always seek, and learning should always involve, a response to God.

To begin with teaching, the Bible makes some startling pronouncements. God says to Moses:

SEE, I HAVE CALLED BY NAME BEZALEL, THE SON OF URI, THE SON OF HUR, OF THE TRIBE OF JUDAH. AND I HAVE FILLED HIM WITH THE SPIRIT OF GOD IN WISDOM, IN UNDERSTANDING, IN KNOWLEDGE, AND IN ALL KINDS OF CRAFTSMANSHIP, TO MAKE ARTISTIC DESIGNS FOR WORK IN GOLD, IN SILVER, AND IN BRONZE, AND IN THE CARVING OF WOOD, THAT HE MAY WORK IN ALL KINDS OF CRAFTSMANSHIP. AND BEHOLD, I MYSELF HAVE APPOINTED WITH HIM OHOLIAB, THE SON OF AHISAMACH, OF THE TRIBE OF DAN; AND IN THE HEARTS OF ALL WHO ARE SKILLFUL I HAVE PUT SKILL, THAT THEY MAY MAKE ALL THAT I HAVE COMMANDED YOU (EXODUS 31:2-6).

The assertion is clear. Whatever their parentage or their apprenticeships may have had to do with it, they were at the same time given their abilities by the Lord. The Spirit of God was the source of their artistic skills.

Was this a once-only instance of divine intervention in the interest of building the tabernacle in the desert? Our tendency to split life into the sacred and the secular encourages this interpretation, but this is one more place where we need an alternative consciousness. It is our sinful tendency to independence that moves us to exclude

God from His world as effectively as we can. However, human giftedness is always taught by the Spirit of God. "Behold, all souls are mine" (Ezekiel 18:4). He who creates them also gifts and teaches them. All teaching ultimately involves the action of God Himself. A growing realization of this will promote a closer relationship to Him in our lives.

Isaiah says about farming what Exodus says about craftsmanship:

GIVE EAR AND HEAR MY VOICE, LISTEN AND HEAR MY WORDS. DOES THE FARMER PLOW CONTINUALLY TO PLANT SEED? DOES HE CONTINUALLY TURN AND HARROW THE GROUND? DOES HE NOT LEVEL ITS SURFACE, AND SOW DILL AND SCATTER CUMMIN, AND PLANT WHEAT IN ROWS, BARLEY IN ITS PLACE AND RYE WITHIN ITS AREA? FOR HIS GOD INSTRUCTS AND TEACHES HIM PROPERLY, FOR DILL IS NOT THRESHED WITH A THRESHING SLEDGE, NOR IS A CARTWHEEL DRIVEN OVER CUMMIN: BUT DILL IS BEATEN OUT WITH A ROD, AND CUMMIN WITH A CLUB. GRAIN FOR BREAD IS CRUSHED, INDEED, HE DOES NOT CONTINUE TO THRESH IT FOREVER. BECAUSE THE WHEEL OF HIS CART AND HIS HORSES EVENTUALLY DAMAGE IT, HE DOES NOT THRESH IT LONGER. THIS ALSO COMES FROM THE LORD OF HOSTS, WHO HAS MADE HIS COUNSEL WONDERFUL AND HIS WISDOM GREAT (ISAIAH 28:23-29).

This does not mean that a farmer does not learn from his father or the county agent. But the God who uses seeds to create plants and parents to produce offspring is, in the final analysis, both the Creator and the Teacher.

Proverbs says the same thing about administrative skill, as wisdom says, "Counsel is mine and sound wisdom; I am understanding, power is mine. By me kings reign, and rulers decree justice. By me princes rule, and nobles, all who judge rightly" (Proverbs 8:14–16). Wisdom here is probably the second Person of the Trinity, who is both the Wisdom and the Word of God. The message is plain. God is not an absentee landlord or a watchmaker who leaves his product to tick away on its own. He is mysteriously but intimately involved in the skills of management and ruling.

When Jesus called His twelve apostles to prepare them for being the foundation stones of His church, He invited them into a three-year program of schooling in which they lived and worked with Him, and He taught them. In a more general invitation He calls those who labor and are heavy laden to come to Him, and to learn of Him (Matthew 11:28–30). But He is the one "in whom are hid all the treasures of wisdom and knowledge" (Colossians 2:3). Even though we do not recognize or believe it, the imparting of any and all learning is related to Christ. Teaching is His work. Paul's prayer for the Colossians was that "you may be filled with the knowledge of His will in all spiritual wisdom and understanding, so that you may walk in a manner worthy of the Lord, to please Him in all respects, bearing fruit in every good work and increasing in the knowledge of God" (Colossians 1:9–10).

To suppose that these and similar passages can be limited to so-called "spiritual" things is to perpetuate the idolatrous dualism that is rampant in the church today and that cuts the nerve of her effectiveness in a neo-pagan world. All that exists goes on existing only at the bidding of the Word of the living God. He does not maintain the world just because He happened to make it. He likes it, and He maintains it to reveal Himself and to provide humans, who bear His likeness, with a medium for responding in worship and service to Him. All teaching, in the final analysis, is His work. A growing awareness of that reality produces in our hearts a deepening awe of and longing for God. It is part of the alternative consciousness we so deeply need to cultivate today.

Does this mean that God teaches only Christians and not others? Surely not. Paul was speaking to pagan Greeks in the Areopagus when he said, "In Him we live and move and exist." When Solomon wanted to build the temple of Jehovah, he asked Huram, king of Tyre, to send him the needed timber because the Tyrians knew how to cut lumber better than the Israelites did. Huram also sent Huram-abi, the son of a Danite woman and a Tyrian father, to do the bronze casting and other craft works needed. It was not only to Jewish farmers that God taught the skills of raising crops, nor was it only to Israelites that the wisdom to govern was granted from the Lord.

Perhaps our evangelical tendency to think of ourselves as God's favorites and to minimize His relationship to other humans partakes more of the spirit of Jonah's enmity for the Ninevites than it does of God's love for the world. It is true that non-Christians fail to recognize the source of their gifts. Christians often do too. That doesn't negate the character of the giftedness God provides to His human creatures. It does make the failure to recognize the gifts a heavier burden on our souls. One of the most shocking realizations on the day of judgment will probably be the discovery that the mental ability that enabled one to excel in the academic, political, professional, or business world was an ongoing gift of God. Sin leads us to suppress this knowledge (Romans 1:18). Teaching, then, is always the work of God, whether it is done directly or through the medium of a human teacher.

If teaching is basically the work of God, does learning also always involve Him? Does the Bible speak to this question? Everyone knows that children use their mental shovels to scoop up learning with an eagerness that outshines almost any adult's and that, unhappily, seems to deteriorate once they get into school. In Matthew 18, in His sermon on relations within the kingdom—a sermon of which two-thirds deals with children—Jesus commands His disciples not to stumble or despise children. He underlines the latter prohibition with three powerful reasons. The children have angels who are deeply and constantly concerned with their welfare. Those angels have immediate and continual access to the presence of the Father. So both the Father and the angels are concerned for the children. Thirdly, the Shepherd of the sheep is equally concerned. The learning they do as they gobble up their world and bond to their parents is one which is enabled by the Lord's own interest in them. Learning is not automatic or mechanical in human children. It is a gift very graciously given to almost every child who is born.

This conclusion is fully supported by other Scriptures. Jesus calls people to take His yoke upon them and learn of Him (Matthew 11:29). In His high priestly prayer, Jesus said, "And this is eternal life, that they may know Thee, the only true God, and Jesus Christ whom Thou hast sent" (John 17:3). Properly knowing anything in the creation ultimately involves knowing the Creator. In our sinfulness we vigorously suppress this truth, but that does not change it. Life does not come apart into an upper, spiritual, and a lower, natural level. It is not a double-decker dome-car on the railway line to heaven. Life is whole. Human existence is integral. We are not rational souls imprisoned in animal bodies to be set free at death from physical confinement. We are whole beings, and every aspect of our lives is immediately and directly involved with the living God who created and sustains us.

All true learning, then, is not only enabled by God; it is at the same time a learning to know God. We learn to know God through the Bible and through the Person of Jesus Christ. Christians often forget, however, that there is a third way in which God makes Himself known to us.

FOR SINCE THE CREATION OF THE WORLD HIS INVISIBLE ATTRIBUTES, HIS ETERNAL POWER AND DIVINE NATURE, *HAVE BEEN CLEARLY SEEN, BEING UNDERSTOOD THROUGH WHAT HAS BEEN MADE,* SO THAT THEY ARE WITHOUT EXCUSE (ROMANS 1:20, ITALICS ADDED).

It is through the quickening power of the Holy Spirit that we can come to know God through the Bible and its message of the saving lordship of Jesus Christ. But it brings no honor to the Holy Spirit if we then proceed to treat the ordinary school studies, which are derived totally from the created world, as if they had nothing to do with God. They are laden with meaning because they are all part of God's way of giving Himself to us, of making Himself known to us. We refuse our birthright and willfully go about as paupers if we insist on regarding ordinary things as unholy. Later we will discuss the ways in which the school subjects reveal the Lord; for now it is enough to assert that we can know Him in and through them.

This is such a radical idea that it may need more explanation and defense. Is it really possible to grow in the knowledge of God through the study of His creation, which provides the material for the school curriculum? Think first of Adam in the Garden of Eden and of God's asking him to name the animals. Of this incident Alexander Schmemann says:

NOW, IN THE BIBLE A NAME IS INFINITELY MORE THAN A MEANS TO DISTINGUISH ONE THING FROM ANOTHER. IT REVEALS THE VERY ESSENCE OF A THING, OR RATHER ITS ESSENCE AS GOD'S GIFT. TO NAME A THING IS TO MANIFEST THE MEANING AND VALUE GOD GAVE IT, TO KNOW IT AS COMING FROM GOD AND TO KNOW ITS PLACE AND FUNCTION WITHIN THE COSMOS CREATED BY GOD.

TO NAME A THING, IN OTHER WORDS, IS TO BLESS GOD FOR IT AND IN IT. AND IN THE BIBLE TO BLESS GOD IS NOT A "RELIGIOUS" OR A "CULTIC" ACT, BUT THE VERY *WAY OF LIFE.* GOD BLESSED THE WORLD, BLESSED MAN, BLESSED THE SEVENTH DAY (THAT IS, TIME), AND THIS MEANS THAT HE FILLED ALL THAT EXISTS WITH HIS LOVE AND GOODNESS, MADE ALL THIS "VERY GOOD." SO THE ONLY *NATURAL* (AND NOT "SUPERNATURAL") REACTION OF MAN, TO WHOM GOD GAVE THIS BLESSED AND SANCTIFIED WORLD, IS TO BLESS GOD IN RETURN, TO THANK HIM, TO *SEE* THE WORLD AS GOD SEES IT, AND—IN THIS ACT OF GRATITUDE AND ADORATION—TO KNOW, NAME, AND POSSESS THE WORLD. ALL RATIONAL, SPIRITUAL, AND OTHER QUALITIES OF MAN, DISTINGUISHING HIM FROM OTHER CREATURES, HAVE THEIR FOCUS AND ULTIMATE FULFILLMENT IN THIS CAPACITY TO BLESS GOD, TO KNOW, SO TO SPEAK, THE MEANING OF THE THIRST AND HUNGER THAT CONSTITUTES HIS LIFE (*FOR THE LIFE OF THE WORLD,* P. 15).

An apt description of the task of the school is that the Christian school's business is to teach children to name the animals—that is, to lead them to know God in and through His creation. This does not mean that the schools should impart some new mystical theological concepts about God. Nor does it mean that they lay primary emphasis on morality in connection with each subject, although there is an ethical aspect to the study of each. That ethical aspect should be presented at appropriate times, but it is not the primary concept in view here. To know God means to be in a relationship to Him in which we are penitent, believing, and obedient. It means that God comes to dwell with us in new and wonderful ways. The assertion here is that the study of the created world can— and is meant to—contribute directly and powerfully to a deepened relationship to Him.

The Bible indicates that nothing is more important than the knowledge of God. "And this is eternal life, that they may know thee, the only true God, and Jesus Christ whom Thou hast sent" (John 17:3). John Calvin began his *Institutes of the Christian Religion* with the assertion that the two most important kinds of knowledge in the world are the knowledge of God and the knowledge of ourselves. But, he continued, these two kinds of knowledge are so closely connected that it is difficult to know which one comes first. In other words, we cannot know who we are unless we know God; if we know God, we will know who we are. This means that the study of psychology is inseparable from the knowledge of God. However, humans are the crown of God's creation, and what is true of us as creatures is also true of the rest of creation. It also is a channel through which we can know and serve God. If we fail to use it in this way, we have missed its main point.

Does it burden the study of ordinary subjects to attach this sort of spiritual significance to them? Does this cast a somber pall over the school studies? Far from it! It opens a door in the wall and lets the light begin to shine in! To see ordinary facts as carriers of meaning is to see them irradiated with holy light and transformed into soul-satisfying food for the heart. The reason we hesitate is that we are thinking within modernity's false fields of perception. We are thinking with the mind of the flesh and not that of the Spirit. As we begin to see learning in its true light, it does not lose interest; it gains it. Studies become Jacob's ladder with a constant two-way concourse of revelation and response. They become part of the treasure in heaven on which we are to set our hearts.

The most serious heresy during the first two centuries of the Christian church was gnosticism. One of its worst features was its denigration of the creation. The gnostics regarded the physical world as dirty and removed it, in their thinking, as far as possible from contact with God. Today, in a somewhat altered form, we are seeing a revival of that heresy. In the introduction to Paul Brand and Philip Yancey's *Fearfully and Wonderfully Made*, Yancey quotes G. K. Chesterton's comment that in the Middle Ages Christians could not see nature as part of God's self-revelation because nature was stained with pagan religions and mythologies. So Christians had to go into the desert where there were no flowers and into caves where there were no stars to get in touch with God. Nature had been severed from contact with God. Yancey continues:

TODAY A SIMILAR PROCESS IS TAKING PLACE. THE CREATED WORLD HAS LOST ITS SACREDNESS. CHRISTIANS HAVE ABANDONED IT, NOT TO PAGANISM, BUT TO PHYSICS, GEOLOGY, BIOLOGY, AND CHEMISTRY. WE TOO HAVE CLEAVED NATURE FROM THE SUPERNATURAL (P. 10).

What all this means is that none of us could teach or learn anything if God were not immediately involved in the process at each moment. We live and move and have our being in Him. If He were to withdraw His Word for one instant we would simply cease to exist. Eugene Peterson puts it this way:

THE WORD THAT GOD SPEAKS ORIGINATES, INITIATES, SHAPES, PROVIDES, ORDERS, COMMANDS, AND BLESSES.

GOD'S WORD IS THE CREATIVE MEANS BY WHICH EVERYTHING COMES INTO EXISTENCE. THE WORD OF GOD CONSTITUTES THE TOTAL REALITY IN WHICH WE FIND OURSELVES. EVERYTHING WE SEE AND FEEL AND DEAL WITH—SEA AND SKY, CODFISH AND WARBLERS, SYCAMORES AND CARROTS—ORIGINATES BY MEANS OF THIS WORD. EVERYTHING, ABSOLUTELY EVERYTHING, WAS *SPOKEN* INTO BEING (*WORKING THE ANGLES*, P. 33).

The implications for Christian schooling are far-reaching, for both the students and their teacher. For the students it means that the study of the various subjects and skills can open out into an experience of communion and fellowship with Him and with each other. The possibility is breathtaking, almost too good to be true. It could mean a new experience of the presence and working of the Holy Spirit. It would involve love, joy, peace, and mutual servanthood and upbuilding. It would introduce a new experience of thankfulness into the classroom. With that would come a new experience of prayer and praise as part of ordinary daily life as much as of specifically religious practices.

To those of us who have been involved in the nitty-gritty of the average classroom, this sounds too ideal to be possible. It is not something that can be brought about through a new teaching technique. It will not happen in one day, one week, or even one year. Its accomplishment will be the quiet work of the Holy Spirit and will come gradually as teacher and students learn to pray and work together in new ways. It will not mean abandoning, in any measure, the goal of the fullest evocation of our students' gifts, though it will doubtless broaden the kinds of learning that take place in the classroom. It will not be a self-conscious process of developing a spirituality in which we can take pride. It will not involve a mechanical and manipulative alteration of classroom processes. Like Jesus' parables, it will be like an attractive series of stories that contain hints, for those students who are moved to learn more, of how to go further in relating to God. It will certainly make prayer and mutual helpfulness more than formal and occasional exercises in the classroom.

The implications for the teacher are equally far-reaching. She cannot begin to develop this sort of classroom unless she herself has grown to know God in an intimate, trustful, and obedient fashion. If the Lord's part in teaching and learning are not home ground for her, she will not be successful in leading students to see them that way. It will make teaching a prophetic ministry in which the weakness of the human teacher will become repeatedly the contact point through which the living God can make His strength perfect. It will mean she will have to become a person of prayer and faith more than ever before. But she will be able to, because the promise of God's strength always accompanies His command to serve in His appointed way.

If the part that God plays in human teaching and learning is to be realized, we will have to give up our convenient habit of splitting the study of so-called secular subjects away from communion with the living God. We will have to seek the renewal, by the transforming of our minds, that will give us entrance into the rich excitement of learning in the presence and with the blessing of the Lord himself. Then we can begin to bear more effective witness to a world that has shut God out of its thoughts. We have lived long enough in a compromising cooperation, in thought and action, with that world. We need to cultivate an alternative consciousness.

NOTES

PRAISE AND THANKSGIVING

5

We have been considering what might be called some foundational facets in the diamond of Christian schooling. These have included a look at the modern consciousness and the postmodern consciousness and how they contrast with a biblical Christian consciousness. Then we considered the idea that both teaching and learning are dependent directly on the living God, whether in Christians or in others. Accustomed as we are to thinking in a thoroughly secularized culture and to expecting the solutions to our educational problems to depend on scientific and technological breakthroughs, the chapters above may well have seemed overly idealistic. Can the Christian school become this different from the secular one and still fit its graduates to function in today's culture? The answer to that question will depend directly on the vision of Christian education that is developed in the faculty, administration, and constituency of any given school. Moses, Daniel, and Paul all knew the intellectual perspective of their times at what we would now call a university level, yet they also knew a great deal about the world that their contemporaries did not know. A Christian school can be very different from its secular counterparts and yet fit its students to contribute to both church and culture. It is a matter of vision. Before leaving this section, however, it will be worth our while to consider one further foundational facet.

In the light of the paragraph above, it will not seem surprising if this further facet of Christian schooling sounds farfetched and improbable. The contention is that prayer and thanksgiving should come to be seen as serious and valuable work in the school, perhaps the most important and God-pleasing of all the school's activities. This does not mean adding a new class or unit to the curriculum. It will not change the studies to be pursued as much as it will undergird them with a new foundation and infuse them with a new spirit. This can happen only as the Holy Spirit works in the hearts of teachers and students to develop an alternative consciousness.

Can praise be work? Preposterous! Biblical praise is identified with spiritual things. It involves prayer, singing, meditation, and perhaps a message, but it would seem to be at the other end of the ski run from work. Work is much lower on the scale. It is grubby, leaving grime under the fingernails. Or it is intellectual, involving stressful thinking without any guarantee of success. Work is certainly a far cry from the praise of God.

Or is it? The angels in the temple at the time of Isaiah's ordination to prophetic ministry would have been incensed if you had told them they should get busy and do something worthwhile. You might well have found yourself propelled roughly into the next county by the brush of an angel's wing. Each angel had six wings: "with two he covered his face, and with two he covered his feet, and with two he flew. And one called out to another and said, 'Holy, Holy, Holy, is the Lord of hosts, The whole earth is full of His glory' " (Isaiah 6:2–3). They were completely absorbed in the work of worshiping and praising God. The mystery of God's being is unsearchable even to the angels. No creature will ever be able to plumb the depths of His essence. At the same time, no work is so well expended or so richly rewarded as the effort to know, serve, praise, and thank the living God.

WHAT IS WORK?

To the modern secular mind, work has nothing to do with spirituality, although religious people obviously do engage in it. To the modern person work is what we do during the week so that we can relax and have pleasure on the weekend. Pleasure is the real goal of life, and work is the way to achieve it. Possessions are also of the highest importance to people today, and work is the way to increase our possessions. Power, over nature and over people, is another primary modern goal, and work is the way to increase our power. But all this has nothing to do with God or His praise— hence the urgent need for Christians to develop a new way of perceiving the world and their work. The mind of the flesh finds it impossible to conceive of praise as work that has infinite value and unending reward. This is why non-Christians often make fun of heaven as a place where people just sing and play harps. That prospect isn't appealing to the mind that thinks of work only as the key to pleasure, possessions, and power. To that mind God isn't involved in those transactions at all. But Christians are called to have the mind of the Spirit, under the influence of which, work and praise appear in a very different light.

Our problem in identifying work with praise is that the concept of work has become so thoroughly secularized that we have to strain to connect it with anything spiritual. This shows the extreme dualism of modern Christian thinking. The Bible does not have this problem. Work was ordained for humans before the fall in the Garden, so it is not the result of sin, even though sin has complicated it endlessly. The human work of procreation and stewardship was itself a form of worship and service to God (Genesis 1:26–28). The New Testament parallels this concept in Romans 12:1–2: "I urge you, therefore, brethren, by the mercies of God, to present your bodies a living and holy sacrifice, acceptable to God, which is your spiritual service of worship." It is in our bodies that we do our work. Clearly, then, the work our bodies do (including our brains) is to be in the worship and thus the praise of God. In this light it is not hard to see why both the Psalms and the book of Revelation make so much of the redeemed human activity of praising God. The Westminster Catechism, one of the great products of the Reformation, begins with the question, "What is the chief end of man?" The answer is, "Man's chief end is to glorify God and to enjoy Him forever." It appears, then, that we need to reverse the concept that puts praise and work at opposite ends of the spectrum. Praise is work, and the best work is praise!

The Bible is not short on support for this alternative view of work. As noted above, the angels in Isaiah 6 were absorbed and fulfilled in their work of praising God. Angels did it again in Luke 2:13–14, where we read, "And suddenly there appeared with the angel a multitude of the heavenly host praising God, and saying, 'Glory to God in the highest, and on earth peace among men with whom He is pleased.'" Jesus did not avoid work; it sustained him. "Jesus said to them, 'My food is to do the will of Him who sent Me and to accomplish His work'" (John 4:34). "My Father is working until now, and I Myself am working" (John 5:17). He also laid upon His disciples the necessity of working. "We must work the works of Him who sent Me, as long as it is day; night is coming, when no man can work" (John 9:4). The idea recurs: "Work out your salvation with fear and trembling; for it is God who is at work in you, both to will and to work for His good pleasure" (Philippians 2:12–13), and again: "And for this purpose also I labor, striving according to His power, which mightily works within me" (Colossians 1:29). These injunctions are not limited to what might be called "spiritual" work: "Whether, then, you eat or drink or whatever you do, do all to the glory of God" (1 Corinthians 10:31); "And whatever you do in word or deed, do all in the name of the Lord Jesus, giving thanks through Him to God the Father" (Colossians 3:17). As we come to realize that dividing our works between the secular and the sacred is contrary to the teaching of Scripture, it becomes apparent that a Christian and a secular definition of work are poles apart.

WHAT IS THE VALUE OF WORK?

To modern people, work is often of negative rather than positive value. Many people do not like the work they do to make a living. Even when they see it as worthwhile, their appreciation goes no further than the belief that their self-worth is enhanced or defined by their work. This may explain a comment that a service station owner made to me. He said he and his wife had decided to do some traveling and other non-work-related activities now rather than after retirement. The reason he gave was that so many of his customers died very soon after they retired. If our work is all that supports our self-concept, then ceasing work may come near to ending life. It takes more than work to make life worth living.

For a Christian, work is related to self-identity also, but in a different way. The Christian's identity is found in bearing the image of God. As she does her work, whatever it is, in the loving service of God, she becomes identified with the God whose image she bears. She hears His, " Well done, thou good and faithful servant," and she is rewarded with the "eternal weight of glory which is far beyond all comparison" (2 Corinthians 4:17). Work is valuable to the Christian because the stewardly exploration and management of the creation leads to growth in the likeness of God. It is thus a form of praise and worship of the highest order.

Thomas Merton captures the difference between the two kinds of work in his discussion of the false self and the true self. He suggests that the false self thinks its drives and desires are the source of its reality. It thereby becomes the slave of those drives and desires. Then the more it can fulfill its felt needs, the more it thinks of itself as mature. He goes on to say that the false self is driven by its fear of death and its need to affirm itself. The result is that it tries to dominate or placate every person or thing it encounters, and that this sort of conduct is reflected in the characteristics of society. Merton's concept of the true self is quite different. It does not have to dominate in order to be someone. It is quite active, but its activity differs from that of the false self:

THE DIFFERENCE IS THAT ITS DOING IS MOTIVATED BY LOVE. . . . THEREFORE . . : THE LIFE OF THE TRUE SELF IS FREE . . . THE TRUE SELF DOES NOT ASSERT ITSELF OVER AND AGAINST THE WORLD AS OBJECT, NOR DOES IT SEEK TO POSSESS THE WORLD . . . IT APPREHENDS THE WORLD MORE AS A LIVING EXPRESSION OF BEING, OF LOVE, OF GOD (THOMAS DEL PRETE, THOMAS MERTON AND THE EDUCATION OF THE WHOLE PERSON, PP. 325 FF.).

What Merton has grasped here is a definition of selfhood that conforms to the great laws of love to God and neighbor. It is a concept radically at odds with the individualistic, consumer-oriented quality of personhood in modern Western culture. It suggests the need for an alternative consciousness.

Merton applies his distinction between the false and the true self to education by asserting that education ought to contribute to the development of true human selfhood. But it cannot do this if it merely provides factual knowledge. Such knowledge does not call on its recipient for any personal involvement. It is cold and lifeless. It does not lead to realizing one's true selfhood. That only happens as the self meets its life-giving source, the Creator, who has revealed Himself in the creation. "True self-realization is a creative, life-affirming event in which the self and its life-giving source meet"(Ibid., p. 41). What Merton is saying fits well with Calvin's statement that the two most important kinds of knowledge are the knowledge of God and of oneself, and that the two kinds are so closely related that it is hard to tell which comes first. The problem is that we have not thought of schooling as primarily involved in the development of true self-knowledge. This is because we have not thought of school as a place where we are meant to come face to face with the living God in and through His creation and so grow in His likeness. To achieve the kind of Christian schooling that leads to Merton's objective of self-discovery or self-realization, praise and thanksgiving will need to become part of the school experience.

PRAISE, THANKSGIVING, AND PRAYER.

Before discussing praise and prayer separately as work, it may be well to consider their mutual incorporation in prayer. To do so, we may need to rethink our concept of prayer. Our most common tendency is to think of it as a shopping list with which we come to God for the fulfillment of our perceived needs. This is petitionary prayer. But there are other kinds as well. Prayer can be repentance, intercession, worship and adoration, an expression of faith, or even meditation. Prayer at its best is actually a way of life. Henri Nouwen, in *Reaching Out*, describes the entrance into the Christian life in its relation to God as a move from illusion to prayer (pp. 80 ff.). Much of human life lived apart from the guidance and power of the Holy Spirit is spent in illusory thinking about the past, the future, and even the present. When we come into redeemed fellowship with God, life becomes an ongoing friendship with Him, a friendship that fulfills the New Testament injunction to pray without ceasing. This doesn't mean we are always saying prayers; it means that life is lifted into communion with God. Prayer can take place without verbal expression. Praise and thanksgiving are important elements in this sort of prayer life.

C. S. Lewis provides an illustration of prayer in this mode. Discussing prayer as worship or adoration, he mentions his friend's suggestion, that such praying should begin where one is. His friend was referring to the pleasure of washing his sweaty hands and face in a little waterfall. Lewis continues:

THAT CUSHIONY MOSS, THAT COLDNESS AND SOUND AND DANC-
ING LIGHT WERE NO DOUBT VERY MINOR BLESSINGS COMPARED
WITH 'THE MEANS OF GRACE AND THE HOPE OF GLORY.' BUT THEN
THEY WERE MANIFEST. SO FAR AS THEY WERE CONCERNED, SIGHT
HAD REPLACED FAITH. THEY WERE NOT THE HOPE OF GLORY,
THEY WERE AN EXPOSITION OF THE GLORY ITSELF.

YET YOU WERE NOT—OR SO IT SEEMED TO ME—TELLING ME
THAT "NATURE," OR "THE BEAUTIES OF NATURE," MANIFEST THE
GLORY. NO SUCH ABSTRACTION AS "NATURE" COMES INTO IT. I
WAS LEARNING THE FAR MORE SECRET DOCTRINE THAT *PLEA-
SURES* ARE SHAFTS OF THE GLORY AS IT STRIKES OUR SENSIBIL-
ITY. AS IT IMPINGES ON OUR WILL OR OUR UNDERSTANDING, WE
GIVE IT DIFFERENT NAMES—GOODNESS OR TRUTH OR THE LIKE.
BUT ITS FLASH UPON OUR SENSES AND MOOD IS PLEASURE (*LETTERS
TO MALCOLM, CHIEFLY ON PRAYER*, P. 90).

Lewis continues his discussion by telling how he now
tries to make *every* pleasure into a channel of adoration.
He doesn't mean simply by giving thanks for the experience, but something more. He describes the way in which
praise and thanksgiving can become a form of prayer without our even saying words to express them:

IT IS POSSIBLE TO "READ" AS WELL AS TO "HAVE" A PLEASURE.
OR NOT EVEN "AS WELL AS." THE DISTINCTION OUGHT TO BECOME,
AND SOMETIMES IS, IMPOSSIBLE; TO RECEIVE IT AND TO RECOGNIZE ITS
DIVINE SOURCE ARE A SINGLE EXPERIENCE. THIS HEAVENLY FRUIT IS
INSTANTLY REDOLENT OF THE ORCHARD WHERE IT GREW. THIS SWEET
AIR WHISPERS OF THE COUNTRY FROM WHENCE IT BLOWS. IT IS A
MESSAGE. WE KNOW WE ARE BEING TOUCHED BY A FINGER OF THAT
RIGHT HAND AT WHICH THERE ARE PLEASURES FOR EVERMORE. THERE
NEED BE NO QUESTION OF THANKS OR PRAISE AS A SEPARATE EVENT,
SOMETHING DONE AFTERWARDS. TO EXPERIENCE THE TINY THEOPHANY
IS ITSELF TO ADORE (IBID., P. 91).

CAN WORK BE PRAISE, AND PRAISE WORK?

The answer is a resounding yes! It takes, however, a
transformed perspective to appreciate this fact. As long

as we think of work in secular terms, the curse of sin is bound to render it tiring at best and meaningless at worst. It is only in the light of a passage such as the following that the identification of work with praise begins to make sense for us: "And whatever you do in word or deed, do all in the name of the Lord Jesus, giving thanks through Him to the Father" (Colossians 3:17). Christ identified His work with His Father's, and all He did was to the praise of His Father (John 5:17). We are to do the same. If everything we do is done in the name (i.e., the character, the identity) of the Lord Jesus Christ, then it will assuredly be a form of praise to God, of worship directed to Him.

In fact, praise is the highest form work can take. Modern people speak of their work as their vocation, the way they earn their living. But the root of the word *vocation* is the Latin word for *calling*. Our calling is to praise God with our whole being. Praise is not merely a matter of bowed head and bent knees. It is as much works as words. It is the real goal of human life. It is not wearying but invigorating. However, we will not see it this way until we have some experience of the transformation that comes with the renewing of the mind spoken of in Romans 12:1–2. The work of praise is part of eternal life. It does not cease with physical death but goes on forever. There is no exhausting the knowledge of God that lies out there ahead of us. As the early church fathers pointed out, we cannot know God in His essence; we know Him in His actions. And we will be able to go on learning more of Him through all eternity without ever knowing Him in the fulness of His essence.

THANKSGIVING AS WORK

Psalm 100:4–5 links praise and thanksgiving: "Enter into His gates with thanksgiving, and His courts with praise. Give thanks to Him; bless His name. For the Lord is good; His lovingkindness is everlasting, and His faithfulness to all generations."

Hebrews 13:15–16 parallels the psalm: "Through Him then, let us continually offer up a sacrifice of praise to God, that is, the fruit of lips that give thanks to His name. And do not neglect doing good and sharing; for with such sacrifices God is pleased."

The crucial importance of thanksgiving is shown in the first chapter of Romans. There the appalling catalog of loosened sinfulness is preceded by these words, "For even though they knew God, they did not honor Him as God, or give thanks; but they became futile in their speculations and their foolish heart was darkened." Thanklessness was like the first break in a snow crown, which precipitates a vast avalanche down the side of the mountain. The urgency of thankfulness is reiterated: "Be anxious for nothing, but in everything by prayer and supplication with thanksgiving let your requests be made known to God. And the peace of God, which surpasses all comprehension, shall guard your hearts and your minds in Christ Jesus" (Philippians 4:6–7). It is emphasized again: "As you therefore have received Christ Jesus the Lord, so walk in Him, having been firmly rooted and now being built up in Him and established in your faith, just as you were instructed, and overflowing with gratitude" (Colossians 2:6–7). Thankfulness is a vital component of Christian life and work.

How This Relates to Christian Schools

The curriculum of the Christian school, and of the secular school as well, for that matter, is made up entirely of the creation. But God did not breathe the creation into being in His sleep or make it with no discernible purpose. The Bible tells us that He made it for the specific purpose of revealing Himself to us (Romans 1:20; Psalm 8:1; Psalm 19:1–6; Job 42:5–6). It also tells us that He formed it, and continues to form it, so that it can be a channel for our loving service to Him and our communion with Him. Both these purposes have been largely forgotten in the church today. Hence work has become something secular for us.

If the creation reveals God and is a channel for our response to Him, how can our research into it and our use of it be anything else than a way of glorifying, praising, and thanking Him? Yet research and use sound strangely like knowledge and skills. These are at the heart of education in anyone's terms. If the knowledge of God is eternal life (John 17:3), and the Christian school is concerned with the creation that reveals Him, then the work of studying, when guided by the Holy Spirit, cannot but turn into worship, service, and praise to God. We can begin here in the classroom an endeavor that will go on into the world to come. Then the praise that is said to be so much a part of the life to come will begin to find its way back into the experience of the Christian schoolroom today. This puts a very high value indeed on what often seems the ordinary work of learning the *a-b-c*'s. And it calls for a level of knowing God and walking with Him that demands exemplary Christian teachers. Students will learn to serve, worship, and praise God in their everyday schoolwork when they are led by teachers who have learned to do that themselves. Then the Christian school will become what it is meant to be, and its graduates will be prepared to witness actively in the world with their lives and words. The students' work of praising God in their studies will turn those studies from drudgery into delight. This is an important part of the vision we need for genuine Christian schools.

NOTES

PART II

A
BASIC
CHRISTIAN
PHILOSOPHY

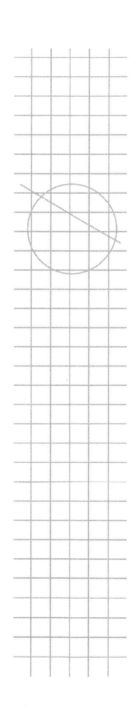

A CHRISTIAN PHILOSOPHY? 6

Some years ago my wife and I watched with apprehension the early stages of the construction of a vacation cabin. Located on a hillside and lacking a basement, it was supported on a number of posts and beams. The cross-bracing was minimal, and the whole effort looked distinctly risky. Evidently the county building inspector thought so too, for in a short time a red "Stop Work" sign was posted on the building. Ultimately the whole structure was removed and replaced by a prefabricated building that satisfied the building code.

Foundations are important in building projects, whether they are made of lumber or of intangible ideas. This is as true in Christian schooling as it is in any other endeavor. The question that immediately rises is, What sort of foundation is needed for a school?

The answer, most simply stated, is a worldview. Questions of curriculum selection and teaching methods, personnel and administrative decisions, the control and direction of the endeavor—all will be answered on the basis of the founders' worldview.

However, worldview is seldom thought of as important in connection with school. This is because worldview, in any society, is usually held unconsciously. It is assumed that everyone understands, in a given place and historical period, how to do the basic things that keep society going. Christians today assume they understand how to start and maintain a Christian school. They seldom realize how many of their ideas on the subject are derived from modern society and not from the Bible. Yet worldview influences every development in a community. We noted earlier the difference between the Japanese and the Canadian ways of bathing a baby, and we saw that this difference reflects differing worldviews in the two societies. The same authors continue by pointing out differences in the way land ownership is viewed by the northern Canadian Indians and the southern Canadian white population. Southern Canadians, like most of us in the United States, treat land ownership as a matter of private and personal possession, but the Indians have a totally different outlook. They do not believe in privately possessing land or in selling it. "The land is our mother. You wouldn't sell your mother, would you?" Worldview is pervasive and powerful.

Since worldview is usually held below the level of consciousness, however, it would be more precise to suggest that the foundation of a Christian schooling project should be a Christian philosophy. When an underlying worldview is brought up into the daylight of consciousness and worked out logically into a set of concepts, the result is a philosophy. We will look later at the question of whether the search for a Christian philosophy can be defended biblically, but let us tentatively adopt the position that a Christian philosophy can be developed and can provide a basis for working out the details of a Christian educational program. First, however, we need to look at the historical background of twentieth-century Western philosophy and the problems Christian worldview has undergone during that history.

THE LOSS OF A CHRISTIAN WORLDVIEW

Ever since the Tower of Babel incident, God has been unwilling to allow humans to put together a unified view of life and the world unless they will listen to His Word. The Greeks, for example, could not get their worldview unified. They had a two-level view of reality. They believed that the physical world was not nearly as important as the unseen world of ideas that lay behind it. Physical things such as trees and houses, chairs and beds, even human bodies, were relatively insignificant because they were not permanent. Behind them lay a realm of eternal ideas of which the physical things were merely temporary embodiments. This led the Greeks to the conclusion that human reason was the divine element in people and that the human mind was imprisoned in the physical body. This dualistic approach to reality is known as the Form/Matter viewpoint. It arose from two religions in ancient Greece, the dark nature religion of the Earth Mother and the more idealistic religion of the Olympian gods. The nature religion found expression in the Matter side of the dualistic approach. The human body stands on top of "Mother Nature" and is, at death, pulled back into it. (It isn't very nice, after all, to stand on your mother.) The eternal idea side was allied to the Form side of the dualistic viewpoint. The Greeks could never discover how to relate their two levels of reality effectively. They thought the body was composed of square atoms, and the soul, or reason, of round atoms. When a person died, the square atoms separated at the joints, and the round atoms escaped into the realm of the eternal ideas, whereas the body went back to the earth from which it had come. The Greeks never achieved a unified concept of total reality.

The Hebrews, of course, had an entirely different perspective. They believed in a living God who was active in, but also transcendent over, the world of ordinary things. They believed that humans had sinned against God but that God was intent on a program of redemption for His creation. With the life, death, and resurrection of Jesus, the components of the Christian worldview—creation, fall, and redemption—were complete and available for the New Testament church to recognize and work out into an elaborated view—a philosophy.

The difficulty was that for the first three centuries the church was fighting for its life, on the one hand against the heresy of gnosticism and on the other against the religion of the Roman Empire. At first the number of educated Christians was small, but as academics came to Christ, they tended to think in terms of the prevailing Greek philosophies and to attempt to reconcile those philosophies with the revelation contained in the Bible. Saint Augustine, for instance, great church father that he was, was fairly deeply influenced by the theories of Plato, which came to him through the writings of Plotinus. Thus Augustine developed a derogatory view of the body and physical labor and thought of sexual relations as less than pious.

As the centuries passed, this dualistic view became more and more firmly fixed in Christian theology. It is known as Scholasticism. In the thirteenth century, when the universities for medicine and law were being established in western Europe, a fresh crisis in thought patterns arose. The works of Aristotle, who was much more empirical than Plato, reached western Europe in this century by way of the Arabian scholarly community. The question of whether Christian thinkers could work with the views of Aristotle was settled by Thomas Aquinas of the University of Paris. He held that it was permissible to follow Aristotle in the realm of ordinary things such as arithmetic, science, and politics, but not in the upper realm of spiritual things like salvation, heaven, and hell. Thus he divided reality into a lower area of Nature and an upper area of super-Nature, or Grace. Catholic theology held that human reason had not been damaged by the fall into sin but that the human will had suffered, resulting in the loss of the extra gift of grace that had been present in Adam and Eve in their innocence. So Thomas divided reality into the realms of Nature and Grace. In the lower area of Nature, all one needed was a logical mind. One could have this whether one was a Catholic, a Jew, a Muslim, or even an atheist. Only in the upper area of Grace were the Bible, Christ, and the Church needed. Thus the medieval period of history found western Europe saddled with a dualistic perspective. Even the Reformation, which promised at first an escape from Thomism into a unified perspective of Grace alone and Scripture alone, turned out to be unable to liberate the church from its dualism. Melancthon and Beza, the men who established the schools for Luther and Calvin, did so on the basis of Thomistic philosophy, or Scholasticism. The records of the early American colleges show the enduring presence of this line of thinking.

As the Enlightenment and the scientific revolution swept over the Western world, interest in the upper area of Grace progressively weakened. Though many of the early scientists were personally Christians, rationalism became the prevailing worldview, and the academic world moved away from religion. Francis Schaeffer says that Nature ate up Grace. It might seem that this development would have opened the way for a unified field of knowledge. But God is not so easily circumvented. Two poles of thought developed in Western society. On the one hand, the science pole, which dealt so successfully with the physical world, came to be seen as the key to understanding all of reality. However, this view led to the conclusion that humans were nothing but high-class animals and that there was no freedom in human life. Many non-Christian thinkers rejected that conclusion and developed the pole of the autonomous human personality as the key to understanding the world. The two poles were mutually exclusive. One could not hold to both at once. Yet there seemed no place on the spectrum between them where the tension could be removed by a unified view that contained both extremes. Now the modern Western world found itself burdened with the Nature/Freedom perspective but unable to integrate the two.

Beginning with the Enlightenment in the early eighteenth century, a period of deep confidence in the power of human reason gripped the Western world. This mood prevailed for two centuries, countered to some extent by the rise of romanticism. The two centuries of rationalism saw the development of the modern dualism of Nature/Freedom but also witnessed the ultimate abandonment by modern philosophers of the attempt to sketch a comprehensive concept of metaphysics or reality. This led Schaeffer to the remark noted earlier, that in the middle of the twentieth century there was more real philosophy among the poets and singers than among the professional philosophers. So the twentieth century has come to be known as the irrational century, not because philosophers no longer think logically but because their field of interest has shifted from metaphysics to epistemology and axiology.

In epistemology one of the most important figures has been John Dewey. One of his major contributions has been the conclusion that truth does not exist "out there" in reality but consists entirely of concepts reached by thinkers using the scientific method. Since such concepts are always subject to revision by new scientific developments, truth has become totally relativized. In the field of axiology the major shift has been to existentialism, which asserts that humans are condemned to the task of establishing their own values. The problem is that they have no way of knowing whether the values they affirm are really valid. In the end all humans experience death, a fact which suggests that the whole business of human life is a bad joke anyway.

In this century the concepts of truth and value as absolutes have been so severely undermined that there is no longer a prevailing consensus on either topic. As we enter the twenty-first century, the powerful current of postmodernism is sweeping Western thought. Postmodernism not only denies absolute truth and value but now undermines confidence in the independent existence of human personality itself.

The Christian church has not done well in responding to these developments. Powerful theologians like Karl Barth have been few and far between, and even Barth had some very serious problems in dealing with philosophy. Christian philosophers have been even fewer, and no integral, large-scale Protestant Christian philosophy has appeared to challenge the direction of secular thought. Most Protestant and Catholic scholars hold to neoscholasticism or neo-Thomism, a modernized form of the Grace/Nature perspective. It can be argued that neo-Thomism has an Achilles heel that renders it incapable of confronting modern secular thought patterns effectively. According to neoscholasticism, only the Grace side of the Grace/Nature view needs the Bible, the Holy Spirit, and Christ for a proper level of understanding. The Nature side simply needs a clear, logical mind. Earlier, this logical mind was supposed to justify a series of logical arguments for the existence of God. But the Enlightenment emphasis on rationalism increasingly pushed God out of the public area of demonstrable facts into the private sphere of personal values.

The arguments for God's existence carry little weight in the modern mind. The playing field has been rendered uneven. What has made it so is the assumption that all humans have a sort of neutral common sense or rationality that lets them understand the world without reference to God. This assumption violates the biblical revelation that the fall of humans in the Garden of Eden affected their reason as well as everything else. Reason is always dependent on the deeper faith commitment of the heart, either to the true God or to some idol. In subscribing to the commonsense perspective referred to just above, Christians have given away the philosophic game before it begins. A lonely voice for a distinctive Christian philosophy can be found in a recent book by Roy Clouser, *The Myth of Religious Neutrality*.

JUSTIFYING THE SEARCH FOR A CHRISTIAN PHILOSOPHY

To many Christians it may seem that the very title of this chapter is a contradiction in terms. There are Christian colleges and universities where philosophy is taught as a strictly secular subject. It is the study of humanity's efforts to understand the world by means of human logic, but it is separated from Christianity by a watertight wall. The introduction of concepts like revealed truth is considered illegitimate. In this view the consideration of faith as the source of knowledge, or of biblical concepts like creation, fall, and redemption as primary, is not admitted, for these belong to theology, not to philosophy. Faith is personal, while learning is intellectual, and, like Kipling's East and West, "never the twain shall meet."

There are doubtless other Christians who feel that the Bible itself forbids any attempt to delineate a Christian philosophy. "See to it that no one takes you captive through philosophy and empty deception, according to the tradition of men, according to the elementary principles of the world, rather than according to Christ" (Colossians 2:8). Doesn't such a verse clearly warn Christians to stay away from philosophical speculations? No, as a matter of fact, it doesn't. Notice the last phrase, "rather than according to Christ." The suggestion is, clearly, that there is such a thing as a philosophy according to Christ. Indeed, how could it be otherwise, when "all the treasures of wisdom and knowledge" are hidden in Him (Colossians 2:3)? What is forbidden is accepting the "wisdom" of men who "suppress the truth in unrighteousness" (Romans 1:18). One could wish that the early church had been more mindful of that prohibition.

It may well be that philosophy has been ruled off limits for Christians more because thinking is difficult than because it is sinful. There are several reasons why the effort to avoid it is mistaken. To begin with, the church has espoused a philosophy since the early centuries. It has not been, as we have seen, a thoroughly biblical philosophy, but it has accompanied the church through almost two millennia. If tradition means anything, we should hesitate on this basis alone to condemn the effort to develop a Christian philosophy.

Furthermore, the very etymology of the word carries a hidden endorsement of such an effort. The word *philosophy* means "the love of wisdom." The Bible is clear in its insistence that Christians ought to pursue and love wisdom. For example, Wisdom, speaking in Proverbs 8:10–11, says, "Take my instruction, and not silver, and knowledge rather than choicest gold. For wisdom is better than jewels; and all desirable things cannot compare with her." The New Testament is no less emphatic that Christians ought to seek and love wisdom. In this sense to be a Christian is, by definition, to be a philosopher.

Again, to insist that philosophy is a secular pursuit with which the gospel has nothing to do is to acquiesce in a form of dualism that is destructive of Christian truth. If Christianity has nothing to say in the study of philosophy, then we have identified an area of life and thought over which Christ is not the Lord. This possibility we must reject, for Christ is Lord of all. And if He is not the Lord of philosophy, then something else is. It might be human reason, or the scientific method, or some other created thing. But to allow such a position would be to endorse a form of idolatry. Once again, we are driven back to the position that as Christians we should develop a biblical philosophy.

Finally, Christians today are quite willing to accept the existence of worldviews and to hold that there is a Christian worldview. Remember that worldviews are deeply ingrained and are usually held below the level of consciousness. They shape our lives far more fully than we realize. But when we lift them to the level of consciousness and work them out in a system of thought, we produce a philosophy. To accept the legitimacy of a worldview is to be already halfway to justifying the development of a philosophy. For all these reasons, it is legitimate for Christians to work at one.

It should be noted that recent years have seen a significant development of interest in philosophy in the United States, particularly among Christian scholars. However, this new interest has yet to produce a distinctive Protestant Christian philosophy. Most Protestant scholars seem to be satisfied with the Roman Catholic philosophy of neo-scholasticism.

It is high time that Christians insist on the idea that faith is foundational to knowledge and that God's self-revelation in the Bible and in creation, climaxing in the incarnation of Jesus Christ, ought to be given serious consideration in a time when hope itself has become a victim of the pressures of modernity. An excellent discussion of this whole question is found in Lesslie Newbigin's *The Other Side of 1984* and *Foolishness to the Greeks* as well as in his other recent publications. The chapters below are offered in an effort to respond to this need.

BASIC ELEMENTS IN A CHRISTIAN PHILOSOPHY

This brings us to a quick sketch of the usual components of the discipline of philosophy. A word of defense is called for first. The vast majority of Christian scholars, Roman Catholic and Protestant, operate today on a neoscholastic basis. That is, they assert the validity of explanations of ordinary things on the basis of human reason without either limitations or enablement from a transcendent, living God. At the same time they hold that spiritual things must be understood by faith in God's revelation. However, they are thus inescapably dualistic. Against such a majority it must seem presumptuous for a book like this one to propose an integral Christian philosophy when the author is not a recognized or specialized philosopher.

My defense is that the ideas outlined below are not my inventions. They are rooted in the viewpoint of the Dutch statesman, theologian, and philosopher Abraham Kuyper as developed in this century by Herman

Dooyeweerd and Th. Vollenhoven. Their viewpoint is in turn rooted in the work of Calvin, Augustine, and St. Paul and in the Old and New Testaments. The entire philosophy goes by the name of the Cosmonomic philosophy or the Philosophy of Law. In my efforts over the past several decades to understand the task of the Christian school, I have found nothing as helpful as this philosophy. So I offer what I have to say in the hope that it may at least be charitably considered and in the desire that it may be of some help to others struggling with the nature and content of Christian schooling.

A brief description of the usual contents of a philosophical system will provide a road map for what will follow in this section. George R. Knight defines the three basic categories of philosophical studies as

(1) METAPHYSICS, THE STUDY OF QUESTIONS CONCERNING THE NATURE OF REALITY; (2) EPISTEMOLOGY, THE STUDY OF THE NATURE OF TRUTH AND KNOWLEDGE AND HOW THESE ARE ATTAINED; AND (3) AXIOLOGY, THE STUDY OF QUESTIONS OF VALUE (PHILOSOPHY AND EDUCATION, P. 9).

Knight then divides metaphysics into four sections: cosmology, theology, anthropology, and ontology. The word *metaphysics* comes from two Greek words meaning "beyond physics," and metaphysics has to do with speculation about the nature and meaning of reality. Cosmology deals with the beginning, the makeup, and the development of the universe. Theology, which secular philosophers would usually reject from their studies altogether, deals with questions about God, and anthropology takes up those about humanity. Ontology comes from the Greek word for "being" and speculates about the nature and meaning of existence.

Epistemology has to do with what is true, what we know, and how we know it. Axiology includes both ethics, or what is good, and aesthetics, or what is beautiful. It will be included below but with some hesitation. The problem for me at this point lies in the assumption that the facts of reality can be adequately discussed separately from their meaning or value. This is one of the major deceptions with which the Enlightenment has burdened modern people. Facts are supposed now to be public and value-free, or meaningless. Values are private and entirely relative. To accede to this division is to be caught saying that God made a world which is meaningless or that He is stupid. So the question isn't whether there are such topics as ethics and aesthetics but whether it is legitimate to separate them from our understanding of reality. God hasn't made, and He doesn't maintain, anything in the world that is without meaning and beauty. Humans, in our sinfulness, have made things meaningless (this is the Old Testament concept of "vanity") and ugly, but God does not hold His world together in that way. We will consider this question further below.

A CONCLUDING CHALLENGE

Before leaving the topic of this chapter, a few comments on the urgency of seeking a Christian philosophy are in order. Not only is it possible to seek a Christian philosophy, it is most urgent that we do so, given the cultural situation in the late twentieth century. Let me offer three reasons.

First, theology does not take the place of philosophy. Since the Middle Ages theology has been considered the queen of the sciences. Many Christian thinkers today seem still to hold that view. While theology is indeed a science, the sciences do not have a queen; they have a king. That king is Jesus. However, theology is not geared to answering the questions with which philosophy deals. While theology does comment on metaphysics, epistemology, and axiology, its main emphasis is on the story of God's redemptive activity in human history. Philosophy deals with a more varied domain. While it is important that we make sure our Christian philosophy is consonant with our biblical theology, it is not wise to try to make theology answer

the questions of philosophy. We need to seek biblical answers to those questions, but we do not need to put our
theology on the rack to force it to deal with the central
issues of philosophy. Philosophy provides an overview
within which we can locate and pursue the various sciences, including theology.

Further, it is important that we pursue a Christian
philosophy because evangelical Christians have come to
be known as people who tend to avoid deep and serious
thinking. There are even groups of Christians who seem
to pride themselves on their anti-intellectualism. "All I need
is my Bible and a fence post to lean against while I study
it." It is, of course, true that there is more to a Christian
perspective than rational propositions. Even theology cannot be reduced to mere propositional statements. Faith,
and the knowledge it begets (Hebrews 11:4), cannot be
limited to what can be explained rationally. There are
mysteries in the incarnation, in redemption, and in the
human personality itself that quickly exceed the reach of
empirical evidence and human logic.

This does not mean, however, that Christians are free to
ridicule or de-emphasize the importance of human reason.
Under the guidance of the Bible and the Holy Spirit, we need
to use it just as thoroughly as we possibly can. Recent books
on the direction of Christian higher education in the United
States give discomforting evidence that Christian academics
are following the direction of secular scholarship in ways
that threaten the loss of the distinctiveness of Christian
higher education. We need to do more thinking, and that
should lead to the more careful delineation of a Christian
philosophy.

Finally, if we fail to seek an integral Christian philosophy, we will condemn ourselves to operating out of
an unrecognized, but no less dangerous, dualism. We will
seek answers in theology where we can find them, but in
other areas we will be subject to secular, non-Christian

presuppositions. By doing this, we will ensure our failure to bear witness to the total lordship of Christ, which is our privilege and our duty as Christians. Thus there are powerful arguments for the pursuit of a Christian philosophy.

THE WORD OF GOD 7

"THE WORD OF GOD CONSTITUTES THE TOTAL REALITY IN WHICH WE FIND OURSELVES."

EUGENE PETERSON

Walter Brueggemann has asserted that the American church today is so deeply involved in the American ethos of consumerism that it is virtually unable to believe or to act. "Our consciousness has been claimed by false fields of perception and idolatrous systems of language and rhetoric." A little later he says the following, quoted earlier in the Introduction:

THE TASK OF PROPHETIC MINISTRY IS TO NURTURE, NOURISH, AND EVOKE A CONSCIOUSNESS AND PERCEPTION ALTERNATIVE TO THE CONSCIOUSNESS AND PERCEPTION OF THE DOMINANT CULTURE AROUND US (*THE PROPHETIC IMAGINATION*, PP. 11, 13).

If he is correct, it will not seem strange that a proposal for a Christian philosophy should begin with a very unusual approach to the nature of the world in which we find ourselves.

Today's North American Christians have all grown up with a consciousness thoroughly interpenetrated by the modern scientific view of the world. We see it as a vast and complicated mechanism composed of atoms and molecules operating under the guidance of "natural laws." It affords us both dangers and rich possibilities. We use our thinking powers to avoid the dangers and to secure as much as possible of the treasure hidden in the physical universe. But the world is, in Peter Berger's words, a world without windows. Nothing transcendent enters into it or escapes from it. Christians profess to believe in creation, but for all practical purposes their perception of the world differs very little from that of the secular world around them.

The Christian worldview includes three strands, the first of which is creation. A Christian philosophy, therefore, begins with the assertion that all of reality has its being in and through the Word of God. Everything that exists has been spoken into being by the Lord. The biblical account of the creation in Genesis says repeatedly, "and God said," followed each time by the assertion that what He said came into being. As Virginia Stem Owens says,

WE SPEAK WORDS; GOD SPEAKS THINGS. HE OPENS WHAT WE SUPPOSE TO BE HIS METAPHORICAL MOUTH, AND OUT TUMBLE TREES, VIRUSES, MOONS. FROM HIS LIPS POUR BLOOD AND WATER AND WISPS OF CLOUDS. TSETSE FLIES AND PTARMIGANS TRIP FROM HIS TONGUE. WHEREAS WE CAN ONLY SAY "IS" OR "EQUALS," HE UTTERS THE ESSENTIAL VERB "BE." LET THERE BE. HE MEANS WHAT HE SAYS AND SAYS WHAT HE MEANS (*GOD SPY*, P. 59).

A Christian philosophy begins with the Word of God. A proper apprehension of it involves us immediately in an alternative consciousness. In this chapter we will look at what the Word of God is, what it does, what it says to us, and how it comes to us.

WHAT IT IS

Most Christians, when asked to define the Word of God, would reply, the Bible. And they would be right but only partially so. This isn't all that the Bible says in answer to the question. The Bible is the Word of God written. Jesus is also the Word of God. He is the Word of God living. Yet the Bible goes even further in its use of the term:

BY THE WORD OF THE LORD THE HEAVENS WERE MADE, AND BY THE BREATH OF HIS MOUTH ALL THEIR HOST. HE GATHERS THE WATERS OF THE SEA TOGETHER AS A HEAP; HE LAYS UP THE DEEPS IN STOREHOUSES. LET ALL THE EARTH FEAR THE LORD; LET ALL THE INHABITANTS

OF THE WORLD STAND IN AWE OF HIM. FOR HE SPOKE, AND IT WAS DONE; HE COMMANDED, AND IT STOOD FAST (PSALM 33:6-9).

And again we read:

HE SENDS FORTH HIS COMMAND TO THE EARTH; HIS WORD RUNS VERY SWIFTLY. HE GIVES SNOW LIKE WOOL; HE SCATTERS THE FROST LIKE ASHES. HE CASTS FORTH HIS ICE AS FRAGMENTS; WHO CAN STAND BEFORE HIS COLD? HE SENDS FORTH HIS WORD AND MELTS THEM; HE CAUSES HIS WIND TO BLOW AND THE WATERS FLOW. HE DECLARES HIS WORDS TO JACOB, HIS STATUTES AND HIS ORDINANCES TO ISRAEL (PSALM 147:15-19).

Clearly the Word of God is more than a book. One problem with restricting the definition of the Word of God to the Bible is that the Bible *is* a book, and we unconsciously think of a book as something we can master, manage, and control. But we cannot master the Word of God. We are not permitted to stand above it and evaluate it before deciding whether we will obey it or not. We cannot even hear it until we are prepared to obey, no matter what that obedience may entail. In John 7:17 Jesus conditions our knowing whether His teaching is from God upon our being willing first to do His will. Think also of the story of the boy Samuel and the voice that sounded to him like Eli's. It was not until he was taught to say, "Speak, Lord, for thy servant is listening" (1 Samuel 3:9) that God gave him the message. In Hebrew, "to listen" means to be prepared to obey.

So what shall we say the Word of God is? Hebrews 4:12 speaks of it as living and powerful. Hebrews 1:3 says that Christ, who is the Word of God, "upholds all things by the word of His power." Perhaps a valid definition would be that the Word of God is God's self-giving power expressed in creating, upholding, and redeeming the world. It is His self-disclosure to His human creatures. By means of it, He gives Himself to us and so opens the way for our optimum fulfillment. In creating, upholding, and redeeming us and revealing Himself, He expresses His love, even to the extent of undergoing crucifixion in the Person of the incarnate Son for the redemption of the world we plunged into ruin by our declaration of independence from God.

WHAT IT DOES

The first thing the Word of God does is to give being to all that is. Nothing exists except at the Word of the Lord. The hymnwriter says:

> TO ALL LIFE THOU GIVEST,
>> TO BOTH GREAT AND SMALL.
> IN ALL LIFE THOU LIVEST,
>> THE TRUE LIFE OF ALL.
>
> WALTER CHALMERS SMITH

Even nonliving things have their being only at His Word. And of humans, Paul says in Acts 17:28, "in Him we live and move and exist." If He were to withdraw His Word, nothing would continue to *be*. We can be thankful that God does not take vacations! We can be awed as well at the nearness of God to us in our ordinary, everyday activities, none of which would be possible if He were not upholding us by His Word. And we can be amazed at the depth of our human depravity that causes us to think of our world's going on simply as the result of natural law.

It is important to note that the doctrine of creation is not simply the proposition that the universe began, not through chance evolutionary progress, but through the deliberate creative activity of a personal Creator. Creation is once and always. That is, the ongoing reality in which we find ourselves is not simply the result of some imagined natural law. It is, it always is, the immediate result of the creative power of God's Word. In the words of Jonathan Edwards, "God's *preserving* created things in being is perfectly equivalent to a *continued creation*, or to

His creating those things out of nothing *at each moment of their existence*" (quoted in Owens, *God Spy*, p. 58). What is commonly thought of as belief in creation today is probably more often a form of deism, the view that says God wound the universe up like a clock and then left it to operate on its own from that point on. Here again a Christian philosophy necessitates an alternative consciousness, with consequences that are far-reaching.

God's Word does more than give being. It sets limits and provides life. Apple seeds do not produce plum trees. They grow up into apple trees, and they do this at the Word of the Lord. Horses beget horses, and humans have human babies. This is not the consequence of "Nature" and "natural law." It happens according to His Word! Life, whether vegetable, animal, or human, is not the result of blind chance. It is given by the Word of God, and it is maintained in the same way. God formed the first man of the dust of the ground, but it was His breathing into the man's nostrils the breath of life that made him a living being. The same is true of every living thing born since then, and also of the moment-by-moment maintenance of life in living things at all times. A thoughtful contemplation of this reality can do wonders for our humility and our awe, reverence, and love for God.

Once again, God's Word imposes demands on His creation. God has a covenant with the creation (see Genesis 9:15 and Jeremiah 33:25), and the creation obeys that covenant implicitly. The salmon return from the ocean to spawn in their birth streams, and the butterflies and birds home over thousands of miles of land and water, all at the Word of the Lord. It is only in the human community that there is disobedience to that Word. The Word calls on us in that community to love the Lord with all our heart, soul, mind, and strength and to love our neighbors as ourselves. We do not do this, and our failure is the occasion for the whole redemptive activity of the Lord that culminated in the death and resurrection of Christ and will be completed one day by His return in glory.

There is one more phase to what the Word does. It not only imposes demands; it provides the enablement to fulfill them. Created things obey their covenant with God by the power that His Word provides. Humans, if and when they respond to God's good commands, do so only in the power of His Word, incarnate in Jesus Christ and communicated to us by the Holy Spirit. Herein lies the promise and the comfort of the gospel. God not only calls on us to love Him; He promises to put love, His love, into our hearts by the Holy Spirit (Romans 5:5). Sin has a powerful hold on us, but God's grace is stronger yet.

WHAT IT SAYS

When we talk of the message of God's Word, we think first, and properly, of the Bible. But we need to recover the understanding that the creation speaks as well. Blinded by the Enlightenment concept of "Nature" and "natural law," Christians today have lost almost all sense of the power of creation to reveal God. We are experiencing, in a different and modern way, a rerun of the gnostic heresy which, in the early centuries, made Christians feel that the physical world was dirty and thus far-distant from God. Notice, however, that when Psalm 147 spoke of God's speaking the snow into falling and of His melting it by His Word (in the Chinook wind), it went right on to speak of His giving His word to Jacob (in the Old Testament). There was no "speed bump" between those last verses. God speaks in the creation as really as He does in the Bible, though not in the same way. The Bible provides us with theological propositions; the creation reveals the power, love, and faithfulness of God and thus calls us to know and respond to Him. Creation really does speak of the Lord, as Psalm 19 and Romans 1:20, among other passages, say so plainly.

What does the Word—in the creation, in the Bible, and in the Person of Christ—say to us? It speaks both positively and negatively. On the positive side, among numerous answers that could be given, perhaps as acceptable as any is that it tells us of the greatness of God. That message resonates, for example, through the second half of Isaiah:

ALL FLESH IS GRASS,
AND ALL ITS LOVELINESS IS LIKE THE FLOWER OF THE FIELD.
THE GRASS WITHERS, THE FLOWER FADES,
WHEN THE BREATH OF THE LORD BLOWS UPON IT:
SURELY THE PEOPLE ARE GRASS.
THE GRASS WITHERS, THE FLOWER FADES
BUT THE WORD OF OUR GOD STANDS FOREVER.

ISAIAH 40:6B-8

THE EVERLASTING GOD, THE LORD
THE CREATOR OF THE ENDS OF THE EARTH
DOES NOT BECOME WEARY OR TIRED.
HIS UNDERSTANDING IS INSCRUTABLE.

ISAIAH 40:28B

I AM THE LORD, THAT IS MY NAME;
I WILL NOT GIVE MY GLORY TO ANOTHER,
NOR MY PRAISE TO GRAVEN IMAGES.

ISAIAH 42:8

IS THERE ANY GOD BESIDES ME,
OR IS THERE ANY OTHER ROCK?
I KNOW OF NONE.

ISAIAH 44:8B

I, THE LORD, AM THE MAKER OF ALL THINGS,
STRETCHING OUT THE HEAVENS BY MYSELF,
AND SPREADING OUT THE EARTH ALL ALONE.

ISAIAH 44:24B

I AM THE LORD, AND THERE IS NO OTHER,
THE ONE FORMING LIGHT AND CREATING DARKNESS,
CAUSING WELL-BEING AND CREATING CALAMITY
I AM THE LORD WHO DOES ALL THESE.

ISAIAH 45:6B-7

Sidney Lanier, a southern poet at the time of the Civil War, captured this concept powerfully in this stanza from a longer poem "The Marshes of Glynn":

AS THE MARSH-HEN SECRETLY BUILDS ON THE WATERY SOD,
BEHOLD I WILL BUILD ME A NEST ON THE GREATNESS OF GOD:
I WILL FLY IN THE GREATNESS OF GOD AS THE MARSH-HEN FLIES
IN THE FREEDOM THAT FILLS ALL THE SPACE 'TWIXT THE MARSH AND
    THE SKIES:
BY SO MANY ROOTS AS THE MARSH-GRASS SENDS IN THE SOD
I WILL HEARTILY LAY ME A-HOLD ON THE GREATNESS OF GOD:
OH, LIKE TO THE GREATNESS OF GOD IS THE GREATNESS WITHIN
THE RANGE OF THE MARSHES, THE LIBERAL MARSHES OF GLYNN.

The positive message of the Word of God is that God is a great God. He is great in His love, wisdom, power, and goodness. He is great in creating, in upholding His creation, and in redemption. He is altogether unique. There is no other god like Him.

On the other hand, the Word of God has a negative message as well. It is a corollary of the positive message. Contained in the first two of the ten commandments, and enunciated in many other Scripture passages, it is this: Don't serve the idols. Worship God alone. Don't let any idol take His place.

The tragic story of Israel in the Old Testament illustrates the importance of this message. The Israelites had difficulty, after the Exodus and even before it, in limiting their allegiance to the Lord alone. In the end, after the kingdom was split, both halves went into captivity in punishment for the same sin. They insisted upon trying to serve both God and the idols, and the Lord would have none of it. After the return they did not turn to the local idols any more, but they stressed the letter of the Old Testament revelation and missed its spirit so thoroughly that, when the Messiah came, they did not recognize Him (John 5:37–39). This was simply a new form of idolatry. The New Testament vigorously repeats the lesson: don't worship or serve the idols.

How is it with the church today? Not as good as it may seem. We tend to identify idolatry with physical objects worshiped in third world countries. Actually, Western culture is rife with idolatry, and Christians are often involved in it without being aware of the problem. Jacques Ellul speaks, for instance, of facts as the great modern Moloch or idol.

> AT THE PRESENT TIME THE FACT, WHATEVER IT IS, THE ESTABLISHED FACT, IS THE FINAL REASON, THE CRITERION OF TRUTH. ALL THAT IS A FACT IS JUSTIFIED, BECAUSE IT IS A FACT. PEOPLE THINK THAT THEY HAVE NO RIGHT TO JUDGE A FACT—ALL THEY HAVE TO DO IS TO ACCEPT IT . . . MODERN PEOPLE ARE READY TO FALL DOWN AND WORSHIP FACTS. EVERYONE TAKES IT FOR GRANTED THAT FACT AND TRUTH ARE ONE; AND IF GOD IS NO LONGER REGARDED AS TRUE IN OUR DAY IT IS BECAUSE HE DOES NOT SEEM TO BE A FACT (*THE PRESENCE OF THE KINGDOM*, P. 37).

This is the idol of scientism. But, as Walsh and Middleton point out, technology, democracy, and economics are also idols. They have come to take the place in people's hearts that should be reserved for God alone. Note the quotation from Walter Brueggemann at the beginning of this chapter, in which he says that "our consciousness has been claimed by false fields of perception and idolatrous systems of language and rhetoric." Again, Virginia Stem Owens says,

WE HAVE FAILED TO SEE THAT BY CONSUMING THE FRUITS OF A SCIENCE THAT DENIES THE PERMEATION OF MATTER WITH MEANING, WE TOO HAVE ACQUIESCED IN A SCIENCE THAT LEAVES THE WORLD FOR DEAD (GOD SPY, P. VIII).

Think in this connection of our Lord's words to the wind and the waves when the disciples woke Him because they feared they were going to drown in the storm on the lake. He did not treat the wind and waves as though they were dead. Here's a final excerpt, this time from Dorothy Sayers:

IT WAS LEFT FOR THE PRESENT AGE TO ENDOW COVETOUSNESS WITH GLAMOR ON A BIG SCALE AND TO GIVE IT A TITLE THAT IT COULD CARRY LIKE A FLAG. IT OCCURRED TO SOMEBODY TO CALL IT ENTER-PRISE. . . . THE CHURCH SAYS COVETOUSNESS IS A DEADLY SIN, BUT DOES SHE REALLY THINK SO?. . . AND ARE YOU AND I IN THE LEAST SINCERE IN OUR PRETENSE THAT WE DISAPPROVE OF COVETOUSNESS? (THE WHIMSICAL CHRISTIAN, PP. 167-168)

Idolatry is as much a problem in modern Western culture as it was ancient Israel. Perhaps because it is so difficult to recognize, it is more of one.

How It Comes to Us

The Word of God is God's powerful way of revealing and giving Himself to His human image bearers in and through His creation. In each way God's Word comes to us—the creation, the Bible, and the Person of Christ—it comes through the power of the Holy Spirit. Someone has called attention to how the story of the wise men in the gospels illustrates this threefold coming. The wise men were led to Palestine by a star, a part of the creation. They went, unwisely, to Herod in Jerusalem to inquire after the new king of Israel. Herod, one of the most jealous mon-archs in history, kept a straight face and asked the as-sembled rabbis where the Messiah would be born. They told him, on the evidence of the Scripture, that the place was Bethlehem. So the wise men were led by the creation and by the Scripture. And finally, in Bethlehem, they bowed before the incarnate Word of God. Thus God's Word had come to them in the creation, the Bible, and the Person of Christ—just as it comes to us. As Eugene Peterson puts it, the total reality that we inhabit is the Word of the living God (*Working the Angles*, p. 33).

The implications of this element in a Christian philosophy are far-reaching, particularly for the Christian school. Everything we have for curriculum has been created by the Word of God, yet we see it and teach it as if it had some existence of its own and was related to God only in the far-distant past of the first creation. If we are even to begin to treat the curriculum properly, we will have to experience a radical alteration of consciousness ourselves and then seek to induce it in our students.

This, then, is a Christian philosophical answer to the question, What is the nature of reality? It isn't atoms and molecules of matter, as naturalist philosophy claims. It isn't eternal ideas or truths, as the idealists held. It isn't the two-truth platform of neo-scholasticism, with the physical side understood by human reason, and the spiritual side by faith. Things are the way they are, and they continue to be that way, only because they are created and continually held in being by the Word of God. In Him we "live and move and have our being" (Acts 17:28), whether we are Christians or not. The usefulness of words lies in communication. This means that God intends to speak to us in and through the creation if only we have our hearts open to hear. We might well put over the schoolroom door the message Moses heard as he neared the burning bush, "Take your shoes off; the place where you are standing is holy ground" (Exodus 3:5). This doesn't make the schoolroom somber and oppressive. It can make it a place of the greatest freedom and happiness. "In thy presence is fullness of joy; In Thy right hand there are pleasures for evermore" (Psalm 16:11). If as Christian teachers we can internalize this alternative consciousness and begin to communicate it to our students, the possibilities of Christian schooling are genuinely breathtaking.

CREATION 8

A Christian view of cosmology begins with the revealed concept of creation. It ends there, too. It starts with
the first creation and concludes with the completion of
the new creation, when the ruin introduced into the first
is finally fully repaired on the basis of Christ's redemptive
work and through His return in glory. The gospel begins
with the creation, too, for the good news is not simply the
story of the salvation of human souls. It is the story of
God's restoration of the creation to His original intention
for it. Creation is also the first element in a Christian
worldview. As that worldview is worked out in a Christian philosophy, it is understandable that creation will be
a primary element there as well.

WHAT IS THE CONCEPT OF CREATION?

It would be difficult to find a Christian who doesn't believe in creation, wouldn't it? Well, yes and no. It depends on
what you mean by creation. If attitudes and actions mean
anything, there are a good many professing Christians who
are really deists, believing God started the world—wound it
up like a clock, went back to heaven, and left it to work by
itself. The concept fits nicely with the viewpoint of the Enlightenment, for it leaves ordinary things to be investigated
without any interference from God.

The concept of creation has two sides. On both sides
creation is the work of the Word of God. The first side has
to do with the origin of the universe. The Christian view is
that God spoke the universe into being at the beginning.
Nine times in the Genesis account of creation, we read the
words "God said." Each time some new phase of the creation takes place. The whole activity was the work of the

Word; all creation was spoken into being. Eugene Peterson expresses the idea in these words:

GOD'S WORD IS THE CREATIVE MEANS BY WHICH EVERYTHING COMES INTO EXISTENCE. EVERYTHING WE SEE AND FEEL AND DEAL WITH—SEA AND SKY, CODFISH AND WARBLERS, SYCAMORES AND CARROTS—ORIGINATES BY MEANS OF THIS WORD. EVERYTHING, ABSOLUTELY EVERYTHING, WAS SPOKEN INTO BEING. "FOR HE SPOKE, AND IT CAME TO BE; HE COMMANDED, AND IT STOOD FORTH," PSALM 33:9 (WORKING THE ANGLES, PP. 32-33).

The other side of the concept has to do with the ongoing process of creation. This is the part that deists leave out. It is often spoken of as the doctrine of providence, thus losing some of its sharpness. Creation is a once-and-always concept. The continuance of the universe at this very moment is just as much the work of God's Word as the original creation was. Colossians 1:17 says of Jesus Christ, who is the Word of God, "in Him all things hold together." Hebrews 1:3 says that He "upholds all things by the word of His power." You are able to read these words only because the page and the print, your eyes and your mind, are held in being moment by moment by the power of God's Word!

As noted in the last chapter, Jonathan Edwards, the eighteenth-century American theologian, put the concept in words which, if allowed to simmer on the back burner of one's mind, can powerfully illuminate the idea and open new vistas in one's vision: "God's *preserving* created things in being is perfectly equivalent to a *continued creation*, or to his creating those things out of nothing *at each moment* of their existence" (Quoted in Owens, *God Spy*, p. 58). When this understanding of the biblical doctrine of creation grips one's heart, the nearness of God and His involvement in the ordinary affairs of each day become awesome. Praise and thanksgiving begin to well up out of what before was a dry segment of the heart.

WHAT MEANING DOES THE CREATION HAVE?

Actually, the heading above is not put in the best way, but the best way needs some explanation before it will be easily understood. Creation does not *have* meaning so much as it *is* meaning. Creation isn't something that has existence whether it is meaningful or not. Creation is an expression of the Word of God. It wouldn't be there if God didn't keep on speaking it into being. It is not substance to which God adds meaning. It is itself a message. God is talking to us in and through it. Creation isn't part of God— that would be pantheism—but God doesn't talk nonsense either. As Virginia Stem Owens puts it, God says what He means and means what He says. Our task is to perceive the meaning that creation is.

Creation, then, reveals God. That is its nature and purpose. In our diseased imagination, we have turned it into a great grab bag of "natural" resources to be utilized for our private purposes if we can break the codes and make it serve us. The Bible, on the other hand, is perfectly clear that God made the creation as a medium for communicating with us. "For since the creation of the world His invisible attributes, His eternal power and divine nature, have been clearly seen, *being understood through what has been made*, so that they are without excuse" (Romans 1:20, emphasis added). During his call to the prophet's office, Isaiah heard the angels calling out, "Holy, Holy, Holy, is the Lord of hosts, the whole earth is full of His glory" (Isaiah 6:3). Psalm 8 begins, "O Lord, our Lord, how majestic is Thy name in all the earth, who hast displayed Thy splendor above the heavens!" Psalm 19 proclaims, "The heavens are telling of the glory of God; and their expanse is declaring the work of His hands." Perhaps the most powerful passage on this topic is the one in Job 42:5–6. Job had encountered devastating deprivations. His three friends and Elihu had all failed to help him. Then God talked to him for what we call four chapters. The Lord did not talk about what we would think of as spiritual topics. His whole address was concerned with the creation: the earth's origin, the oceans and floods, the stars, lightning and rain, and the animals. When He finished, Job said, "I have heard of Thee by the hearing of the ear; but now my eye sees Thee; therefore I retract, and I repent in dust and ashes"(Job 42:5–6). That would be quite a conclusion for students to reach in a high school natural science lesson, wouldn't it? Yet it is clearly the message we are meant to derive from the power of creation to reveal the Creator.

There is more to the reality that creation reveals God than may at first occur to us. God's being is a complete mystery to us. We have no way to discover what He is like. Science is totally at a loss here. God is personal, and persons can be known only if they are willing to reveal themselves to us. God did not have to make Himself known to us. He freely chose to make the world the way He did as a means of revealing Himself to us. Before Adam sinned in the Garden of Eden, he could name the animals. That is, he could see in each creature what God was saying about Himself. After he sinned, he could no longer do that. So God gave His written Word in the Old Testament. But we didn't understand that either. Then He took the ultimate step. In the Person of His Son, the Lord Jesus, He entered the world to redeem it. On the human side Jesus was fully and truly human. On the divine side He was fully and truly God. Yet He was one Person, and He perfectly revealed the Father. Here was God's self-revelation in creation at its peak.

We have not yet plumbed the depths of this awe-inspiring mystery of God's self-revelation. It provides the supreme illustration of biblical love. James E. Martin says that biblical love "is a freely chosen act of self-enslavement, or self-determination, for the good of the beloved" ("Toward an Epistemology of Revelation" in *The Reality of Christian Learning*, Heie and Wolfe, ed., p. 151). This love came to its climax in the sufferings and death of Christ.

What God is like shows itself most clearly there. That means that the rest of the creation, of which Christ, the God-man, is the pinnacle, also reveals the love of God. Thus we need, as will be discussed later, to be aware of and provide for the place of love in learning.

Illustrations of God's self-revelation abound in ordinary affairs. One of the responsibilities and delights of the Christian school teacher is to perceive new illustrations. For example, Tom Howard says:

IT IS HARD TO SEE OURSELVES AS WALKING DAILY AMONG THE HALLOWS—THAT IS, AS CARRYING ON THE COMMONPLACE ROUTINES OF OUR ORDINARY LIFE IN THE PRESENCE OF MIGHTY MYSTERIES THAT WOULD RAVISH AND TERRIFY US IF THIS VEIL OF ORDINARINESS WERE SUDDENLY STRIPPED AWAY.

TAKE SOMETHING LIKE GETTING MEALS, FOR EXAMPLE. THIS IS ONE OF THESE COMMONPLACE ROUTINES. WE DO IT THREE TIMES A DAY, MORE OR LESS, AND WE ARE PROBABLY THINKING MAINLY OF GETTING THE RICE KRISPIES BOX OPEN, OR THE PLASTIC OFF THE BOLOGNA, OR THE FROZEN SPINACH INTO THE SAUCEPAN. THERE IS NO RELIGIOUS MUMBO JUMBO THAT ATTENDS THE GETTING OF MEALS. WE WOULD LOOK BLANKLY AT ANYONE WHO SUGGESTED THAT WE WERE DOING SOMETHING EUCHARISTIC THERE ON THE FORMICA ALTAR IN THE KITCHEN. WHAT? EUCHARISTIC? AND YET WE ARE. THE POINT IS THAT WE HAVE NEVER THOUGHT OF IT THAT WAY. WE SING IN CHURCH TO A GOD WHO DWELLS "IN LIGHT INACCESSIBLE HID FROM OUR EYES," AND WHO WAS KNOWN TO HIS FOLLOWERS IN THE BREAKING OF BREAD (HALLOWED BE THIS HOUSE, PP. 3FF).

The story Howard apparently has in mind is that of Easter Sunday morning. Two brokenhearted disciples were walking home to Emmaus from Jerusalem on the morning of the resurrection. They were utterly despondent. Their sky had fallen on them. Jesus, who they had supposed was the Messiah, was dead. As they walked, a stranger joined them with the comment that they looked depressed and a question as to what was wrong. Their response was, "Are you the only one visiting Jerusalem and unaware of the things which have happened here in these days?" His response "What things?" shows the amazing magnitude of God's sense of humor! He was the one the things had happened to. So they told Him about the crucifixion, and how they had hoped Jesus was Israel's redeemer, and even about the rumor of the resurrection. He chided them for their unbelief in the prophets and began telling them about Himself in the Old Testament. When their road turned off and He would have gone on, they invited Him in for the night. At the table He blessed the food and handed it to them, and their eyes were opened to who He was. Then He disappeared from their sight. Howard continues:

> BUT NEVER IN A THOUSAND MEALTIMES DOES IT OCCUR TO US THAT HE CAN BE KNOWN IN OUR ORDINARY, DAILY BREAKING OF BREAD. THAT'S ONLY IN CHURCH, AND THERE IT ISN'T LITERAL ANYWAY. WE'RE JUST GETTING BREAKFAST HERE. WHAT DO YOU MEAN, EUCHARISTIC? (IBID., PP. 9-10)

There are many other illustrations like this; we just haven't been in the habit of looking for them. C. S. Lewis, for instance, says:

> WE MAY IGNORE, BUT WE CAN NOWHERE EVADE, THE PRESENCE OF GOD. THE WORLD IS CROWDED WITH HIM. HE WALKS EVERYWHERE INCOGNITO. AND THE INCOGNITO IS NOT ALWAYS HARD TO PENETRATE. THE REAL LABOR IS TO ATTEND. IN FACT, TO COME AWAKE. STILL MORE, TO REMAIN AWAKE.

Further illustrations will be found in the chapter "Meaning Restored to the School Subjects" in the next section.

There is also a second side to the meaning of creation. It is not only a medium through which God speaks to us; it is the medium through which we respond to Him in praise, worship, and service. We act this reality out, probably almost always unconsciously, whenever we partake of the Lord's Supper in church. We take a little piece of bread and a small cup of wine or grape juice, or we drink from a common cup, and we say we have had communion with God. Through something as material as bread and wine? Of course. But that is only the tip of the iceberg. The entire creation is meant to be sacramental. Our handling of it is either in reverent obedience to God in Jesus Christ or in rebellious independence while we serve some idol of our own choosing. This is why Romans 12:1–2 calls us to present our bodies a living sacrifice. All we do consists in a handling of the creation, and it is all meant to be in the service of God. "Whether, then, you eat or drink or whatever you do, do all to the glory of God" (1 Corinthians 10:31). "And whatever you do in word or deed, do all in the name of the Lord Jesus, giving thanks through Him to God the Father" (Colossians 3:17).

Without adding to the list of sacraments, this can very well be termed the doctrine of the sacramentality of the creation. In my experience no one expresses it more clearly than Alexander Schmemann:

> IN THE BIBLE THE FOOD THAT MAN EATS, THE WORLD OF WHICH HE MUST PARTAKE IN ORDER TO LIVE, IS GIVEN TO HIM BY GOD, AND IT IS GIVEN AS *COMMUNION WITH GOD.* THE WORLD AS MAN'S FOOD IS NOT SOMETHING "MATERIAL" AND LIMITED TO MATERIAL FUNCTIONS, THUS DIFFERENT FROM, AND OPPOSED TO, THE SPECIFICALLY "SPIRITUAL" FUNCTIONS BY WHICH MAN IS RELATED TO GOD. ALL THAT EXISTS IS GOD'S GIFT TO MAN, AND IT ALL EXISTS TO MAKE GOD KNOWN TO MAN, TO MAKE MAN'S LIFE COMMUNION WITH GOD. IT IS DIVINE LOVE MADE FOOD, MADE LIFE FOR MAN. GOD *BLESSES* EVERYTHING HE CREATES, AND, IN BIBLICAL LANGUAGE, THIS MEANS THAT HE MAKES ALL CREATION THE SIGN AND MEANS OF HIS PRESENCE AND WISDOM, LOVE, AND REVELATION: "O TASTE AND SEE THAT THE LORD IS GOOD" (*FOR THE LIFE OF THE WORLD,* P. 2).

In this light, one begins to see why Jesus said that to receive a child in His name was to receive Him (Matthew 18:5) and that feeding the hungry, giving drink to the thirsty, clothing the naked, or visiting the sick or imprisoned was equivalent to doing those things to Him personally. Our handling of the creation is always a response to God, whether we realize it or not. School lessons can be done, not for a grade or for the teacher or one's parents, but for the Lord. When done for Him, they can receive the most glorious reward available to humans, the Father's "Well done, thou good and faithful servant." All of life can be lived this way. Creation is, much more truly than we have dreamed, sacramental. It is a channel for communion with God.

OUR PERCEPTION OF THE CREATION

Belief in myths is not limited to third world countries and backward societies. Modernity is crowded with them, only they are not called myths, so modern people think of themselves as majestically enlightened! One of the worst myths of the Enlightenment is that the only way to know anything properly is through the scientific method. Only science, it is supposed, can give us the truth as modern people. The problem with this view is that it completely ignores the foundational experience of reality that every human being has. This prescientific experience is given to us by God. It is whole, rich, and meaningful if we are prepared to see it that way. God has made the world and us in such a way that the world speaks to us of Him and is the channel through which we can commune with Him. Scientific discoveries are on a second level. They are legitimate, useful, and blessed if they deepen our love, awe, and respect for God. They are evil if they do the opposite.

More than one thinker has suggested that there are a number of levels of value or realms of meaning in our experience of the creation. Paul W. Taylor identifies eight basic areas or points of view: moral, aesthetic, intellectual, religious, economic, political, legal, and etiquette or custom. These, he says, apply to all people. Other, nonbasic realms of value relate to particular groups within a society, a professional team, for instance, or a political party, or the armed forces ("Realms of Value," in *Theories of Value and Problems in Education*, Philip G. Smith, ed., p. 49).

Philip Phenix takes the position that humans are creatures who can experience meanings and that "general education is the process of engendering essential meanings." Then he develops six realms or fundamental patterns of meaning. (1) Symbolics is the realm of language, mathematics, and other symbolic forms such as body language, through which meanings find expression. (2) Empirics includes the sciences of the physical world, nonhuman living things, and humans. Here meanings are probable empirical truths. (3) Esthetics includes the arts. (4) Synnoetics is the realm of "personal knowledge," a type of direct awareness. (5) Ethics is the realm of moral meaning or obligation to act. (6) Synoptics is the realm of all-inclusive, integrating meanings like philosophy, religion, and history. (*Realms of Meaning*, pp. 5–7) These two systems of classification illustrate ways in which reputable educators identify meaning with the process of education.

The Dutch Christian philosopher, Herman Dooyeweerd, offers another method of classifying meanings. He believes that meanings are aspects, or modes, of human experience and that each realm has its own principle or law. (Phenix would agree with both these points.) Dooyeweerd thinks that the Word of God, passing like a beam of white light through the prism of time, spreads out into fifteen aspects of human experience, much as a prism reveals the range of colors contained in light. Each aspect of meaning is present in every thing, person, event, or thought that a human encounters in life. Each aspect is created by God's Word and has its own core meaning, or law. The aspects are: numerical, spatial, movement, physical, biological, sensory, logical, historical, linguistic, social, economic, aesthetic, justitial, ethical, and fiduciary or confessional. This is the perspective to be followed in this book. It is not inerrant or unchangeable, but it offers a helpful way of understanding our experience in the light of the Bible.

The next section will cover in more detail the relation of these aspects of experience to the school subjects. At this point, two other ideas should be mentioned in connection with the aspects. One is their relation to the ancient philosophic question of the one and the many. The other is their place in the origin of isms.

From ancient times the question of whether reality is one thing or many things has persisted, usually without a satisfactory answer. The previous illustration may show how the aspects, or modalities, help to provide a Christian answer.

As the illustration suggests, the Word of God is the unifying element in all of reality. It is one, and it constitutes the total reality in which we find ourselves. However, we can discover a number of different sides or meanings to reality, so there is some sort of pluralism in the world. If we think of the Word of God as a beam of light passing

Word of God

through a prism and spreading out into a whole spectrum of meanings, we may have found a biblical way to connect the one and the many. Each of the aspects can be made into a study or a discipline on its own, though care must be taken lest the coherence of the experience be lost. The study of a discipline, then, really consists in trying to understand the law of the Lord for that particular side of our experience. Such study can, and is meant to, feed back into our hearts to deepen our love, awe, and respect for the living God. The tragedy is that scientific inquiry has been turned to the very opposite use. It has served to lead people to think that there is no god responsible for the world. But it does not need to lead that way.

The other topic, the origin of isms, flows from the question of what happens if a person does not believe in God at all. Then the inquirer will seek for some aspect of experience that can serve as a foundation for all the others, something that is independent itself and that all the other aspects depend on. Different thinkers have chosen different aspects, but each one turns into an ism that is not big enough to support the whole structure of human experience. Here the old story of the blind men and the elephant comes to mind. Each blind man handled a different part of the elephant, and each thought he had discovered the nature of the beast. Tail, leg, body, and trunk led to the identification of the elephant with a rope, a tree, a wall, and a snake. So in modern times, Marx has identified the economic aspect as

FAITH-THEOLOGY, BIBLE
MORAL-ETHICAL VALUES
JURIDICAL-POLITICAL SCIENCE
AESTHETIC-FINE ARTS
ECONOMIC-ECONOMICS
SOCIAL-SOCIOLOGY
LINGUAL-LINGUISTICS
HISTORICAL-HISTORY
LOGICAL-LOGIC
SENSITIVE-PSYCHOLOGY
BIOTIC-BIOLOGY
PHYSICAL-CHEMISTRY
KINEMATIC-PHYSICS
SPATIAL-GEOMETRY
NUMERICAL-ARITHMETIC

the essence of reality. Skinner would suggest the biological aspect, Freud the sensory, and others different aspects yet. But none is large enough to provide a foundation for the whole of our experience of reality. Neither Marxism, Freudianism, Skinnerism, nor any of the other possible isms, is sufficient. Only the Word of the Lord is large enough.

The significance of the aspects for the schooling of Christians will be discussed in Part 3, Chapter 15. Here it is sufficient to remind ourselves that it is not only possible but required that we should see the creation as sacramental, as the medium through which God reveals Himself to us and through which we render loving service to Him and to our neighbors. Creation by the Word of the Lord is basic to our cosmology as well as to our salvation.

ANTHROPOLOGY   9

Anthropology is a well-established discipline in universities today, but it is not usually considered a part of technical philosophy. Secular philosophers do not deal with theology and anthropology as separate divisions. Theology has long been omitted because it is not considered an appropriate field for scientific investigation. Anthropology regards humans as the highest dimension of the animal world because of the theory of biological evolution. In an effort like this one to outline a Christian philosophy, however, both theology and anthropology deserve inclusion. Already in the preceding chapters the presence of a theological foundation is obvious. Theology as a discipline would be treated as a study of the pistical, or faith dimension of human experience. Anthropology, on the other hand, deserves separate treatment because of the importance of humans, in the light of revelation, in the entire cosmos—hence this separate chapter on anthropology.

Cosmology, as a division of metaphysics, deals with the origin, nature, development, and purpose of the universe. The word *cosmos* is almost a direct transliteration of a Greek word and means an orderly, harmonious, and systematic universe as contrasted with the word *chaos*. Since we have dealt with the cosmos extensively in the previous chapter on creation and will touch on it further, there is no need for a separate chapter on cosmology. But there is a need for one on humans.

A discussion of humanity in biblical light, while beginning with creation as treated in the previous chapter, also inescapably involves the topics of sin and redemption. The treatment here will consequently begin with the creation of the human race and with God's intention for humans, then pursue the topics of the fall and redemption, both in relation to humans themselves and to the creation as a whole.

THE CREATION OF HUMANS: THEIR NATURE AND CALLING

In a time when the magnitude of the universe is so much better known than in former centuries, it may seem strange that a Christian cosmology should lay major stress on the tiny planet we call Earth. Such an emphasis is not really strange; virtually all philosophical thinking engages in it. From the Christian standpoint, it is justified by the fact that God has personally entered into humanity in the person of His Son, Jesus, and that humans bear God's likeness. In any case, a Christian philosophy is concerned primarily with the environment and the inhabitants of this planet. The environment includes the geological and geographical characteristics that render Earth a suitable habitat for its living occupants. Among those occupants there are three major divisions—plants, animals up to humans, and humans themselves. However arrogant this elevation of humans to a special place of authority and responsibility may seem to some modern thinkers, it is supported by very ancient tradition and by the biblical assertion that humans bear the image of almighty God and are called to a far-reaching stewardship over the globe they inhabit.

Leaving aside the whole question of how God brought the solar system and the earth into existence, there is no question that Scripture asserts that the original human pair were a very special creation. Their specialness can perhaps best be described in terms of their relationships. Humans have relationships with their environment, with each other, and with God, relationships that cannot be attributed to any other group in earth's population. Humans enjoy a measure of superiority and control over the earth and its life forms that is not rivaled by any of the animals. Indeed, with the smashing of the atom and the development of gene alteration, there are solid grounds today for questioning the wisdom and the ethics of the extent to which that control has been pushed. But obviously it is only humans who can exercise this sort of control. Humans also have very special relationships with each other. They are bound together by ties of family, clan, race, and nation; they suffer deeply from isolation in solitary confinement. They are clearly social beings. More, they are beings capable of a special relationship to God Himself. They are made in His image and likeness, which clearly establishes, for humans, the possibility and the responsibility of a friendly, dependent, and serving relationship to the living God. The fact that this relationship has been turned into enmity toward God is, in biblical purview, the reason why social and environmental relationships have suffered so severely among humans.

What does it mean to be made in God's image? Does the image consist in some created feature of the human being? Berkouwer refers to Schilder in insisting that the image is something active rather than static in humans. People were created, and continue to be created today, with qualities that enable them to mirror or reflect what God is like:

> THE ACTUAL IMAGE IS FOUND IN THE *USE* OF THESE CREATED QUALITIES IN AN ACTIVE AND DYNAMIC SERVICE OF GOD. THUS AND ONLY THUS CAN MAN REFLECT GOD, MIRROR GOD, BE IN GOD'S IMAGE. THE IMAGE OF GOD DOES NOT CONSIST OF QUALITIES IN THEMSELVES, BUT IN CREATED MAN'S LIFE . . . IN ACTION, AND IN FUNCTIONING (*MAN: THE IMAGE OF GOD*, P. 55).

The only two New Testament references to humans' bearing the image of God support this view. In Ephesians 4:24 and Colossians 3:10, the qualities of righteousness, holiness, and true knowledge are identified with the renewal of the image of God in people. Knowledge in biblical terms is not the mere accumulation of information but the doing of the truth (1 John 1:6). It is clear that the image is something active, something lived out in the ordinary affairs of everyday life.

Mark Fakkema, a very active mid-century advocate of Christian schooling, suggested an illustration of creation in God's image that helped many of his listeners. He compared the nature of humans to a receptacle filled with reflective liquid like quick-silver and balanced on a very narrow raised support. As long as it stayed in balance, it would reflect accurately any star or cloud in the sky above it. The name he gave this apparatus was "original IMAGE" to suggest that humans have a two-sided nature. On the one hand, they are like a mirror, which automatically reflects whatever is placed before it. On the other hand, they possess a kind of independence that makes them capable, within strict limits, of being creative themselves. The "original" is in small letters because humans are not creative in the absolute sense, as God is. God creates by simply speaking; we must have tools, materials, time, and skills to do so. But there is something God-like in the human capacity for creating or being original.

The illustration can be pushed even further by suggesting that the mirror is held in balance by two equal forces, one operating at each end. On the *IMAGE* end is the force of "ought to," because a mirror ought to give back just what it receives. On the *original* end, is the force of "want to" because people are made in such a manner that they can want to do what they ought to do. Granted, historical examples of this kind of human living are few. Adam and Eve before the fall, and Christ in His incarnate life on earth are the only fully accurate examples. Jesus especially fulfills the figure. He said His meat was to do the will of Him who had sent Him. He wanted to do the

Father's will just as thoroughly as He was responsible to do so. Thus He could respond to Philip's question by saying, "He who has seen Me has seen the Father" (John 14:9). The problems of our first parents began when they decided they did not want to do what they ought to do. Genesis 1 and 2 express their calling:

AND GOD BLESSED THEM; AND GOD SAID TO THEM, "BE FRUITFUL AND MULTIPLY, AND FILL THE EARTH, AND SUBDUE IT; AND RULE OVER THE FISH OF THE SEA AND OVER THE BIRDS OF THE SKY, AND OVER EVERY LIVING THING THAT MOVES ON THE EARTH" (GENESIS 1:28).

THEN THE LORD GOD TOOK THE MAN AND PUT HIM INTO THE GARDEN OF EDEN TO CULTIVATE IT AND KEEP IT" (GENESIS 2:15).

Implicit in the command to rule over the creatures and to cultivate and keep the garden lies the responsibility to create human cultures and to protect the environment. Humans were made stewards of the earth to work it in love for God and for each other.

What this means is that a calling from God is not limited to ministers or missionaries. Every human, and therefore all the more every Christian, is called by God to live all of life in the service of the Lord and for the advancement of His kingdom. The creation provides the materials we are given to work with. Our environment in the created world, our time, our bodies, minds, and hearts with their skills and potentials—all have been provided as the channels through which to express our love for God and our neighbors (Romans 12:1–2; 1 Corinthians 10:31; Colossians 3:17). This is the second side of the purpose for which God made the creation. On the one hand it reveals God; on the other it is the medium through which we worship and serve Him. What a difference it would make to the church's witness to the world if Christians were to live out their calling more consistently.

To analyze this calling in terms of modern life, one could say that Christians are called to understand the creation, to shape and use it in love for God and neighbor, and to enjoy it. Understanding it means seeing it not as the source of pleasure, possessions, and power for our selfish uses, but as a book in which God tells us about Himself and a means through which we fulfill our stewardship to Him. We act as stewards as we shape and use the part of the creation that He puts under the care of each of us. And we are meant to find our true joy in such service. Hence the answer to the first question in the Westminster Catechism, "What is the chief end of man?" is, "Man's chief end is to glorify God and to enjoy Him forever."

THE FALL: HUMANITY'S DECLARATION OF INDEPENDENCE

The first strand in a Christian worldview is creation. The second is the fall of humanity and with it the bondage of the entire creation. This is the Achilles' heel of all nonbiblical worldviews. The problem with modern prescriptions for curing humanity's ills is their failure to recognize their radical alienation from the living God, their only source of life. This problem is a failure to face up to the reality of human sin. The topic of the fall can be considered conveniently under the subheads of the temptation and the fall itself.

It is significant that the temptation came from outside our first parents. The idea of rebelling against God did not occur to them on their own but was introduced by a third party. The devil, speaking through the serpent, told them that they could not trust God and that disregarding His prohibition would make them like gods themselves. In this the devil was, so to speak, a ventriloquist. The suggestion was that he, the devil, occupied a position outside the creation and independent of God. If the human pair would obey his suggestion, they too could become independent, outside the limitations of creaturehood. The problem is that the devil wasn't outside creation at all. No creature can escape creaturehood. The devil talked as if he were outside when he was really inside. Our first parents' effort to get outside ended with them still inside but with their faces in the mud. They were still creatures in the entirety of their being, as they must always be.

WHEN THE WOMAN SAW THAT THE TREE WAS GOOD FOR FOOD, AND THAT IT WAS A DELIGHT TO THE EYES, AND THAT THE TREE WAS DESIRABLE TO MAKE ONE WISE, SHE TOOK FROM ITS FRUIT AND ATE; AND SHE GAVE ALSO TO HER HUSBAND WITH HER, AND HE ATE (GENESIS 3:6).

The temptation was three-pronged. The first prong was the lure of pleasure, the second was possessions, and the third was wisdom or power. The same three temptations appear in our Lord's confrontation with the devil in the wilderness subsequent to His baptism by John the Baptist, and in the Apostle John's definition of the world in 1 John 2:16—"the lust of the flesh, the lust of the eyes, and the pride of life." There is a tired and tragic sameness about temptation all the way through the Bible.

The key to understanding the essence of the temptation lies, as Schememann has pointed out, in the fact that this was the one tree in the garden that God had declared off-limits to Adam and Eve. He had not blessed it to them. They were now trying to get from the forbidden tree things that can come only from God through the blessed creation. Pleasure, possessions, and power are not wrong in themselves. If we receive them from the Lord through the creation, they are blessings. When we attempt to get them from the creation without recognizing their origin in God, the creation instantly becomes an idol (Romans 1:25), and idols never fulfill their promises. They always enslave.

Slavery is precisely what followed. Human beings are constituted in such a way that they cannot exist without some value center that functions like a ship's rudder in directing the path they travel. Religion, even though its existence is denied, is essential to their very being. They either serve the living God in Jesus Christ, or they serve some created thing, material or immaterial, that takes the place of the true God. We are most familiar with this in addiction to liquor or in substance abuse, but the phenomenon is universal. All humans, if they do not serve God in Christ, are addicted to something in the creation. The problem with all addictions is that they absorb the heart's entire capacity for attachment, and there is no room left to love God or neighbor.

The change that followed the declaration of independence was far-reaching indeed. The seeds of physical deterioration and death were sown. The friendship with God that had been their most precious possession was now gone. God had become Enemy No. 1. They hid from the sound of His voice when He walked in the garden in the cool of the day. Their relation to each other was broken. They became ashamed of their nakedness and tried to hide their vulnerability from each other with garments of leaves. Their relation to the creation was broken as well. The animals now feared them, and the ground bore weeds and thorns. Their very consciousness of themselves was now shadowed by a self-contradictory sense of alienation. Mind, heart, emotions, will—all were infected. Their self-awareness took on the heavy burden of guilt. They knew they were in the wrong.

Nor was this a temporary condition. Having stepped off the cliff on which they had enjoyed fellowship with God, they could not now reverse their situation. They had no strength left to try to correct the problem. If help was to come, it must come from outside. The devil had bound them with cords of their own choosing, and they were helpless to free themselves.

REDEMPTION:
THE THIRD STRAND IN A CHRISTIAN WORLDVIEW

Help did come for them and for us. It came, amazingly, from the very source they had despised and rebelled against, from the God who had created and who continued to love them. The Bible is the written account of God's redemptive activity, centering in the Person of Jesus Christ, the incarnate Word of God. The story of God's condescending grace and love in Jesus is the most beautiful and most powerful in the world. It is the gospel, the good news.

To understand the Gospel it is necessary to understand the biblical concept of representation as well as the two-fold problem under which humanity suffers. First, there is the matter of representation. At the culmination of redemptive history, Christ came into our humanness as a baby born of the Virgin Mary in Bethlehem. He came as the representative of all those people who would put their trust in Him for the help they need. As Adam represented the entire human race in his sin, so Christ represented all His people in His saving work (1 Corinthians 15:22, 45–49). In our arrogant independence we resist the idea that we were included in Adam's sin. It is healthful to remember that if we refuse to be counted in Adam, we cannot consistently ask to be counted in Christ.

To understand the gospel, we also need to recognize our real need. We have two problems. One is that we are basically not very nice people. When there is scarcity, as in a gasoline shortage, our selfishness is sure to assert itself. We are involved in a bad kind of life. Additionally, we have, so to speak, spit in God's face by declaring that we can do better for ourselves than He can. We are guilty before Him, and we have no way of clearing away that guilt.

Christ's redemptive work addresses both these needs. In His life, He provided the good kind of human life that we lack. For instance, He was baptized by John the Baptist with a baptism unto repentance. He had no sins of His own to repent of; He was repenting for us. So Peter speaks in Acts 5:31 of Christ's giving repentance and forgiveness of sins. Again, Christ went from the baptism to the temptation in the wilderness. This is the real story of David and Goliath. He was tempted not only in His own person, but as our representative. Where Adam failed, He held steady. He repulsed each temptation that Adam gave in to. And He did it on our behalf. Hence 1 Corinthians 10:13 can promise us a way to escape temptation. All of Christ's life was lived to the Father's glory in order to provide a reservoir of healthy and holy generic human life from which we are privileged to draw by the activity of the Holy Spirit. This is why the New Testament speaks of Christ's living in us by the Holy Spirit. So Christ met our first need.

The second need—deliverance from guilt—He met on the cross. Schilder suggests in his three volumes on *The Trial, Sufferings, and Death of Jesus Christ Our Lord* that the real key to Christ's suffering on the cross was His loss of the sense of His Father's approval. All through His life He could do without anything else, but He could not do without that. On the cross He lost it. All the other sufferings of that day culminate in this. In His agony He cried out not, "My Father," but "My God, My God, why hast thou forsaken me?" He was, as Schilder puts it, walking the very floor of hell. Yet even in that deepest depth of suffering, He would not relinquish His belief that He was the Son of God. Schilder says it was as if a hand came up out of hell and rested on the steps of God's throne, insisting, "I am your Son, even though I have lost all consciousness of it." (I think it is legitimate to say that the Father and the Spirit were also experiencing, in a way we cannot begin to penetrate, a tearing within the Trinity.) And the Father, pleased with Christ's sacrifice, raised

Him from the dead and thereby proclaimed the efficacy of His saving work (Romans 1:4). Thus Christ dealt with the guilt side of our need.

How, then, do sinful humans come to enjoy the benefits of Christ's redemption? They do so by identifying with Him as their representative. They do not do so by cleaning up their act first. They have no power to clean themselves up. They come in all their weakness and defilement, and entrust themselves to His powerful, cleansing, saving hand. From their standpoint, the steps are repentance (a change of mind about themselves and about God) and faith. From God's side, the transaction takes place through the power of the Holy Spirit, who enters into the human heart and joins the sinner to Christ as a member of the new race.

There is something mysterious here. The theologians call what takes place the mystical union. The sinner is made new when Christ actually comes to dwell in him or her by means of the Holy Spirit. The Jerusalem Bible translates John 15:4 thus: "Make your home in me as I make mine in you. . . . " The New Testament bends over backward to illustrate this miraculous transfer. Christ is the vine, we are the branches. Christ is the Shepherd, we are the sheep. He is the Head, and we, the Body. He is the Bridegroom, and we, the bride. So the new birth is not simply a legal transaction; it is a vital or living union forged between Christ and the individual person whereby Christ's righteous standing and His generic human life become available to the forgiven sinner. It is, indeed, the best story in the world. It is the gospel.

NOTES

The division of philosophy that deals with knowledge is called epistemology. This is an area where the Christian community is in desperate need of a return to biblical foundations. We have been carried far from our anchorage by the influence of the Enlightenment. Francis Bacon, the father of the Enlightenment, told his followers to forget about speculation on the meaning and purpose of things and simply pursue facts. His point was that facts give power, and in the early-morning euphoria of the scientific revolution, this line of thought seemed so persuasive that facts without any meaning or significance became the central definition for knowledge. In a long and tortuous retreat from biblical foundations, the church has agreed to restrict herself largely to "spiritual" knowledge, which is afforded by the Bible. In ordinary things, most Christians hardly question the validity of the idea that science alone can establish the truth.

Epistemology has been one of the two most prominent areas of philosophical investigation during this century. Philosophers have largely abandoned the effort to sketch a map of the nature of reality and have put their efforts into epistemology and existentialism. In epistemology John Dewey has been the leading American thinker. It seems strange that while Christians generally have little sympathy for Dewey's conclusions, they continue to be satisfied in everyday affairs to believe that science really does identify the truth. Dewey concluded that there is no such thing as absolute truth. The only absolute he would agree to was that there are no absolutes! He has had a deep and lasting influence on American public education. Dewey held that we make truth by using the scientific method and that, if it works, the truth we make is reliable until science alters it. No one who believes the Bible could concur, yet there is little stir in the church over the basic question of reliable knowledge except in spiritual matters. There are few things that the church needs as badly as a new Christian epistemology.

THE PROBLEM IN MODERN EPISTEMOLOGY

To understand the need for a clearer Christian view of knowing, it is helpful to look at the problem of knowing as it has developed from the Enlightenment. The Enlightenment, as we saw in Part One, was an eighteenth-century attempt to use human reason to establish a clear understanding of reality. Enlightenment thinkers put their confidence in the scientific method. Casting a backward glance, they felt that the ages before them were shrouded in the darkness of superstitious trust in revealed truths from the Bible. By contrast theirs was an age of new light—hence the name Enlightenment. The dominance of this viewpoint has led to the eighteenth and nineteenth centuries being called the period of rationalism.

The problem with this new outlook lay in the nature of scientific knowledge. Science can deal only with the quantitative; empirical investigation is limited to what can be measured. Qualities, such as meaning or purpose in life, or even many aspects of sound and color, cannot be measured scientifically. This recognition led to the modern division between nature and freedom. Nature is determined. It is investigated by science, and lacks freedom because it is always ruled by the so-called "laws of nature."

Many modern thinkers, quite apart from any Christian perspective, resisted the determinism of natural law with its implication that humans are simply high-level animals. They opted, instead, for confidence in the autonomy of the human person. Modern thinking has vacillated ever since between these two poles, science and personal human autonomy.

Immanuel Kant, a German philosopher who lived through the last three quarters of the eighteenth century, gave an explanation of the Enlightenment perspective that has endured ever since. He called the empirical world "the world of phenomena." Everything in the empirical world is controlled by law and hence excludes any freedom. It is the area explored and defined by the scientific method. However, Kant wanted at the same time to preserve a place for values, morality, and meaning. He called their realm "the noumena." This is the realm of things in themselves, and it includes the possibility of freedom. It is also the realm of religion.

The problem is, how do we form a concept of knowing that can embrace both freedom and determinism? Scientific knowledge is determined; it contains no freedom. The knowledge of values or purpose or beauty involves freedom. But no concept can embrace both what is free and what is not free. This tension has led to the modern concept that the only really reliable knowledge is scientific. It has pushed religious concepts off into the private or relative sphere. Thus modern epistemology is plagued with a serious difficulty: it has no way to include religious or moral concepts within the sphere of valid knowledge.

A CHRISTIAN SOLUTION TO THE PROBLEM OF KNOWING

James E. Martin, in his article, "Toward an Epistemology of Revelation" (*The Reality of Christian Learning*, Hiei and Wolfe, ed.) has offered an intriguing answer to the modern problem of epistemology. It is an answer that has exciting and promising implications for Christian schooling. The explanation below is heavily dependent on his article.

Martin holds that there is no way to invent a concept that can combine what is free and what is not free in a logical statement. His solution is to introduce the idea of *imaginative insight*. This he identifies with the biblical idea of "mystery," a secret previously unknown but now revealed.

As a psychologist, Martin seeks the key to knowing in the mysterious process of coming to know another person. We can know something about another person from the scientific standpoint, but real knowledge depends on the other person's willingness to reveal himself or herself. Only when that willingness is present can we really know another person. This is why the Bible speaks of sexual intercourse, the most intimate inter-relationship of a man and a woman, as knowledge (Genesis 4:1).

Martin notes that we are at this point close to the heart of the biblical revelation. Knowing God depends on His making Himself known to us. We are also close to recognizing the place of love in true knowledge. God created the world freely and in love. He continues to love it and to maintain it by His powerful Word. He does this in order to make Himself known to His human creatures and to provide them with a way to respond to Him in awe, love, praise, and service.

This understanding of knowledge reaches its climax in the incarnation of Jesus Christ. The Son of God, who is utterly free, came down into human nature, which is determined or bound by God's laws for the various aspects of human life and experience. He came to make God known to us. What empirical observation can never discover, God in love revealed to humans in the person of Christ. The self-revelation culminated in a ghastly event that was at the same time the culminating revelation of God's character, His free self-giving for the benefit of humans. Human reason cannot construct a concept of God. Logic cannot penetrate the mystery of Christ's dual nature in one Person. But imagination can by faith receive this knowledge. That is knowledge indeed!

This biblical understanding of knowing is far-reaching. Reality itself can be known only in this way. Martin says:

At this point, it becomes clear not only that we cannot provide a justification of or foundation for our
knowledge of reality, but that we do not *need* to. That
responsibility is not ours; it belongs to the self-revealing
reality whose presence and activity we must await. Our
responsibility is to be prepared to receive whatever is
revealed ("Toward an Epistomology of Revelation," in *The Reality
of Christian Learning*, p. 150).

Creation serves to reveal God. It is His good pleasure
that we should come to know Him through it. This is exactly what the Christian school should be promoting in
the minds and hearts of its students.

This understanding of creation has implications for
our evaluation of science, but it says nothing against our
practice of it. Martin continues, "The one-sided view of
nature articulated by the natural sciences, when taken
alone, is an essentially false vision" (pp. 150–151). Kant's
methodology cannot give us true knowledge of reality.
Only in the light of revelation can we perceive the world
as a "freely chosen act of creation." Only so can we begin
to understand the real meaning of the creation. Its real
meaning, not in a pantheistic but in a transcendental sense,
is God Himself. This does not mean that Christians should
abstain from doing science but that they do it correctly
only when the knowledge they gain feeds back into their
hearts to deepen their awe, love, praise, and service of God.

James Loder spends an entire book developing the
understanding that learning to know something is always
an event that includes an imaginative leap, an "Aha syn-
drome" of insight. For example, he says:

No matter how one searches with penetrating
conscious analyses to make logically tight connec-
tions, the insightful resolution to conflict is always
a gift that takes awareness by surprise. . . . This striking discontinuity at the critical juncture of the
knowing event suggests intentionally cooperative

INTERVENTION FROM A REALM OF REALITY BEYOND CON-
SCIOUSNESS ITSELF (*THE TRANSFORMING MOMENT*, P. 41).

In other words, God Himself is the Author of our
knowing, whether in the realm of crafts (Exodus 31:3–6),
ruling (Proverbs 8:15–16), farming (Isaiah 28:23–29), or
anything else. Today's world is in desperate need of a new
epistemology. Christians have it in their power to provide
one. Will we awake soon enough to do so?

FAITH AND KNOWLEDGE

Supposedly, one of the greatest victories of the Enlightenment was to set knowledge free from the supersti-
tions of the Middle Ages and of the church. Empirical
knowledge, or knowledge based on the experience of the
senses and logical deductions from it, was now the new
light for the world. Faith in revealed truth or theological
dogma was no longer to have any legitimate place in reliable human knowledge. The success of this viewpoint has
forced Christians in recent centuries to be concerned with
the problem of how to integrate faith and learning.

The irony here lies in the very nature of the question,
How do you integrate faith and learning? Questions have
an unnoticed way of including the limits of their possible
answers. For instance, it is unwise to accept the question
Have you stopped beating your wife? since either answer
will involve you in trouble. The question about integrating faith and learning is flawed because it implies that faith
and learning can be separated. The reality is that there is
no possibility of learning without faith. If one does not
believe the axioms and postulates, one cannot do geometry. Yet the axioms and postulates are too simple to be
proved; they must be presupposed. Roy Clouser has demonstrated in *The Myth of Religious Neutrality* that there is
not a single theory in mathematics, physics, or psychology that does not depend on some presupposition that is

regarded as independent of all else and on which all reality is supposed to depend. These presuppositions function like the tenets of a religion, though they may include no formal worship and may name no god. They are beliefs, not proven realities. Thomas Kuhn in *The Anatomy of Scientific Revolutions* and Michael Polanyi in *Personal Knowledge* have disturbed the scientific world in recent decades with their demonstrations that there are no scientific theories that do not have personally biased elements in their foundations.

The reality is that it is impossible to learn anything without some element of faith. Hebrews 11:3 can be cut off after four words, "by faith we understand," and be entirely dependable. There is no knowledge that does not depend on faith. The question is, In the light of what faith are you doing your learning? Is it in the light of faith in Jesus Christ as the Truth, or in the deceptive illumination of some idolatry like the primacy of numbers, or of some human faculty like reason? Thus a Christian epistemology begins with the recognition that learning and knowledge for all people, not just for Christians, begin with faith of one kind or another.

THE NATURE OF KNOWLEDGE

A Christian view of knowledge departs radically from accepted modern views in its definition also. Modern people assume that knowledge is the passive accumulation of information, as in a computer database, or the practiced acquisition of some skill, like driving an automobile. In the Christian view, knowledge is active. The truth must be done to be known. Genuine knowledge, since it is always knowledge of something created and upheld by God, inevitably demands a response, an answer to the God who speaks to us in His creation. "If we say that we have fellowship with Him and yet walk in the darkness, we lie and do not practice the truth" (1 John 1:6). "Outside are the dogs and the sorcerers and the immoral persons and the murderers and the idolaters, and everyone who loves and practices lying" (Revelation 22:15). Truth telling and lying are not things we say; they are things we do! When we act in dependence on God, we do the truth; when we act independently, we lie.

A second distinctive in a Christian view of knowledge is that knowledge that does not include love is not true knowledge. For example, A. A. Van Ruler says: "It is in the love of God that I discover my fellow man; it is in the love of God that I discover the whole of created reality." And again:

> LOVE GIVES LIFE TO ALL THINGS. IT GIVES MORE THAN LIFE; IT GIVES REALITY. LOVE CREATES. THINGS RECEIVE REALITY AND WORTH ONLY WHEN MEN LOVE THEM. THE WORLD IS CREATED, AS IT WERE, ONLY WHEN IT IS LOVED. IT IS SAID OF GOD THAT HE CREATED THE WORLD. THIS IS SO BECAUSE HE LOVED THE WORLD. IN AND THROUGH LOVE, THE WORLD FIRST BECAME REAL. MAN IS NOW CALLED TO SHARE IN THIS CREATIVE ACTIVITY OF GOD. MAN, TOO, MUST BEGIN TO LOVE THE THINGS GOD CREATED. ONLY THEN DO THEY BECOME REAL TO HIM. AND THEN HE, TOO, BECOMES MORE THAN AN EMPTY SOUND (*THE GREATEST OF THESE IS LOVE*, PP. 10-11).

Parker J. Palmer, in his book *To Know As We Are Known: A Spirituality of Education*, makes the point that just as it is in love that God knows us, so it must be in love that we know each other, any part of the created world, or God Himself. Creation reveals God; hence any true awareness of a created thing carries the obligation and privilege of a loving response to the God we are called to love with all our heart, mind, soul, and strength.

A third distinctive of a Christian epistemology is that knowledge is personal. Cows and cats, dandelions and daisies, don't know; people do. We do not know another person merely by acquiring a set of statistics. We know a person only when she is willing to reveal something of herself to us. So Martin says that "knowledge of persons is grounded first in the autonomous act of self-disclosure on the part of the persons who may be known." This is the distinction we make between knowing about God and knowing God. We can know God only when He reveals Himself to us. The exciting thing is that this is exactly what He is doing in the creation, culminating in the incarnation and the redemptive suffering of the Lord Jesus. Christian knowledge is vastly different from what is commonly thought of as knowledge today. Martin is right when he says, "An epistemology which makes room for persons—for self-revelation and love—is long overdue" ("Toward an Epistemology of Revelation" in *The Reality of Christian Learning*, pp. 151–152).

George R. Knight lists the following sources of knowledge: the senses, revelation, authority, reason, and intuition (*Philosophy and Education*, pp. 22–25). Of these, modern people hold that knowledge acquired through the senses and cultivated through reason is the only genuinely reliable kind. The problem here is that modern people fail to recognize that they are always influenced by presuppositions, of which they are usually quite unconscious, and that, as Pascal said, the heart has reasons that the head knows nothing about. John Van Dyk, a Christian philosopher from Dordt College, asserts that God did not give us "reason" as a dependable identifier of the truth. He gives us understanding, but that only by the Holy Spirit and in the light of the Bible. Reason is an apostate idol served by people who do not want to be subject to the governance of the God who reveals truth.

Revelation is the only sure ground for knowledge. Revelation begins in the creation itself. God made it the way He did in order to reveal Himself to us. But the knowledge found in the creation must conform to that revealed in the Bible. Again, the Bible's revelation must be centered in Jesus Christ, who is the Truth. The Pharisees thought the Bible was the final revelation.

They completely misunderstood it because they failed to recognize that it spoke of Jesus (John 5:37–39). It is quite possible today to perpetuate the Pharisees' mistake and to suppose that if we have a good grasp of the Bible we automatically know the truth. There is an intuitive or mystical element in true knowledge that we disregard at our peril. The letter still kills; it is the Spirit that gives life (2 Corinthians 3:6).

TWO LEVELS OF KNOWLEDGE

Knowledge comes to us first of all in an integrated, holistic form in our ordinary daily experience. This knowledge is concrete, not abstract; practical, not theoretical; and unified, not fragmented analytically. This naive experience is so common to us that we hardly think of it as knowledge at all. Yet it is our most basic form of knowledge. It is the gift of God to each human being, though it is limited for some handicapped individuals. God made and holds the world together, and He holds our minds in such a condition that we experience our world in a way that makes sense to us and that we recognize as our own knowledge. It comes in a richly textured fabric that includes a variety of aspects or modes of experience, as we have seen earlier.

When we use the logical capacity God has given us, it is possible to analyze our naive experience into its various parts and to analyze each aspect of experience in isolation. When we thus practice theoretical thought, we acquire scientific truth. Scientific knowledge is the second kind of knowledge that is accessible to us. Discovering it is an important part of fulfilling the calling that God gave us to have stewardly dominion over the creation. However, particularly because science has opened a treasure chest of technological improvements in our lifestyle, science poses an alluring snare. It can easily become an idol to which we look for the solution of our problems and the supply of our needs. Rather, we ought to look to God to meet our needs through science. C. S. Lewis alludes to this danger in *The Abolition of Man*: "Perhaps, in the nature of things, analytical understanding must always be a basilisk which kills what it sees and only sees by killing" (p. 90). Virginia Stem Owens recognizes the danger as well:

> FOR EVER SINCE THE AGE OF NEWTON AND THE CLASSICAL LAWS OF PHYSICS, CIVILIZED FOLK HAVE AGREED THAT MATTER IS ESSENTIALLY A MANIPULABLE MACHINE. NO "SPIRIT" OR KNOWLEDGE WAS OBSERVED TO INHABIT MATTER, REGARDLESS OF THE PSALMIST'S ASSERTION THAT THE HEAVENS PROCLAIM THE GLORY OF GOD, THAT THE DAY POURS FORTH SPEECH AND THE NIGHT DECLARES KNOWLEDGE. AND CHRISTIANS, AS CREATURES OF THEIR CULTURE, HAVE BEEN CONTENT TO BUMP ALONG WITH NEWTONIAN LAWS OF MOTION, ADDING AN OCCASIONAL VAGUE REFERENCE TO EINSTEIN AND THE RELATIVITY OF TIME AND SPACE. . . . WE HAVE FAILED TO SEE THAT BY CONSUMING THE FRUITS OF A SCIENCE THAT DENIES THE PERMEATION OF MATTER WITH MEANING, WE TOO HAVE ACQUIESCED IN A SCIENCE THAT LEAVES THE WORLD FOR DEAD (*GOD SPY*, P. VIII).

Our Lord's response to the storm when He was wakened by the frightened disciples is an interesting witness to how differently He saw the created world. He told the wind and waves to be quiet, and they were!

Scientific knowledge is valid and important, provided it feeds back into our hearts to promote there our love, reverence, and awe for the God who gives it meaning. Otherwise it becomes an idol that enslaves and ultimately destroys us.

FACTS AND TRUTH

In summary, a comment on facts and truth is needed. Modern people suppose that if they have the facts about a given thing, person, or event they have the truth. They forget that facts are not meaningless or value free, and that if we do not associate the meaning with the fact, we do not have the truth. Since every fact involves a created thing, and since all creation bears witness to the living

God, every fact points ultimately to Him who is the Truth (1 John 14:6). The Truth is a Person. This is just as true of the arithmetic fact that $2 + 2 = 4$ as it is of the biblical doctrine of salvation. Every created thing bears witness to its Creator and to His "eternal power and godhood" (Romans 1:20). Value-free or meaningless facts are not the truth, however scientifically sound they may seem. Only Christ is the Truth. However, when we attach their God-given meaning to what we call facts, then they bear witness to Christ and become a part of His truth.

Values and Beauty 11

Ethics and aesthetics, or values and beauty, are the two subdivisions of the philosophical area called axiology. They are approached here with a measure of hesitation because it is dangerous to suppose that it is possible to separate values and beauty from created things. This separation, whereby axiology forms a separate category from metaphysics, may well have risen from the incurable dualism of Form/Matter in the Greek worldview. That worldview could let metaphysics deal with material things and axiology with the eternal Forms, or Ideas. Such a separation is not valid. God does not create things that have no value or meaning. All He creates reveals Him and exists only at His Word. Because it reveals Him, it has meaning or value. Hence we ought not to think of created things as if they could have an existence in themselves without any meaning or value. Unhappily, this is the way modernity looks at reality. It is even the way many Christians look at reality, but it is a mistaken understanding. With this protest, and because ethics and aesthetics are usually treated as a separate category in philosophy, they are discussed separately in this chapter. It is possible to separate them from metaphysics logically but not actually.

Ethics deals with questions of values, morality, and right and wrong. It is closely related to meaning. In today's world facts are thought to be neutral or meaningless. They are thought not to carry within them any demand for response from the human knower. This is a false and damage-laden consequence of Enlightenment thinking. Aesthetics is concerned with questions of beauty and ugliness. It is the domain of the arts but is at the same time important in everyone's human experience. We will consider it after looking at values.

VALUES

Western culture is virtually dead in the water today over the values issue. There is little cultural consensus about what is true or false, good or bad, valuable or worthless. Postmodernism, in fact, denies the very existence of truth and goodness as absolutes. The violent separation of fact from value that originated in the Enlightenment has led to a pervasive cultural consciousness that facts are public and absolute (until changed by science) while values are private and relative. One may opt for any values one chooses. All that is forbidden is the criticism of anyone else's values. The fear of court challenge has made Christian values an especially restricted topic in public schools, yet our society has no other commonly accepted set of value positions. The Enlightenment has at this point exhausted its originally inherited array of values and is now revealing its inherent emptiness. For practical purposes, the whole concept of values seems to be up for grabs. The implications for the culture in terms of marital and family breakdown, drug addiction, malfeasance both public and private, and random violence are sobering indeed.

Values are, of course, still discussed in academia. In the secular world two principal perspectives prevail: objectivism and subjectivism. The objectivist position is that values exist but are affective, or emotional. They are not rooted in facts, which are scientifically established and provide the only way to express genuine knowledge. Facts tell us what is; values, what ought to be. It is impossible, however, to get an "ought" out of an "is." Science can't tell us, for instance, why it is wrong to torture. Since science cannot deal empirically with questions of value, the objectivist provides no bridge between facts and values.

A poignant illustration of this dilemma is seen in the perplexity of G. E. Moore, a brilliant British philosopher of the early 1900s. Moore was an ethicist. He spent his life studying what is "good." Near his death he expressed the conclusion he had reached in words that sound like total double-talk. "I am absolutely convinced," he said, "that good does not exist, and yet it most certainly is." What he meant was that as a scientist he could not identify or define the "good," while as a human being he was completely confident that such a thing as good exists. This is a prime example of an unsatisfactory dualism. In the light of the Bible, one must say that it demonstrates the judgment of God. He will not let humans put their world together if they will not listen to His Word.

The other secular perspective is that values are subjective. Humans create them, and there is no one correct or absolute set of values. What is right for you may not be right for me. At the level of social life, this can make for embarrassing and uncomfortable separations between individuals. At the higher social levels of business and government, it can lead to gross injustice and to genocide. What happens, practically, is that "might becomes right." Those with the money or the power determine what is right. People either submit or are liquidated. The objectivist is impaled on the two horns of the dilemma created by the separation of facts from values. The subjectivist is lost in the wasteland of values clarification without any objective or absolute standard as a reference point for identifying values.

In biblical perspective values do exist and they are absolute. They are created by God, and they run through every part of our life and experience. They cannot be separated, except for purposes of discussion, from any side of reality. Just as nothing in our world exists by itself, but all things are held in being by the power of God's Word (Colossians 1:17; Hebrews 1:3), so values are created by God and are subject to Him. They do not exist in and by themselves. Good is not approved by God because it is good, for then there would be some standard of goodness even above God. Rather, good is good because it pleases God. The ultimate meaning of true value is that God says a thing or an act is good or that He says of our service, "Well done."

Now perhaps we can see how disastrous is the separation of facts from values. If facts are neutral, they make no demands on us. They are simply something we can use, if we are clever or powerful enough, to our own advantage. But if God created them and if they reveal Him, then there isn't a single fact in our experience that does not call on us for a response. God is talking to us in His created world. The least we can do is to recognize His involvement, to stand in deeper awe of Him, and to give Him our thanks and praise. This means that once we have come to God through Jesus Christ, even the ordinary experiences of life can be channels through which we come to know God better.

The reason why what we call "facts" have value is that they are created and upheld by God's Word and He likes them. He likes them because they reveal Him and are channels through which we can respond to Him. In Genesis 1 the expression "and God saw that it was good," or its equivalent, occurs seven times. God was pleased with His self-expression in the world He had formed. He liked it. He still does. That is why the world continues to exist. Capon says that the world

> . . . REMAINS OUTSIDE THE COSMIC GARBAGE CAN OF NOTHING-NESS, NOT BECAUSE IT IS SUCH A SOLEMN NECESSITY THAT NOBODY CAN GET RID OF IT, BUT BECAUSE IT IS THE ORANGE PEEL HUNG ON GOD'S CHANDELIER, THE WISHBONE IN HIS KITCHEN CLOSET. HE LIKES IT; THEREFORE IT STAYS. THE WHOLE MARVELOUS COLLECTION OF STONES, SKIN, FEATHERS, AND STRING EXISTS BECAUSE AT LEAST ONE LOVER HAS NEVER QUITE TAKEN HIS EYE OFF IT, BECAUSE THE *DOMINUS VIVIFICANS* HAS HIS DELIGHT WITH THE SONS OF MEN" (*THE SUPPER OF THE LAMB*, P. 5).

We have noted in an earlier chapter that God has enabled us, as humans, to experience His creation under a number of different aspects, or in various modes. This is an appropriate place to note that our moral responsibility differs in the different aspects. The cosmonomic philosophy recognizes the difference by distinguishing between laws and norms. At the lower level of the numerical through the sensory or the psychical aspects, Dooyeweerd speaks of God's laws. The law of gravity and the laws of thermodynamics are illustrations. These are the areas that Enlightenment thought, in its desire to escape its obligations to the Creator, calls "the laws of Nature," or "natural law." In these aspects of quantity, space, movement, physical laws, biology, and even feeling, we are not given liberty to disregard or violate the laws. We do not defy the law of gravity without severe consequences. We have little or no control over our breathing, our blood circulation, or our digestion. Even feelings are not good or bad in themselves, though our response to them may be right or wrong. What we are responsible to do in this area is to respond with awe, love, praise, and service to the wonder of God's creative wisdom, power, and love.

In the aspects of experience above these, Dooyeweerd speaks of norms. The Lord has built His law into each of the upper nine aspects. Each has its own core meaning and mode of inquiry, as the earlier ones also do. Our task is to discover, in the light of the Bible, what is the will of God for us in each area and to live it out for His pleasure. For example, the norm for the ethical modality is to love God and our neighbors. We have the freedom to violate the norms, and we frequently do. The world would be a very different place if humans were as faithful to the norms as they are to the laws of the physical creation. Jesus died to forgive our sins and to enable us, by the indwelling power of the Holy Spirit, to grow in such a way that we violate the norms less and less. This is what theologians call sanctification.

Value, then, is inherent in the creation. Nothing God has made is meaningless or value free. Our task is to ascertain the law of the Lord in each aspect of our experience and to live it out. There is an inherent problem for us here. Because of our brokenness through sin, we find self-centered ways of dealing even with the norms of the Lord. We become moralistic and legalistic. We turn God's will for us into merit badges that we wear on a sash like boy or girl scouts. The Pharisees are a prime biblical example of this, and, if we are not afraid to be honest, we are all pharisees at heart. We find ourselves wanting God to give us some quality of spirituality that we can wear like a medal and pride ourselves on, rather than wanting His presence in our lives to direct us in every situation.

This is not the way God means it to be. He does not give us spiritual "things" that become our own in isolation from Him. What He does is to come alongside us, actually to come inside us by His Spirit, and thereby enable us to walk the way Jesus did. He makes His home in us (John 15:4, Jerusalem Bible), not after we have become good enough to deserve it, but when we come in our weakness and acknowledge our need (2 Corinthians 12:8–10). Then we encounter the grace of God. It offends our sinful independence that makes us want to be something on our own. But it sweetly and richly meets our need when we are willing to acknowledge our helplessness and rely on His power.

AESTHETICS

Aesthetics is the branch of philosophy that deals with the nature of the beautiful and with judgments concerning beauty. The word comes from a Greek word denoting sense perception. This derivation suggests that what the artist is trying to do, whether in words, colors, sounds, or crafts, is to make us stop and see what we normally do not see. Our lives are usually so pressured that we see around us only what we need to meet our immediate objectives. While driving on the freeway, we should not be gazing at the scenery. From the biblical standpoint, what we see is of the utmost importance. Hence aesthetics deserves our careful attention. The nature of beauty has undergone long and vigorous debates with no consensus to date. We will not try to enter that area of the subject. Nor will we deal in any detail at this point with the various arts included in aesthetics. Those will be at least touched on below. What we will try is to suggest some ways in which aesthetics is important to all human beings and so is of special importance in Christian schooling.

Music and art as part of the curriculum have long suffered a large measure of disregard in both public and Christian schools. The reason may be, at least in part, the predominant influence of Greek, rational thinking in Western culture. It is hard for westerners to imagine that there is something more to be derived from the "facts" that science deals with than concepts to be studied, memorized, and used in controlling physical and human reality. That such an enlarged possibility not only exists but is of far-reaching importance has special meaning for the Christian school. Irwin Edman holds that the arts "clarify, intensify, and interpret" our experience:

NUANCES OF FEELING, SUBTLETIES OF THOUGHT THAT PRACTICAL EXPERIENCE KEEPS US TOO GROSS OR TOO BUSY TO OBSERVE, THAT WORDS ARE TOO CRUDE TO EXPRESS, AND AFFAIRS TOO CRUDE TO EXHAUST, HAVE IN THE ARTS THEIR MOMENT OF BEING. FOR THESE REASONS, TOO, FOR THE OBSERVER, THEY ARE ABSORBING FLIGHTS FROM LIFE. BUT THEY MAY—IN MAJOR INSTANCES THEY DO—CLARIFY, INTENSIFY, AND INTERPRET LIFE" ("ARTS AND EXPERIENCE," IN ARTS AND THE MAN).

Edman develops this idea as follows. The arts can stop us in the busy course of seeking to fulfill the immediate goals of each day. By arresting our sensations, they intensify our experience. They also clarify it. In ways we are seldom conscious of, our declared independence from God has led to a cruel slavery to objectives like pleasure, possessions, and power. Note that these are the three temptations seen in the garden with Adam and Eve and in the desert with Christ. We have some sort of pattern in life; without it we could not live. But it is shrouded in the fog in which idolatry always involves us. Further, the arts can interpret our experience for us. Edman comments:

> OUR INTELLIGENCE AND OUR HABITS ARE, IN THEIR WAY, ARTISTS. THEY ENABLE US TO RESPOND TO THINGS NOT SIMPLY AS SHEER PHYSICAL STIMULI BUT AS MEANING. THE FINE ARTS SIMPLY ACCENTUATE THE PROCESS OR PERHAPS MERELY ITALICIZE THE PROCESS WHICH ALL INTELLIGENCE EXEMPLIFIES (IBID.).

Edman does not write, so far as I can tell, as a Christian. But his observations make possible an exciting Christian interpretation. Sin has blinded us to the nearness of God in the creation. Our daily experiences, in unrecognized slavery to the Enlightenment idea that facts are neutral or meaningless, have lost almost all sense of God's self-revelation in the ordinary experiences of ordinary life. What the aesthetic aspect of experience can do is awaken us to God's nearness and so deepen our awe, love, praise, and service to Him. This is a side of Christian life that has been virtually lost because we have severed redemption from creation. It needs to be recovered not only by artists but by every Christian. The answer to the Westminster Catechism's first question "What is the chief end of man?" underlines this point. "Man's chief end is to glorify (or beautify) God and to enjoy Him forever." Beautifying God in our lives is the essence of the aesthetic aspect of experience and is the responsibility of everyone.

The Old Testament is full of the assertion that the creation shows God's glory. It needs recovery in our concept of the gospel. In our effort to be spiritual, we have rather effectively neglected the Old Testament in favor of the New. Psalm 19, for example, begins:

THE HEAVENS ARE TELLING OF THE GLORY OF GOD;
AND THEIR EXPANSE IS DECLARING THE WORK OF HIS HANDS.
DAY TO DAY POURS FORTH SPEECH,
AND NIGHT TO NIGHT REVEALS KNOWLEDGE."

Then, because the obligation to put this into human speech lies on us, it continues,

"There is no speech, nor are there words; Their voice is not heard." We are the ones to give expression to this reality, once our hearts have been aesthetically awakened to realize what is going on in the world:

LET THE GLORY OF THE LORD ENDURE FOREVER;
LET THE LORD BE GLAD IN HIS WORKS;
HE LOOKS AT THE EARTH, AND IT TREMBLES;
HE TOUCHES THE MOUNTAINS, AND THEY SMOKE.
I WILL SING TO THE LORD AS LONG AS I LIVE;
I WILL SING PRAISE TO MY GOD WHILE I HAVE MY BEING
LET MY MEDITATION BE PLEASING TO HIM;
AS FOR ME, I SHALL BE GLAD IN THE LORD."

PSALM 104:31-34

The creation, as Calvin Seerveld puts it, is speaking in tongues. It is our task to interpret and express them. The New Testament maintains the same emphasis as the Old. As Seerveld again suggests, our ministry of reconciliation (2 Corinthians 5:19) calls us to see in the creation what sin has clouded over for us as sinners, i.e., the glory of God also in His creating and sustaining work (*Rainbows for the Fallen World*, pp. 38–39).

There is pleasure and playfulness in an aesthetic life. It is imaginative, fanciful, nuanced, and allusive. Proverbs, in the words of Wisdom, justifies such assertions:

THEN I WAS BESIDE HIM, AS A MASTER WORKMAN;
AND I WAS DAILY HIS DELIGHT,

REJOICING ALWAYS BEFORE HIM,
REJOICING IN THE WORLD, HIS EARTH,
AND HAVING MY DELIGHT IN THE SONS OF MEN."

PROVERBS 8:30-31

Perhaps, in biblical perspective, we can push on a little further in the discussion of aesthetics. Because what is good is also beautiful, aesthetics is closely related to ethics. It is a sign of the poverty of our times that we usually think of beauty simply in terms of a pretty scene or an attractive face or figure. We look on the outside, but God looks on the heart (1 Samuel 16:7). The Bible speaks of the beauty or splendor of holiness (Psalm 96:9). What sort of beauty can there be in holiness? To understand, we may need to put on a different pair of glasses. This is part of what Romans 12:2 means by urging us to "be transformed by the renewing of your mind." The mind of the Spirit sees beauty where the mind of the flesh sees none.

To be holy means to be set apart for God, to be His friend, to be absorbed in our fellowship with Him. Actions that we think of as holy are not stepping-stones to make us holy; they are the fruit of an intimate relationship with Him in which we learn to rely on His presence in and with us, and in consequence of which we practice what pleases Him. Because we are sinners, we tend to think of pleasure, possessions, and power as the things worth seeking in life. But these are the things the non-Christian world seeks. Holiness in the sense of a communion with God in our ordinary daily activities is what we are really meant to strive for. This identifies true beauty.

Beauty does not necessarily look pretty. Christ was never so beautiful as when, suffering on the cross the very pains of hell, He did His Father's will and wrought the salvation of His people. In thinking about holiness, we need to be sure we have changed our glasses. The catechism question cited above illustrates this.

C. S. Lewis suggests that beauty, in its depths, is identified with longing. The sight of true beauty stirs a longing in the heart, and all longing is sooner or later related
to a longing for God. That longing lies deep in every heart,
though it is seldom recognized. In *For the Life of the World*
Schmemann speaks of the fact that humans are hungry
beings and that their hunger is at bottom a hunger for
God. The physical hunger is a reminder, almost a sacrament, of heart hunger. The psalmist cries out:

O GOD, THOU ART MY GOD;
I SHALL SEEK THEE EARNESTLY;
MY SOUL THIRSTS FOR THEE,
MY FLESH YEARNS FOR THEE
IN A DRY AND WEARY LAND
WHERE THERE IS NO WATER
THUS I HAVE BEHELD THEE IN THE SANCTUARY,
TO SEE THY POWER AND THY GLORY.

BECAUSE THY LOVINGKINDNESS IS BETTER THAN LIFE,
MY LIPS WILL PRAISE THEE.
SO I WILL BLESS THEE AS LONG AS I LIVE;
I WILL LIFT UP MY HANDS IN THY NAME.
MY SOUL IS SATISFIED AS WITH MARROW AND FATNESS,
AND MY MOUTH OFFERS PRAISE WITH JOYFUL LIPS.

PSALM 63

All this means at least two things for the Christian
school. First, we need to develop a much more aesthetic
approach to the school studies so that they lead students
to an increased awe and love for God. There is an aesthetic
side to every aspect of our experience, and the Christian
approach to schooling needs to pay much more attention
to this than it does now. Second, without neglecting the
aesthetic side of all the subjects, music and art should have
a much more important place in the curriculum than our

money-conscious ways often afford them. C. S. Lewis mentions somewhere that we know very little about heaven except that there are music and silence there, both of which the devil hates. Probably we ought to do more with music and art, not merely as skills in themselves but as doorways through which to introduce students to a richer aesthetic life and to the true beauty of holiness. Knowing God is the most exciting and rewarding life possible for humans. In fact, Jesus identified it with eternal life (John 17:3). But we have to have renewed minds to appreciate this and to begin putting it into practice. Encouraging the renewal of the minds of our students is one of the prime opportunities and responsibilities of the Christian school.

IDOLATRY, DUALISM, AND GNOSTICISM   12

IF I PROFESS WITH THE LOUDEST VOICE AND CLEAREST EXPOSI-
TION EVERY PORTION OF THE TRUTH OF GOD EXCEPT PRECISELY THAT
LITTLE POINT WHICH THE WORLD AND THE DEVIL ARE AT THAT MO-
MENT ATTACKING, I AM NOT CONFESSING CHRIST, HOWEVER BOLDLY I
MAY BE PROFESSING CHRIST. WHERE THE BATTLE RAGES, THERE THE
LOYALTY OF THE SOLDIER IS PROVED, AND TO BE STEADY ON ALL THE
BATTLEFIELD BESIDES, IS MERELY FLIGHT AND DISGRACE IF HE FLINCHES
AT THAT POINT.

MARTIN LUTHER

The quotation above may help to explain the need for this additional chapter in the philosophy section. It does not deal with other sides of philosophy, but rather it attempts to identify some of the places where Christians today are most easily led astray from true biblical wisdom. These places are not new in the history of the church, but they are particularly virulent in today's cultural and intellectual climate. Idolatry, dualism, and gnosticism are problems that all Christians need to be aware of and armed against. Otherwise we will find ourselves holding to the *form* of the gospel but losing its *power*.

IDOLATRY

The seriousness of God's displeasure with idolatry is evident from the fact that, when He gave His law to Moses on Mount Sinai, the first two of the Ten Commandments dealt with idolatry: no gods but God was the first; no graven images, the second. The prohibition against idolatry rings clearly and repeatedly throughout the New Testament as well as the Old. It is a matter about which God is intensely jealous (Exodus 20:5). He is not jealous in the sense we are, afraid that someone else will get some credit or glory that puts us in the shade. Nothing in the creation can do that to God. He is jealous because He loves us and wants the very best for us. Idolatry closes the door to our full development as creatures who bear God's image. So He prohibits it.

What is idolatry then? It is the replacement of the living God with some created thing that a human looks to for guidance, help, or satisfaction. A very clear illustration is found in the story of the fall in Eden. As Schmemann explains it in *For the Life of the World*, the first pair, misled by the serpent, sought pleasure, possessions, and power from the one tree in the Garden that God had not blessed to their use. That is, instead of seeking blessing from God through the environment He had filled for their use, they sought to short-circuit their relation to God and get their blessings directly from His creation. What they sought was not wrong provided that they received it from God through the creation in line with His will. To seek these things from the creation without regard to God's will was idolatry (Romans 1:25). Idolatry is really a creature's declaration of independence from the Creator. What it promises, independence from God, can only be a tragic and heartbreaking illusion and enslavement.

What idolatry does is similar to addiction. In fact, it can be accurately described as a form of addiction. Gerald May lists these characteristics of addiction: tolerance, withdrawal symptoms, self-deception, loss of willpower, and distortion of attention (*Addiction and Grace*, pp. 3-4). Tolerance means that the addict needs more and more of whatever he or she is addicted to. Withdrawal symptoms are the pain and difficulty experienced when the addictive substance is withheld. Self-deception is the addict's inability to recognize his or her captivity, and distortion of attention means that the addict's heart is so filled with the desire for the addictive thing that there is no room left for love to God or neighbor. We are familiar with these symptoms in alcoholics and substance abusers, but May enlarges the addiction field:

I AM NOT BEING FLIPPANT WHEN I SAY THAT ALL OF US SUFFER FROM ADDICTION. NOR AM I REDUCING THE MEANING OF ADDICTION. I MEAN IN ALL TRUTH THAT THE PSYCHOLOGICAL, NEUROLOGICAL, AND SPIRITUAL DYNAMICS OF FULL-FLEDGED ADDICTION ARE ACTIVELY AT WORK WITHIN EVERY HUMAN BEING. THE SAME PROCESSES THAT ARE RESPONSIBLE FOR ADDICTION TO ALCOHOL AND NARCOTICS ARE ALSO RESPONSIBLE FOR ADDICTION TO IDEAS, WORK, RELATIONSHIPS, POWER, MOODS, FANTASIES, AND AN ENDLESS VARIETY OF OTHER THINGS. . . . ADDICTION ALSO MAKES IDOLATERS OF US ALL, BECAUSE IT FORCES US TO WORSHIP THESE OBJECTS OF ATTACHMENT, THEREBY PREVENTING US FROM TRULY, FREELY LOVING GOD AND ONE ANOTHER (IBID., PP. 3-4).

The worst consequences of idolatry are that it robs God of the glory due Him and that it prevents us from fulfilling our potential of loving God and our neighbor. It stunts and deforms our growth and ultimately leads to death. It promises freedom but immediately enslaves us in ways we cannot overcome on our own. God created us to bear His image. Idolatry prevents this and distorts us into the image of the idol we serve. Nothing could harm us more.

The Old Testament world was full of idols, and the Israelites had recurring trouble in their attempts to serve Jehovah and the idols at the same time. Because of this, in the end the nation was carried captive to Assyria and to Babylon. Paul refers to what happened in Romans 1:25: "For they exchanged the truth of God for a lie, and worshiped and served the creature rather than the Creator, who is blessed forever. Amen." Even after the captivity, the tendency persisted, though not now in idolatry to physical images of a god. The Pharisees led the people in an exaltation of the letter of the revealed law to the exclusion of its spirit. As a consequence, at the coming of Jesus, who was the very heart of the message of the Old Testament, they did not recognize Him (John 5:37–39).

The problem for the Christian church today is even worse than it was for Israel, for two reasons. First, there are just as many idols in the world today as there were in ancient Israel. Second, they are more dangerous because they are not recognized as idols. Newbigin points out in *The Other Side of 1984*, for instance, that the Enlightenment has replaced God with "Nature" and "natural law." Scientists, who claim to understand Nature, have become the high priests who can lead people in their understanding of life and the world.

Actually, there are as many idols today as there are things to which we may become addicted. Here are some more examples:

WHEN RICHARD NIXON DECLARED A FEW YEARS AGO THAT THE SPIRIT OF APOLLO ELEVEN WAS ABLE TO BRING PEACE AMONG ALL NATIONS, HIS WORDS BETRAYED A BELIEF IN THE *SAVING* POWER OF TECHNIQUE (B. GOUDZWAARD, *AID FOR THE OVERDEVELOPED WEST*, P. 14).

In a discussion of the inadequacy of the Colorado River to supply all the water needs of the American Southwest, George Sibley said:

BUT THE TRUTH IS, WE WOULD EVENTUALLY HAVE COME UP AGAINST THIS PROBLEM, EVEN IF THE RIVER RAN AN AVERAGE OF 20 MILLION ACRE-FEET, DUE TO THE NATURE OF OUR RELIGION—WHICH WE OF COURSE DENIED AS BEING A "RELIGION" AT ALL, AND THEREBY NEVER EXAMINED FOR FLAWS OF FAITH. BUT OUR FAITH IN TECHNOLOGY, SCIENCE, AND RATIONALIZED ECONOMY HAS A PROFANE AND TRAGIC FLAW: WE HAVE ASSUMED AN INFINITY OF SUPPLY, CAPABLE OF FULFILLING AN INFINITY OF DEMAND, IF WE CAN COME UP WITH THE TECHNOLOGY OF PRODUCTION ("THE DESERT EMPIRE," *HARPER'S*, OCTOBER 1977).

John Maynard Keynes, the renowned economist, added his concurrence (probably unwittingly) in these words:

FOR AT LEAST ANOTHER HUNDRED YEARS WE MUST PRETEND TO OURSELVES THAT FOUL IS USEFUL AND FAIR IS NOT. AVARICE, AND USURY, AND PRECAUTION MUST BE OUR GODS FOR A LITTLE LONGER STILL.

Schumacher, in whose book this quotation was included, adds:

That avarice, usury, and precaution (i.e., economic security) should be our gods was merely a bright idea for Keynes; he surely had nobler gods. But ideas are the most powerful things on earth, and it is hardly an exaggeration to say that by now the gods he recommended have been enthroned (E. F. Schumacher, *Small Is Beautiful*, p. 93).

Still another witness is Dorothy Sayers:

It was left for the present age to endow covetousness with glamor on a big scale and to give it a title that it could carry like a flag. It occurred to somebody to call it enterprise. . . . The Church says covetousness is a deadly sin, but does she really think so? . . . And are you and I in the least sincere in our pretense that we disapprove of covetousness (*The Whimsical Christian*, pp. 167-168)?

But Colossians 3:5 says that greed is idolatry, and the word *idolatry* is a synonym of *covetousness*. Indeed, idolatry is alive and well in the twentieth century. In his recent book *Dining with the Devil*, Os Guinness, while crediting the megachurch movement with great spiritual possibilities, at the same time points out the danger of its involvement in modern forms of management and therapy to the exclusion of the power of the Holy Spirit and the biblical content of the gospel. Idolatry can be hard to recognize.

What we must do with our modern idols is to recognize and renounce them. However, this is not easy. In Chapter 10 of *The Transforming Vision*, Walsh and Middleton provide an excellent discussion of the topic. Their prescription for dealing with the problem is fourfold. First, we must renounce our idols. Second, we must recognize that idolatry always overemphasizes one aspect of our lives to the detriment of others. Third, we must look again at each aspect of our life to find out God's will for our service to Him and our neighbor in that aspect. Finally, Christians must seek a renewal of community that will enable them to fulfill the first three steps.

DUALISM

Dualism is closely allied to idolatry. The earliest form of it is found in the effort to mix the worship of God with that of the idols. Dualism is present when we divide life into two parts, one of which is lived to the glory of God, the other in the service of something created, most frequently today the service of a non-Christian worldview. As an illustration, a story entitled "Oh Say, Can You Ski?" is told of a man who had never been on skis before. His friend persuaded him to put on a pair at the top of the slope, and then the friend gave him a push. Things went well for a short time, but suddenly our victim realized that the skis weren't going in the same direction. He did some lightning calculations and realized that in fifteen seconds he would be covering four acres! So he had to let one ski go. It is impossible to ski very far unless the skis are headed the same way. Life is like that, too.

Illustrations of modern dualisms are abundant. The fact/value split provides one. Facts are supposed to be value free or meaningless; values are private and personal—as if God would ever create something meaningless! Everything He created was for the purpose of revealing Himself to us (Romans 1:20 and Psalm 19, for example). Again, natural and supernatural are separated as if God works miracles but medicine works by natural law without God's involvement. We have lost the sense of God's immediate involvement in the creation. Science is the way we learn about the world; theology teaches us about God. But the Bible says the world was made to talk to us about God. Christians talk about "full-time Christian service" as if these verses were not in the Bible: "Whether, then, you eat or drink or whatever you do, do *all* [emphasis added] to the glory of God" (1 Corinthians 10:31). "And whatever you do in word or deed, do all in the name of the Lord Jesus, giving thanks through Him to God the Father" (Colossians 3:17). There is no such thing as "part-time Christian service" for any Christian. Under that concept, business and religion are in two different spheres, and the Apostles' Creed has nothing to do with the way a corporation should be run. Dualism is prevalent; it is also perilous!

The problem with dualism is that it splits our lives into two parts. In our spiritual life, we acknowledge and serve Christ. In our ordinary life, we use our head. This means that in ordinary things we follow our reasoning power, or culture, or some other idol. God is no more pleased with this than He was with the crass idolatry of the Old Testament Israelites. It is not easy to recognize the areas where we are involved in dualisms. It is even harder to repent of them and be transformed by the renewing of our minds (Romans 12:1–2). But it is what we are called to do, and it is how the highest reward conceivable will become ours: "Well done, thou good and faithful servant."

GNOSTICISM

During the first two centuries of its existence, the church was involved in a life-and-death struggle with enemies outside and inside. Outside, it was the persecutions of the Roman emperors, on grounds that were political and at the same time religious, that threatened the continuance of the new religion. Inside, the worst problem was with the heresy known as gnosticism, a cult that made salvation dependent on special knowledge of spiritual truths unknown to ordinary people. Gnosticism denigrated the physical world as defiled and unwholesome. Only spiritual things were important, and the gnostics knew the secret teachings that led one into the spiritual realm. Today gnosticism is undergoing a revival. Of particular interest to us here is the impact the new heresy has on our view of the creation.

In chapter 4 we noted Philip Yancey's comment that Christians have abandoned the natural world, "not to paganism, but to physics, geology, biology, and chemistry. We too have cleaved nature from the supernatural." A little thought will abundantly confirm what Yancey is saying. We have become so accustomed to thinking in scientific terms of cause and effect, as though an Enlightenment mentality could comprehend the meaning of God's creation in this way, that we have lost the real significance of the creation. The psalmist describes a thunderstorm in this way:

THE VOICE OF THE LORD IS UPON THE WATERS;
THE GOD OF GLORY THUNDERS,
THE LORD IS OVER MANY WATERS.
THE VOICE OF THE LORD IS POWERFUL,
THE VOICE OF THE LORD IS MAJESTIC. . . .
THE VOICE OF THE LORD MAKES THE DEER TO CALVE,
AND STRIPS THE FORESTS BARE,
AND IN HIS TEMPLE EVERYTHING SAYS, "GLORY!"

PSALM 29

Since Benjamin Franklin we think we understand thunderstorms. We explain them to our children in terms of differences in electrical potential between cloud masses or between a cloud mass and the earth, and the glory of the Lord doesn't enter into it at all. This illustrates the appalling loss that modern gnosticism has given us. The creation was made to reveal God to us and to be the channel for our worship and service of Him. We have reduced it to mere matter, and that in a day when the most advanced physicists are saying that they don't really know what matter is and that it seems more like a force or an idea than something substantial! A biblical philosophy begins with creation by the Word of God and thus with the meaningfulness of the creation. That is why gnosticism is such a threat to the true gospel.

Idolatry, dualism, and gnosticism, then, are three of the hot buttons in the Christian church today. They are severe threats to the gospel. They may well account for the small amount of influence the church seems to have on modern culture. We urgently need to be aware of them, to know how to refute them, and then to refuse to practice them.

NOTES

Part III

Content in Christian Schooling

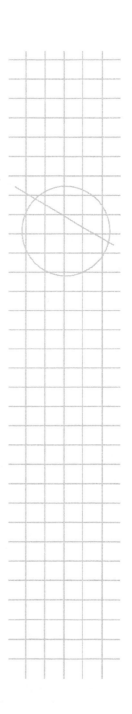

CREATION AND COVENANT

13

As we turn to the practical side of Christian schooling and begin to ask questions about its curriculum, we are immediately confronted by an easily overlooked but startling realization: the school curriculum is composed entirely of the creation. Much of it, from preschool through graduate school, consists of a study of "Mother Nature," as the idolatry of the Enlightenment has taught us to call it. The rest of the curriculum consists of the study of humans in their individual and social lives, their cultures, and their scientific and technological alterations to the original creation. All these educational topics consist of things God has made and continues to maintain and redeem. In our brokenness we think it is easier to study the world if we can divorce it from God, for then it imposes no claims on us. But the reality remains that what we include in the school curriculum is created, maintained, and redeemed by the living God. We study what God has made and holds in being.

The Bible describes the relationship between God and the creation in terms of a covenant. In Genesis 9:9–17, God announces the establishment of His covenant with Noah, his family, all the animals that were in the ark, and even the earth itself. He promises not to inundate the earth with a flood again and gives the rainbow as a sign of His intention. In Jeremiah 33:20 God speaks of His covenant with the day and the night, a reference that ties back to Jeremiah 31:35–36:

THUS SAYS THE LORD,
WHO GIVES THE SUN FOR LIGHT BY DAY,
AND THE FIXED ORDER OF THE MOON AND THE STARS FOR LIGHT BY
   NIGHT,

WHO STIRS UP THE SEA SO THAT ITS WAVES ROAR;
THE LORD OF HOSTS IS HIS NAME: IF THIS FIXED ORDER DEPARTS
FROM BEFORE ME, DECLARES THE LORD,
THEN THE OFFSPRING OF ISRAEL ALSO SHALL CEASE
FROM BEING A NATION BEFORE ME FOREVER.

Job 38–41 in its entirety deals with God's control of the whole creation, including the earth, the seas, the weather, the stars, and the animals. Psalm 36:5–6, 104:19–23, and 145:9 all refer to God's covenant with the creation. These are not references to an absentee landlord. God is intimately involved in the moment-by-moment operation of His creation.

A basic distinctive of a Christian approach to the school studies and, indeed, to the Good News itself, is an adequate understanding of the biblical doctrine of creation. As suggested above, the first strand in the Christian worldview is creation, then the fall, and then redemption. But with regard to creation, most modern Christians could probably with justification be called deists. They disagree with the evolutionists as to how the world got started, but they are content to believe that it carries on now by natural law. Actually, "Nature" and "natural law" are dangerous, destructive modern idols. For practical purposes they have replaced God in the thinking of modern people about the ordinary world. Unhappily, Christians often share this perspective.

The biblical doctrine of creation asserts that all things have been spoken into being by the Word of God. The speaking is a once-and-always speaking! God not only started the world by His Word; He keeps it going in the same manner. If He wanted to stop it, He would not need to do something, but to stop doing something. Jonathan Edwards, as quoted earlier, put it in these words:

GOD'S *PRESERVING* CREATED THINGS IN BEING IS PERFECTLY EQUIVALENT TO A *CONTINUED CREATION,* OR TO HIS CREATING THOSE THINGS OUT OF NOTHING *AT EACH MOMENT* OF THEIR EXISTENCE (QUOTED IN V. S. OWENS, *GOD SPY,* P. 58. ITALICS IN THE ORIGINAL).

The Bible clearly attributes the orderliness and regularity of the ongoing creation to the sole influence of God's Word. Hebrews 1:3 says that "He . . . upholds all things by the word of His power." Colossians 1:17 asserts that "in Him [Christ, the Word of God] all things hold together." Paul applies this to every facet of our lives, including the physical, when he says in Acts 17:28, "in Him we live and move and exist." This biblical revelation of the way things really are is capable of causing a profound change in our way of seeing life and the world when we let the Holy Spirit stir it as it simmers on the back burner of our minds.

All this, and much more, is involved in God's covenant with the creation. He is the faithful God, and the regularities we depend on in the material and the immaterial world are not accidents or the products of mere chance. They are the consequence of the faithful attention of the living God to His creation. The awareness of His nearness and His interest in ordinary things, including ourselves, can both initiate and deepen our communion with Him. This is one of the very special and blessed potentials of a Christian approach to teaching.

This chapter will deal with God's covenant with the creation in the following ways. First, what is the biblical concept of covenant, and what varied forms of it does the Bible reveal? Next, what is meant by God's covenant with the creation? Then, why did God establish a covenant with the creation? Finally, what are some principles for dealing with the idea of covenant in the classroom?

THE BIBLICAL CONCEPT OF COVENANT

A covenant in the Bible represents an agreement between two parties. The parties could be two or more humans, or they could be humans and God. David and Jonathan, for example, entered into a covenant with each other to express their deep friendship. Jacob and his uncle Laban made one, too, though it was expressive of mutual distrust rather than friendship. Covenants of this sort were actually legal instruments. Their establishment usually involved the following steps: the agreement was "cut," God was appealed to as witness or judge, the details of the agreement were specified, an oath was taken, a sacrifice was offered, and a sacred meal was eaten together.

When a covenant was made between humans and God, the agreement became more than a legal arrangement between humans. Now the arrangement was initiated by God, and His will or His law was imposed. In this situation, kingdom was involved as well as covenant. God's lordship made the arrangement a kingdom; His saving purpose was the goal, and His involvement made sure the covenant would be valid. There was no danger of default on God's side. Thus covenant describes the redemptive aspect of the three-fold creation-fall-redemption worldview. In dealing with God's covenant with humans, the Bible speaks of both an old and a new covenant. The old one was "cut" with Israel, the tribe of Abraham. The new one came in with Jesus and reaches out to the entire world.

When God had freely and sovereignly liberated the people of Israel from Egypt, He cut a covenant with them at Mount Sinai. He agreed to be their God if they would observe His commandments, and they undertook to be His people if He would fulfill His promises to them. All the rest of the Old Testament tells the tortured story of their ups and downs in keeping or violating the covenant. Along with their castigation of Israel for its repeated failure to observe the covenant, the prophets announced the prospect of a new covenant. It was promised by God when He said:

BEHOLD, DAYS ARE COMING . . . WHEN I WILL MAKE A NEW COVENANT WITH THE HOUSE OF ISRAEL AND WITH THE HOUSE OF JUDAH. . . . I WILL PUT MY LAW WITHIN THEM, AND ON THEIR HEART I WILL WRITE IT; AND I WILL BE THEIR GOD AND THEY SHALL BE MY PEOPLE (JEREMIAH 31:31, 33).

The New Testament, whose name really means "the new covenant," begins with Jesus' proclamation that the kingdom of God had arrived. Since the King had come, the kingdom had come as well. This new covenant was sealed by Jesus' death on the cross and His resurrection. It is the central message of the entire New Testament.

At its beginning the first-century church was composed of Jews. Soon, however, and largely through the ministry of the Apostle Paul, Gentiles were added. We modern people have the greatest difficulty realizing what a problem this presented to the Jewish Christians. How did the new covenant relate to the old? Was God through with Israel forever? This is not the place to discuss the theological problems involved here. What Paul says in Romans 11 about the future of Israel should be borne in mind, however.

FOR I DO NOT WANT YOU, BRETHREN, TO BE UNINFORMED OF THIS MYSTERY, LEST YOU BE WISE IN YOUR OWN ESTIMATION, THAT A PARTIAL HARDENING HAS HAPPENED TO ISRAEL UNTIL THE FULNESS OF THE GENTILES HAS COME IN; AND THUS ALL ISRAEL WILL BE SAVED. . . . FOR JUST AS YOU ONCE WERE DISOBEDIENT TO GOD, BUT NOW HAVE BEEN SHOWN MERCY BECAUSE OF THEIR DISOBEDIENCE, SO THESE ALSO NOW HAVE BEEN DISOBEDIENT, IN ORDER THAT BECAUSE OF THE MERCY SHOWN TO YOU THEY ALSO MAY NOW BE SHOWN MERCY. FOR GOD HAS SHUT UP ALL IN DISOBEDIENCE THAT HE MIGHT SHOW MERCY TO ALL (ROMANS 11:25-26; 30-32).

One other comment may be helpful here. Just as the responsibilities of Israel under the old covenant were spelled out in detail in the Old Testament and involved every aspect of life, so the will of God for us under the new covenant is made clear in Jesus' preaching of the Sermon on the Mount and in the remainder of the New Testament. No aspect of life today is exempt from the promise and the responsibilities of the new covenant and the kingdom.

WHAT IS GOD'S COVENANT WITH THE CREATION?

The Bible speaks repeatedly of God's covenant with the creation. It is clearly different from either the legal or the Old and New Covenants described above. Here there is a comprehensive imposition of God's will on the world that He has brought into being and maintains. God has imposed His law on every aspect of the creation, and the creation obeys that law faithfully and completely. Hence what we call "natural law" is so reliable that we can learn to manipulate the creation by means of it. Natural law is really God's law. Birds and butterflies home across thousands of miles each year at the Word of the Lord. At that same Word salmon return every four years to spawn in the stream where they were born. The gravity that holds the moon in its orbit or the earth in its circuit of the sun is not an abstract principle; it is a demonstration of the power of God's Word (Hebrews 1:3; Colossians 1:17). This means that God is intensely and continually involved in the operation of the creation every instant of every day. He has not gone back to heaven to let the world operate on automatic pilot. If He is this closely involved with everyday affairs, then it may be possible for people to have contact with God, to commune with Him and serve Him, in the ordinary activities of every day and not only in the spiritual activities of a church relationship. This is clearly what the Bible is telling us. Then school can become a place where students come into contact with God in and through their study of the creation.

WHY DID GOD ESTABLISH A COVENANT WITH THE CREATION?

The next question is, why did God speak the creation into being and impose a covenant on it? What purpose did He have in mind? What value did its realities have for Him? Modern people do not even confront this question, because they have concluded either that God is dead or that He is irrelevant to secular matters. Facts, they assume, have neither meaning nor purpose except as humans utilize them for human objectives. If that were so, it would mean that God made the world without thinking about it.

Christians disagree. They insist that God knew what He was doing. They see at least two purposes in the divine covenant with creation. In the first place, what God had in mind relates particularly to the crown of His creative activity, the human race, which bears His likeness. His goal was to establish an ongoing relationship with human beings. The creation was intended as a medium for that friendship. It was to carry a two-way traffic, revealing God to His people on the one hand, and serving as a channel for their worship and service to Him on the other. Christian schooling endeavors to restore to the realities of the creation their God-intended meaning and thus to use them as a means for bringing students into touch with the living God. The most wonderful thing in life is to know God (John 17:3). Once our relation to Him has been restored through Christ's redeeming work, that is possible.

At the heart of a Christian approach to teaching is the reality that Jesus reveals himself in the creation. For example, the eye of faith perceives him in children: "And whoever receives one such child in my name receives Me" (Matthew 18:5). Again,

FOR I WAS HUNGRY, AND YOU GAVE ME SOMETHING TO EAT; I WAS THIRSTY, AND YOU GAVE ME DRINK; I WAS A STRANGER, AND

YOU INVITED ME IN; NAKED, AND YOU CLOTHED ME: I WAS SICK AND
YOU VISITED ME; I WAS IN PRISON, AND YOU CAME TO ME. . . . TRULY
I SAY TO YOU, TO THE EXTENT THAT YOU DID IT TO ONE OF THESE
BROTHERS OF MINE, EVEN THE LEAST OF THEM, YOU DID IT TO ME
(MATTHEW 25:35-36, 40).

Job 42:5–6, Romans 1:20, Psalm 19, and other Bible references make it perfectly clear that God means us to see
Him in His works. In Revelation 3:20, the risen Christ says,
"Behold, I stand at the door and knock; if anyone hears My
voice and opens the door, I will come in to him, and will dine
with him, and he with Me." Since all the school studies deal
with the creation, each one is a door at which Jesus knocks.
If we have the heart to open the door, He will come in and
meet the deep hunger of our hearts. The school subjects can
be a way of having communion with God if we as teachers
can see and offer that opportunity. Christ's use of the creation in His parables evidences the deep way in which He
saw God revealed in the created world.

A second reason why God established a covenant with
the creation is that the creation has been cursed. This brings
us closer to the theological type of covenant. Creation labors
under a curse because of humanity's declaration of independence from God in the Garden of Eden. Humanity too, of
course, labors under the curse. In this twentieth century,
with our destruction of 187 million people in wars, holocausts, and ethnic cleansings, the burden of our alienation
from God has become almost unbearable. People are more
and more bereft of hope for the progress that the Enlightenment promised. When the twenty-four hour per day
bombardment of entertainment that television and the other
media provide is interrupted, people experience a torpor or
malaise that they do not know how to identify or relieve. We
experience the burden under which the creation suffers because of our sin.

Romans 8:19–21 indicates that God will in due time release the creation from this bondage: "For the anxious longing

of the creation waits eagerly for the revealing of the sons of God" (vs. 19); and "that the creation itself also will be set free from its slavery to corruption into the freedom of the glory of the children of God" (vs. 21). We who belong to Christ today already enjoy, albeit not perfectly, the freedom of the children of God. These verses mean, then, that we have a double reason for being good stewards of the creation. We have the original command of God to look after His creation (Genesis 1:28–29), and we have the added incentive that our freedom in Christ is a promise of ultimate freedom for the entire creation. 2 Corinthians 5:19 says, "God was in Christ reconciling the world to Himself, not counting their trespasses against them, and He has committed to us the word of reconciliation." The freedom we enjoy as Christians is a down payment on the freedom the creation will finally receive. The consummation of the freedom for the creation will take place when Christ returns in glory to the world that rejected Him on His first advent. Thus we can share today in the ultimate reconciliation of the entire creation.

It may even be that the creation as we know it today is illustrative of this coming release. For example, the annual rotation of the seasons reflects something of the pattern of death and resurrection. Each year the wintry death of vegetation is followed by the emergence of new life in the spring. Jesus said that unless a seed falls into the ground and dies, it remains alone, but if it dies it brings forth much fruit. Perhaps in ways such as these God foreshadows, for our benefit, the coming redemption of the creation from its curse. The creation that underlies the school curriculum is rich in lessons about the faithful love of God if we have the heart to watch for them.

A WORD OF CAUTION

What has been said above about the nature of the creation, however, does not mean there should be incessant talking in the Christian schoolroom about God's self-revelation in it. Remember the principle of Jesus' teaching in parables. His stories concerned the creation, and people found them fascinating, but He did not belabor their inner meaning. He said enough so that those who were willing to hear more could perceive His teaching and follow it up. A teacher does not know the spiritual readiness of his students. He helps them to encounter the facts, with enough hints along the way so that those who want to meet Jesus through the facts can do so. The seed he sows may take years to grow and bear fruit. He sows in faith and prays for a harvest.

There is need, then, for a word of precaution here. As Christian teachers we strive to help our students achieve a renewed consciousness, a way of perceiving reality that is radically different from the way in which the modern world sees it. But we ourselves have been indoctrinated since childhood with modernity's perspective, and we are usually quite unconscious of how deeply we have been affected. We have lost a biblical way of seeing the creation. The distinctive capacity of ordinary experience for revealing God and providing a way to commune with and serve Him is no longer our delightful experience. That is why praise to God is seldom drawn from our hearts and lips in connection with the everyday affairs of our lives.

The precaution is, then, go slowly! What we want to convey to our students is not just an ideology or theory of reality. It is an alternative perspective that sees the creation as a channel for relating to the living God. This concerns their active involvement as caretakers as well as healers in and of God's world. This cannot be explained as simply as the proof of a geometric theorem. Our students' reception of this consciousness comes as a gift from God, a work of the Holy Spirit. Unless the Word of God has obtained a firm grip on our own hearts in this area, we will be hard put to convey this new way of seeing things to our students.

The teacher-pupil relationship is preeminently one of master and apprentice. Or perhaps it is even more like the bonding process by which a newly hatched duckling relates to its mother or to some other living thing that intrudes between them. We need to go slowly in our effort to inculcate a biblical vision in the hearts of our students. Only when our own vision has become so transformed that we cannot be silent will it be safe for us to try to communicate it to our apprentices. And when it has us in its grip, we may rest assured that the Holy Spirit will enable us to find appropriate words and methods by which to pass it on.

Since the creation is intended to be a channel for perceiving God and responding to Him (think of the symbolism of bread and wine in the communion service!), the level of our own fellowship with God in and through the creation is of primary importance. One can teach the so-called facts of algebra or chemistry or literature without even being a Christian. But one cannot teach a biblical vision of creation without having an increasingly intimate touch with God Himself in our own understanding of the creation. We habitually separate our spiritual life from our ordinary life. That will not do for a Christian in teaching or in any other life activity. The powerlessness of the Western church against the tidal wave of secularization that has overwhelmed our culture is probably due largely to the dualism we have become accustomed to in most of life. The Christian teacher not only must have a good grasp of the "facts" of her subject; she must also be growing in her fellowship with God in and through that subject. This is a challenge that can be met only through prayer, meditation, Bible reading, other helpful reading, and fellowship with others who are struggling with the same challenge. We cannot teach students to love God in and through the creation unless we have learned to do it ourselves.

A PROBLEM AND A CONCLUSION

There is a problem that must be recognized in this whole discussion of God's covenant with creation. Human sin has introduced irregularities into the situation. God's lawful order for His world is no longer faithfully observed in all respects. In the physical area of the creation, God has not permitted us to interfere with His law. Thus we dare not violate the law of gravity by jumping off the roof. We speak correctly in this area of our experience of the laws of God. In the nonphysical areas of the creation, we can better speak of God's laws as norms for human life, and these are often grievously broken. For example, the norm of love for God and for our neighbor is honored more in its violation than its observance. (It should be noted that violations of the norms are not always visited with immediate consequences. When we disobey the physical laws, we encounter immediate consequences. The effect of violating the norms in the nonphysical aspects of our life and experience will be felt ultimately, but not always in this life.) To accommodate the brokenness in our life in the world, we speak of the law of love as our goal in life. Jesus observed that law without fail, and the promise is that ultimately His church will be purified to the point of a similar observance. In the meanwhile, we speak of the norm of love because that is God's intention for human life. A Christian understanding of life and the world has its foundation in God's covenant with creation.

In conclusion, God's covenant with creation means that no subject in the curriculum can be properly studied or taught without reference to God. He is revealed in each of them, and our handling of them is always a response, either positive or negative, to Him. God's covenant with creation makes it a medium for perceiving and responding to Him. At the same time, it is not wise for a Christian teacher to try to convey these ideas simply as spiritual truths or facts that students should know. The teacher herself needs to be gripped by God's Word in the creation before trying to communicate to her students the possibility of coming to know and serve God even in and through the seemingly secular subjects. That discovery will prove to be, more than anything else could, the key to effective teaching in a Christian school. Students need to experience this renewed consciousness and to be involved in the caretaking and reconciling of the creation, thus learning what it means to glorify God in all their lives. It will not be easy, but it will be infinitely worthwhile.

NOTES

MEANING RESTORED TO SCHOOL STUDIES   14

The discussion of creation and covenant in the preceding chapter brings us to a foundational question on curriculum. What is special about teaching school subjects Christianly? Aren't the studies the same in any school, Christian or secular? Is there a special Christian arithmetic or science or geography? No, God has made only one world that we know of, and it is the same world whether investigated by a Christian or an atheist. (One precaution: the so-called "facts" must be clearly established as facts. People don't always distinguish accurately between theories and facts. When an evolutionary scientist begins to say that the cosmos is all there is, all there ever was, and all there ever will be, as Carl Sagan said on TV, he has left science for philosophy. His scientific credentials give him no right to expect a hearing in philosophy.) Nevertheless, there is a profound difference between the way a Christian should teach any subject and the way an atheist (avowed or practical) would do so. The Christian teacher restores meaning to the study; the secular teacher can give no meaning to neutral facts. Sadly, sometimes Christian schools are not aware of this difference. If they are not, they fail to fulfill the promise of the Christian curriculum.

To understand this distinctive quality of teaching Christianly, we must remember what was discussed in the chapter on the Enlightenment. Francis Bacon introduced a new way of thinking about facts. He urged his fellow scientists to forget about the supposed meaning of phenomena and simply look for physical causes. That would give people value-free or meaningless facts, requiring no commitment or response on the part of the learners.

Facts were simply neutral. Rightly used, they could give great power to people, but they did not mean anything in themselves. Since the truth depended on empirical information and logic, truth was no longer absolute. As science changed, so would truth.

The problem here, from the biblical standpoint, is that neutral facts regarding any thing or event simply do not exist, and they are not, in themselves, the truth. Truth is not neutral information; it is a Person. Jesus said, "I am the Way, the Truth, and the Life" (John 14:6). This does not mean merely that He is the spiritual truth. He is the only truth there is in any part of the created world. By His powerful Word He creates and maintains the world moment by moment. His trademark is on every created thing, visible or invisible. If this is not recognized, the truth has not been fully expressed.

Coming back now to the topic of this chapter, the cosmos of which we are a part has, in its entirety, a purpose, and that purpose gives it meaning or value. It is intended to be a channel for God's self-revelation to humanity and for humanity's friendship or communion with and service to God. To suppose that it can be adequately defined by statements of value-free fact is to lose what is most precious in human life and experience. It is to deny God's existence or to accuse Him of creating a world without thinking what He was doing—and that is sacrilegious.

Before looking more carefully at meaning in creation and in education, there is need for one comment. It is better to say that the creation *is* meaning than to say it *has* meaning. Creation does not exist like a billboard and then advertise some product with a picture. Creation exists only at the Word of the Lord, and the point to its existence is its revelation of God. Creation isn't a substance that would continue to exist if God withdrew His Word. It doesn't exist independently and then point humanity toward God. It exists only by the Word of God with the purpose of revealing God.

The created world not only reveals God; it provides a medium or channel through which we can serve God. The way we think of and use the creation expresses our real relation to God. When we use it as if we were independent of God, we declare ourselves to be little gods. When we use it in love to Him and to our neighbor, it becomes a means of communion with God. We hint at this when we eat a bit of bread and drink a tiny cup of wine or grape juice in church and profess to have had communion with God. But we rarely think of the life-encompassing significance of what we do there. The Eucharist is only the tip of the iceberg. The whole of reality is meant to be seen and used in a similarly meaningful fashion. This doesn't mean that the creation teaches us new propositions about God; that is the province of the Bible. But the creation does call on us to respond to God in awe, love, praise, and service.

Perhaps now the dreadful price of modernity's split between facts and values begins to be apparent. It has reduced our perception of the world and so our conception of the school studies to a purposeless, meaningless collection of objective facts. Those facts are now regarded as keys to our self-centered use of the world. But this is idolatry. This outlook has emptied the creation of significance. But the world does have a purpose; it has meaning and value. The denial of this has, in modern times, been accompanied by an unprecedented development of science and technology and a meteoric improvement in material living standards. While we should give thanks to God for these, they have acted almost like an opiate, blinding us to what we were losing in the process of denying that facts have meaning. The benefits did not depend on the denial of meaning. It would not have been necessary to think that facts are neutral in order to learn how to make life more comfortable. We have made the kind of bargain Faust made with the devil. We have gained physical convenience and comfort at the loss of our souls.

This explains what is distinctive about a Christian approach to the school studies. Neutral facts make no demand on the learner. One's response is conditioned solely on one's personal and selfish interest in the facts involved. The Christian teacher does not provide a new set of facts, but she does something special with them. She reinvests them with their God-intended meaning. In this light, they now demand a response from the student. Learning is translated from a passive and receptive exercise into an active and dynamic one. The examination, through the school studies, of the creation and of people's responses to it becomes a doorway into communion with and service to God. They cease to be secular studies, for they are channels to the knowledge of God, "whom to know aright is life eternal" (John 17:3)! The response they call for involves deepening awe for God, love, praise, and service to Him. There could hardly be a greater gulf between two approaches to "facts" than this.

FURTHER ILLUSTRATIONS

An earlier chapter provided an illustration of the God-revealing quality of the creation. Perhaps some additional examples would be useful here. For me, one of the most inviting and rewarding doors into this new world has been a passage from C. S. Lewis. There Lewis thanks his friend for helping him to learn "the far more secret doctrine that *pleasures* are shafts of the glory as it strikes our sensibility" (*Letters to Malcolm, Chiefly on Prayer*, p. 90). Pleasure does not come, in the final sense, from a tasty delicacy, a cool drink on a hot day, or a heart-warming conversation with a dear friend. Pleasure comes *through* these, not *from* them. Only God makes pleasures (Psalm 16:11; James 1:17). They are direct touches from God Himself on our hearts, mediated by things or people in the creation. The devil misuses pleasures; he does not make them. Bad pleasures, Lewis continues, are

... PLEASURES SNATCHED BY UNLAWFUL ACTS. IT IS THE STEAL-
ING OF THE APPLE THAT IS BAD, NOT THE SWEETNESS. THE SWEETNESS
IS STILL A BEAM FROM THE GLORY. THAT DOES NOT PALLIATE THE
STEALING. IT MAKES IT WORSE. THERE IS SACRILEGE IN THE THEFT.
WE HAVE ABUSED A HOLY THING (PP. 90-91).

Then Lewis goes on to suggest that, while we ought
to give thanks for pleasures, if we really recognize their
Source, the very recognition becomes a prayer of praise,
adoration, and thankfulness without our speaking a word.
This biblical concept can become a doorway into a new
and alternative consciousness! Philip Yancey has said:

DR. BRAND AND I DESIRE THAT THIS BOOK WILL HELP SPAN THE
CHASM THAT FOR TOO LONG HAS SEPARATED THE CREATED WORLD
FROM ITS SOURCE. GOD INVENTED MATTER. HE INVESTED HIS GREAT,
CREATIVE SELF IN THIS WORLD AND, SPECIFICALLY, IN THE DESIGN OF
OUR BODIES. THE LEAST WE CAN DO IS BE GRATEFUL ...YOU MAY FIND,
AS WE DID, THAT THE HUMAN BODY EXPRESSES SPIRITUAL REALITY SO
AUTHENTICALLY THAT SOON THE COMMON STUFF OF MATTER WILL
APPEAR MORE AND MORE LIKE MERE SHADOW (*FEARFULLY AND WONDER-
FULLY MADE*, PREFACE).

Yancey is not suggesting that matter is not real or
that we are not bodies as well as souls, but that matter
without meaning is empty.

In *A Rumor of Angels* Peter Berger cites a number of
instances of what he calls "tokens of transcendence," experiences in ordinary life that go beyond empirical evidence
and scientific explanation. One of these he calls the argument from ordering. He cites the experience of a child away
from home waking in the night and finding himself utterly alone and terrified. He cries out, and it is almost
always his mother who resolves his problem. She comes
into the room, turns on a light, picks him up, and always
says the same thing to him. "Don't be afraid; everything
is all right." The remarkable thing is that the child believes her and goes back to sleep. She has restored his sense

of an orderly world. Berger pursues the incident by asking whether the mother is lying to the child—lying out of love, no doubt, but still lying. Everything cannot be all right unless there is a benevolent Deity in whose hands everything rests. Whether the mother knows it or not, she is bearing witness to God's hold on His creation. For instances in ordinary life that speak tantalizingly of the transcendent, and so of God, Berger's book is a valuable resource.

Robert Capon combines cookery with philosophy and theology in an intriguing manner. He asks the reader to take an onion and, with a sharp knife, remove the outer layer and lay the fragments inside-up on the board. "They are," he says, "elegant company," for with their understated display of wealth, they bring you to one of the oldest and most secret things of the world: the sight of what no one but you has ever seen. This quiet gold, and the subtly flattened sheen of greenish yellow white onion that now stands exposed, are virgin land. Like the incredible fit of twin almonds in a shell, they present themselves to you as the animals to Adam: as nameless till seen by man, to be met, known, and christened into the city of being. They come as deputies of all the hiddennesses of the world, of all the silent competencies endlessly at work deep down things. And they come to *you*—to you as their priest and voice, for oblation by your heart's astonishment at their great glory (*The Supper of the Lamb*, p.12).

The glory does not belong finally to the onion. It is God's glory revealed to the eye of faith through the onion. In another book Capon says that Dante's concept of romantic love is

... ABOUT THE MYSTICAL BODY—THE CITY—THE MYSTERY OF MEMBERSHIP IN EACH OTHER. . . . THE GENERAL IDEA IS THAT THIS ASTONISHING THING OF BEING LIFTED OUT OF ONE'S SELF BY THE MERE SIGHT OF THE BELOVED, THIS ABILITY OF THE BELOVED TO SEEM SO

MUCH MORE THAN FLESH AND BLOOD, HER APTNESS TO COMMUNICATE, TO COME ACROSS HARD, IS A HINT THAT THE WHOLE BUSINESS OF LOVE WAS DESIGNED TO BE A COMMUNICATION. NOT, MIND YOU, THE GIRL'S COMMUNICATION OF SOMETHING *IN HER*, BUT GOD'S COMMUNICATION *THROUGH HER* OF THE MYSTERY OF THE COINHERENCE. SHE IS AN IMAGE, A DIAGRAM, OF THE GLORY OF THE CITY—OF THAT COLLECTION OF CREATED PIECES MADE TO TEND CEASELESSLY TOWARD THE ONENESS OF THE BODY. . . .

OF COURSE, WE USUALLY MISS THE POINT OF IT ALL. WE LIKE TO THINK THAT BEATRICE IS SAYING SOMETHING ABOUT HERSELF, AND WE BEGIN, AFTER THE FIRST WONDER, TO AIM AT HER RATHER THAN THE GLORY BEHIND HER. . . . THEY WERE NOT MEANT *FOR* EACH OTHER; THEY WERE MEANT TO COMMUNICATE THE GLORY *TO* EACH OTHER. THEY ARE NOT GODS, BUT MINISTERS. BEATRICE IS PRECISELY A PRIESTLY FIGURE. SHE IS NOT MY DESTINY, BUT THE AGENT, THE DELIGHTFUL SACRAMENT, OF IT. IF I TREAT HER AS AN END, DELIGHT IS ABOUT ALL I CAN BARGAIN FOR, AND NOT EVEN THAT FOR LONG. IF I TAKE HER AS A SACRAMENT, I RECEIVE, ALONG WITH THE DELIGHT, THE JOY THAT LIES BEHIND HER (*BED AND BOARD*, PP. 65-66).

Perhaps the finest resource for seeing the sacramental aspect of creation is found in Alexander Schmemann's *For the Life of the World*. Here you will find a priceless exposition of how the created world can become for us a Jacob's ladder heavy with two-way traffic—God's self-revelation coming down and our praise and worship going up:

THE FIRST, THE BASIC DEFINITION OF MAN IS THAT HE IS *THE PRIEST*. HE STANDS IN THE CENTER OF THE WORLD AND UNIFIES IT IN HIS ACT OF BLESSING GOD, OF BOTH RECEIVING THE WORLD FROM GOD AND OFFERING IT TO GOD—AND BY FILLING THE WORLD WITH THIS EUCHARIST, HE TRANSFORMS HIS LIFE, THE ONE THAT HE RECEIVES FROM THE WORLD, INTO LIFE IN GOD, INTO COMMUNION WITH HIM. THE WORLD WAS CREATED AS THE "MATTER," THE MATERIAL OF ONE ALL-EMBRACING EUCHARIST, AND MAN WAS CREATED AS THE PRIEST OF THIS COSMIC SACRAMENT (P. 15).

C. S. Lewis reaches the culmination of God's self-revelation in creation with these words:

> NEXT TO THE BLESSED SACRAMENT ITSELF, YOUR NEIGHBOR IS THE HOLIEST OBJECT PRESENTED TO YOUR SENSES. IF HE IS YOUR CHRISTIAN NEIGHBOR, HE IS HOLY IN ALMOST THE SAME WAY, FOR IN HIM ALSO CHRIST ... THE GLORIFIER AND THE GLORIFIED, GLORY HIMSELF, IS TRULY HIDDEN (*THE WEIGHT OF GLORY*, P. 15).

No wonder Robert Browning says:

> EARTH'S CRAMMED WITH HEAVEN,
> AND EVERY COMMON BUSH AFIRE WITH GOD;
> BUT ONLY HE WHO SEES TAKES OFF HIS SHOES—
> THE REST SIT AROUND AND PLUCK BLACKBERRIES.
>
> AURORA LEIGH, BOOK III

CONCLUDING COMMENTS

What has been said above about the meaning of the "facts" does not mean that the teacher must be constantly talking about how the school studies reveal God. If he does, the concept will soon become meaningless to the students. However, as he himself becomes gripped by the wonder of God's self-revelation in the creation, he will find imaginative and intriguing ways to suggest the idea to his students.

One of the major goals of education is the exploration of the creation, but there is more than one way to do it. Modern public schools emphasize the scientific method as the only way to get at the truth. Knowledge that is not scientific is regarded with suspicion. Science, strictly speaking, cannot deal with anything that cannot be quantified or measured. As a result, large areas of truth are inaccessible to the secular school. But the modern mind has been so seduced by the success of science in observable things that it has put its confidence in what is called "science" in other areas of life as well. Hence we have the social sciences, the behavioral sciences, and so on. These purport to present the truth in the secular school, but they offer only a counterfeit kind of truth. Christians often accommodate the gospel to this Enlightenment perspective by saying there are two kinds of truth, secular and spiritual. The Bible, however, does not recognize such a distinction. Christ is the truth in everything, for He is the Creator to whom all creation, mathematical to theological, points.

Their emphasis on science has meant that secular schools highlight logical/linguistic abilities and characterize children as intelligent or not on the basis of their IQ scores. However, it turns out that intelligence comes in a good many other forms than the logical/linguistic one. The IQ, as a result, tends to measure the likelihood of a student's success in school rather than in life.

The problem with the scientific approach to the truth is that, as Doug Blomberg points out, scientific knowing may deepen our understanding of the creation, but it cannot replace it. Scientific knowing is one kind of knowing; but there are a good many others. To limit knowledge to scientific knowledge is to debase and cheapen it, particularly in the light of the God-revealing quality of the creation. Blomberg continues:

> SCIENTIFIC THOUGHT IS ONLY ONE SPECIAL WAY OF KNOWING AMONGST OTHERS; IT IS NOT THE ARCHETYPE OF KNOWLEDGE, TO WHICH ALL OTHER WAYS OF KNOWING MUST ASPIRE, BUT OF WHICH THEY ALWAYS FALL SHORT. OTHER WAYS OF KNOWING ARE NOT UNSCIENTIFIC; AS IF THEY INADEQUATELY MEET THE SCIENTIFIC CANONS: THEY ARE NON-SCIENTIFIC, AND MUST BE JUDGED ACCORDING TO OTHER NORMS (*No Icing on the Cake*, p. 53).

The goal of the Christian school is also the exploration of the creation, but it approaches the creation in a different way. While it presents the so-called "facts" that science has uncovered, it sees them as revealing God and providing channels of service and communion with Him.

In this sort of exploration, the important thing is to identify the gifts a student has and to help the student use them in exploring. Gifts, as the Bible indicates, come in many varieties. There are intellectual gifts, artistic gifts, social gifts, gifts of persuasion and influence, gifts of helping, and many others. Each one opens up a different aspect of the creation and so leads to an appreciation of another side of the Creator. It is important that the Christian school be aware of these differences and provide for each student ways to explore the creation that match his or her gifts.

One way to measure how well a Christian school recognizes and provides for this sort of approach to education is to look at the school's hidden curriculum. Do honors at graduation go mainly to students who have been successful in handling the linguistic/logical approach, which has traditionally been the principal approach? Apart from academics and sports, what evidence is there that gifts in aesthetics, in service, in personal understanding, in concern for the less fortunate, and others are recognized. To what extent are we, as Christian schools, simply following the pattern of the secular schools around us?

There is another side to the importance of gifts in the Christian approach to learning. The secular public school, with its emphasis on the scientific method as the source of truth, is highly individualistic and competitive. (There are some signs of change in this area. For instance, a 1994 book by Thomas J. Sergiovanni, *Building Community in Schools*, presents the urgent need to develop community in schools because community in the general society has become so rare.) An emphasis on the variety of gifts and their value opens the way for the development of a Christian community that is noncompetitive because the contribution of each member is more clearly recognized and appreciated. Humility, that foundational element in the Christian life, is thereby encouraged, and the mutual support that all need is more readily available.

An interesting feature of current educational research is the suggestion that there are multiple intelligences. In *Frames of Mind: The Theory of Multiple Intelligences*, Howard Gardner identifies seven intelligences and hints at more. Blomberg, in addition to theoretical knowing, lists techno-cultural, lingual, social, economic, aesthetic, jural, ethical, and confessional knowing. Clearly, Christian schools need to give attention to these ideas if they are to work out the possibilities of distinctively Christian teaching and learning.

This does not mean that the Christian school will not emphasize academic excellence. For the student with a gift for scholarship, the Christian school will endeavor to provide all the challenge needed for the thorough unfolding of that gift. Daniel, in the university of Babylon, was undoubtedly excellent in the various disciplines taught there, but he put all he learned into a totally different framework from that of his teachers. Moses and Paul had a similar relation to the higher learning of their days. So Christian school students with gifts for scholarship will be challenged to do their best, but scholarly thinking will not be the crowning or the only kind of knowledge in the school. It will be one of the ways in which we can know God and become responsive disciples.

What is distinctive about Christian school teaching is that it restores to the "facts" their God-given meaning. Thus the study of the creation becomes a way of having fellowship with God and serving Him. However, this kind of knowledge cannot be communicated to students in a merely theoretical manner. To be a student is to be an apprentice. The master must experience and practice what he would have the apprentice learn. Hence it is imperative that parents, pastors, and Christian school teachers experience the creation as the voice of the Lord (Psalm 19) and that they respond to Him in their understanding of His world.

Teaching Christianly is a challenging but highly rewarding task. It involves the effort to induce in students' minds and hearts a radically new view of the world we live in. On the teacher's part, it calls for a depth of fellowship with God that we have sorely underestimated. Such teaching is not easy, but it is undergirded by the promise of the presence of Christ and the enablement of the Holy Spirit. How the created subjects can reveal God will be discussed in more detail later. For the moment, it is enough to open a crack in the wall of the created world and suggest something of the glory that lies behind it. In John 17 Jesus identifies eternal life with the knowledge of God, and the Bible clearly indicates that, once we have come to new life in Christ, the created world is replete with God's self-revelation and is a channel for communion with Him. This is a fundamental distinctive of Christian schooling.

Listed below are some useful resources on the meaning of the creation.

RESOURCES ON GOD'S
SELF-REVELATION IN THE CREATION

1. Peter Berger, *A Rumor of Angels*
2. Paul Brand and Philip Yancey, *In His Image; Fearfully and Wonderfully Made*
3. Robert Capon, *The Supper of the Lamb; Bed and Board; An Offering of Uncles*
4. Tom Howard, *Hallowed Be This House* (formerly *Splendor in the Ordinary*)
5. C. S. Lewis, *The Weight of Glory*
6. Virginia Stem Owens, *God Spy: Faith, Perception and the New Physics* (formerly *And the Trees Clap Their Hands*)
7. Eugene Peterson, *The Psalms as Tools for Prayer*
8. Alexander Schmemann, *For the Life of the World*

Notes:

1. This is only a beginning bibliography. As you become aware of how creation reveals the Creator, you will find other resources.

2. The above books are available, as long as they remain in print, through the Alta Vista Bookroom, PO Box 55535, Seattle, WA 98155.

NOTES

Human Experience and School Subjects

15

Human experience is limited, with one exception, to the created world. The exception lies in the human capacity to have touch with God. The Creator is outside His creation, while He is also active within it. Thus our capacity to know Him in Jesus Christ reaches outside the creation. For this reason this capacity is inaccessible to empirical experience and logic, which are the foundation of the scientific method. Science cannot corner God in order to analyze His being. "Can you discover the depths of God? Can you discover the limits of the Almighty" (Job 11:7)? There is mystery here that we can never fully penetrate.

Nevertheless, our relation to God is interwoven with our experience of the creation. As we have seen, the reason why God created the universe at all was to reveal Himself to humans, to make it possible for us to know and respond to Him through it. Once we have come to know God through Christ our Redeemer, the school studies can become doors through which we see God and respond to Him in love and service.

There are at least two ways of knowing the reality in which we exist. One is by analysis—reflecting on observation or experience to find regularities or laws. This is the scientific method. The other and more basic way is through our ordinary experience (sometimes called prescientific). We are so accustomed since babyhood to the second way that we do not usually think of it as a way of knowing reality. However, that is what it is. Actually, it is a gift from God, a way of seeing things that involves all our senses plus our mental, emotional, and spiritual capacities to give us a holistic or unified picture of the world and our life in it.

Our ordinary experience of reality is an amazingly unified combination of a number of different meaning aspects, or ways of experiencing. By means of our logical capacity, we can isolate these aspects, or modes, of our experience. They turn out to be the areas that make up the academic studies, particularly at the university level. They are never listed in the Bible. Hence the list below carries no claim to inspiration. It is a human effort to understand the world in the light of the Bible, and it may need to be altered. But because it has great potential for helping us understand the academic studies, it is presented here. Derived from the work of Dooyeweerd, it is as follows, with a parallel list of school subjects added:

ASPECTS	SUBJECTS
FIDUCIARY (PISTICAL)	THEOLOGY
ETHICAL	ETHICS, MORALITY
JUSTITIAL	CIVICS
AESTHETIC	FINE ARTS
ECONOMIC	ECONOMICS
SOCIAL	SOCIOLOGY
LINGUISTIC	LANGUAGE
HISTORICAL	HISTORY, CULTURE
LOGICAL	REASONING, LOGIC
SENSORY	PSYCHOLOGY
BIOTIC	BIOLOGY
PHYSICAL	CHEMISTRY
KINEMATIC	PHYSICS
SPATIAL	GEOMETRY
QUANTITATIVE	ARITHMETIC

There was a reason for this particular order of the aspects of experience, at least in Dooyeweerd's mind. The reason is too complicated for complete discussion here, but a comment on the lowest three aspects on the list may help to show why he established an order. The quantitative aspect deals with numbers, and a number of points must be established before we can draw a picture of a space. Space is necessary before we can conceive of motion (which is prominent in physics). So each aspect has a dependency relation to the aspects below it.

These aspects are not things but ways in which we encounter God's world. They are not "whats" but "hows." They are full of regularities, or laws, that are maintained moment by moment by the power of God's Word. The initial task of the Christian teacher is to help students begin to think of these regularities as God's laws. While there are times when moral lessons may appropriately be introduced, the first task is to recover the laws from "Nature" and return them to God where they belong. In dealing with them, we are never far from Him, and if, under the influence of His Spirit, we think about them in this way, we will soon find ourselves in an awed and deepening fellowship with Him.

A brief parenthetical comment is appropriate here. The fact that all these aspects of experience are involved in our holistic experience of life and the world because they are all the work of the Word of God may be telling us that our approach to schooling is far too fragmented to provide the best pedagogy. Probably because of the influence of Greek rationalism on Western thinking, we tend to split everything up analytically, including the school curriculum. In reality, as some of the most advanced educational reformers are seeing today, life doesn't come apart like this. We probably need to integrate our curricula much more effectively than we have so far learned to do.

Creation is the first strand of the Christian worldview, and we may experience the creation in at least these fifteen aspects, or modes. Yet the aspects are intricately interrelated. For example, the last aspect on the list, quantity or muchness, appears in each of the other aspects. There are not only smaller and larger numbers in arithmetic; there are also varieties of muchness in geometric or spatial figures. Force and movement, the kinematic aspect, have a muchness side. A billiard ball weighs more than a feather. (We call this *gravity* and thereby manage to lose the Word of God out of the situation.) In the physical or chemical area, too much salt can ruin your supper. In biology, too many goldfish in a small bowl can lead to the death of some. One can feel a little depressed or deeply depressed on the sensory side of experience. A slight mistake in logic may pass unnoticed, while a big one won't. A culture can be relatively Christian or almost entirely secular. Some people use words sparingly, while others talk so much we wish they wouldn't. People with a sanguine temperament are likely to have a full social life; melancholic people may not. On the economic side, populations include the rich and the poor. An artist's painting may have too much or too little of a certain color. Laws may be too severe or too lax. And, while there can never be too much true love, there is frequently too little. Faith, too, can be small or large. The aspects of experience are intimately interrelated. Each one appears in all the others.

At this point we encounter the other two strands of a Christian worldview: this is a fallen world, and it is one redeemed in Jesus Christ. One way of recognizing these two strands can be seen in the fact that the cosmonomic philosophy speaks of laws in the lower six aspects of our experience, but of norms in the upper nine. The upper nine are the particularly human aspects of experience, and it is there that the reality of the fall into sin and restoration in redemption are most apparent. The effect of sin on the creation is evident in the fact that "the whole creation groans and suffers the pains of childbirth together until now" (Romans 8:22), but it does not change the distinction between laws and norms. The regularities that God maintains in the lower aspects are such that we disregard them only at severe risk. Breaking the law of gravity exacts a severe penalty. On the other hand, in the ethical modality the law of the Lord is love, but since the fall we seldom observe this norm with any degree of completeness. We may even disregard it in this life, though the Bible indicates that there will be a day of reckoning in the life to come. Disregarding norms is an expression of our fallenness. We come to observe them, though never perfectly in this life, through the redemptive work of the Lord Jesus applied to our hearts by the Holy Spirit. The norms are the laws of the Lord for the various upper areas. They are His will for our activities in those areas. They are a part of God's covenant with the creation, even though we humans pay little respect to them. We begin to fulfill them only when we are gripped by the Word in its marvelous potency as the grace of God. They are not listed specifically in the Bible, but we can discover them by studying it.

What has all this to do with teaching Christianly? A great deal, but there is no merely technical way of effecting it. When, under the mysterious influence of the Holy Spirit, we become conscious that the laws and norms really belong to the upholding and redeeming Word of the Lord, something remarkable begins to happen in our hearts. We become conscious that the earth really "is the Lord's and the fulness thereof, the world and they that dwell therein" (Psalm 24:1). And with that alternative consciousness comes an upsurge of thankfulness, praise, love, adoration, prayer, and communion with God such as we have not known before.

Take the subject of arithmetic, for example. It is the study closely associated with the quantitative, or muchness, aspect of our experience. It involves the use of numbers. What a blessing it is that we can count, tell time, and make change! These are not accidents, or the chance result of biological evolution. They are gifts from a loving heavenly Father. The constancy of the addition, subtraction, multiplication, and division tables is not a mere chance either. They hold because God is faithful. He both maintains these relationships among numbers and upholds our minds so that we can make use of them. When we work out a problem in arithmetic and get the right answer, we have a good feeling. Often we attribute our success to our own cleverness and make invidious comparisons with others who have difficulty with the problem. Instead, we ought to recognize that the good feeling is a little touch of God's "well done." We have done the problem in keeping with His faithful maintenance of the facts of arithmetic, and we have arrived at His answer. We need to be grateful to Him. (We are so accustomed to a secular view of mathematics that this very suggestion sounds superpious. With caution and time, however, it should be possible to develop in the classroom a thankful awareness of God's involvement even in arithmetic.)

The facts of arithmetic are not different for us than for others, but they now begin to regain their true meaning or value. God made them and He upholds them. He is talking to us in them, and we can begin to see our use of them as service to Him. We can start noticing other mathematical features in the world around us and give thanks. The path that the earth travels around the sun is not a circle but an ellipse. It has the shape of a graph of a quadratic equation. There is an equation for the way sunflower seeds grow in a sunflower. Tree branches do not grow haphazardly, but in a regular mathematical order around the trunk. (Even if they didn't, the element of surprise, of the unexpected, of individuality, also reveals God's greatness.) Modern physicists have come to rely more and more on mathematical formulae in their effort to describe reality. As awarenesses like these grow on us, our hearts will fill with praise and thankfulness. We will learn new levels of communion with God and so of service to Him.

Counting, figuring, and using numbers are never neutral, "objective," value-free activities. They are more than skills to be used to our own advantage. We serve either God or the idols when we do arithmetic or mathematics. What a source of joy it can become to realize that

Christ has made it possible for us to serve God in this way.

There is no merely technical way of encouraging this sort of perception in the hearts of our students. However, as our own perception grows, and with it our love for God, we will be enabled to bear witness to what we have come to see, and we will pray that the Holy Spirit will write some measure of the same experience in the hearts and minds of our students. This is why Psalm 145 is sometimes spoken of as the teacher's psalm:

ONE GENERATION SHALL PRAISE THY WORKS TO ANOTHER,
AND SHALL DECLARE THY MIGHTY ACTS.
ON THE GLORIOUS SPLENDOR OF THY MAJESTY,
AND ON THY WONDERFUL WORKS, I WILL MEDITATE.
AND MEN SHALL SPEAK OF THE POWER OF THINE AWESOME ACTS;
AND I WILL TELL OF THY GREATNESS.

PSALM 145: 4-6

Teaching Christianly is not only a science but also an art, and its effectiveness depends heavily on the level of the teacher's own communion with God. If we can see the Lord in His world, we will find ways to speak of Him. At the same time we will be familiarizing our students with the so-called "facts" of the subjects. And we will be praying and trusting that the Holy Spirit will bring alive in our students' hearts something of the glory that has begun to dawn on us as we see the Lord in the creation and return it to Him in praise and adoration.

From what has been said above, it is clear that the aspects are intricately interrelated. It is also true that they are irreducible to one another. Each has its own inner principle or law from the Word of God that holds it in being. No one aspect can be allowed to dominate the others. Only God is big enough to hold them all in being, and in their interrelationships, without damage to any of them. If, however, people refuse to acknowledge God as the Creator and

Sustainer of the creation, they will not be able to do without something that has an independent status and on which everything else depends. Then they will create an idol or an *ism* out of some one aspect, and in the process they will wrench all the other aspects out of focus. For example, Karl Marx selected economics as the basic element in reality and human history, and the result was Marxism. The misshaping of culture that followed is now apparent to everyone. B. F. Skinner sees the biological human animal as basic to history. Behaviorism follows. Freud saw psychology as central and gave us Freudianism. Any aspect can be turned into an idol. This is what Romans 1:25 warns against. "For they exchanged the truth of God for a lie, and worshiped and served the creature rather than the Creator, who is blessed forever. Amen." We in America are seeing the implementation of historicism, as standards of ethics and morality are being changed by popular vote or Supreme Court edict. Even theology can become an *ism*. We call it Pharisaism, and Jesus warned against it with great severity in John 5:38–40.

In the next two chapters we will look at the other aspects and the related subjects and suggest some ways in which we can restore meaning to the "facts" in these subjects as well.

More Aspects and School Subjects   16

Ordinary or prescientific human experience is a thoroughly unified and yet complex thing. It is so common to us since babyhood that we seldom give it a thought. Modern people especially have difficulty in focusing attention on ordinary experience. They have been thoroughly taught that the only truth to be had is scientific truth. Anything other than scientific truth is automatically shunted aside as primitive, unimportant, and probably superstitious. The reality is that humans all have a remarkably integrated awareness of themselves and their surroundings. This is a gift from God and is renewed to us at each moment of our lives. It is concentrated in the core of our personhood, the heart, out of which, the Bible says, the issues of life proceed (Proverbs 4:23). A renewal of our realization of God's involvement in our ordinary experience is a fundamental element in the alternative consciousness that the gospel brings to us.

As we have seen, it is possible for us, by using our power of logical reasoning, to group the elements of our ordinary experience within a number of aspects, which we deal with in the school subjects. Investigating these aspects is part of our role as God's shop-stewards, responsible for looking after His world. The aspects of experience are not equivalent to the school subjects, but the school subjects look into things in our lives that correspond to certain aspects. The aspects are ways in which we encounter God's world. When we analyze one of them, we develop a science. The analysis is meant to deepen our awe and love and fear of God and thus also to deepen our love for our neighbor.

The correspondence between the school subjects and the aspects is not always one to one. There are subjects like geography, home economics, and physical education that range across several aspects. But there are none that do not connect with at least one side of our experience.

The aspects are intricately interrelated, so that each one appears in all the others. Yet they are irreducible in that none of them can be defined as a division or subset of another. The reason is that each aspect is the work of the Word of God, as is the entirety of our ordinary experience of creation. God has written His law into each side of life as we experience it. When, through Christ's redemptive work, we become aware of this, we learn something of what Psalm 19:7 means by saying, "The law of the Lord is perfect, restoring the soul." Any genuine touch with the living God has a restorative impact on our lives, broken as they are by our sinfulness. When we try to isolate one aspect of experience as the one that dominates all the others, we fall into the error of the blind men who identified the elephant with whatever part each one encountered. Thus we produce modern idolatries like Marxism and Freudianism. Each aspect of experience has a God-given core meaning, or key idea. The interrelationships among the aspects suggest the value of thematic units in school. Unit studies tend to highlight the holistic nature of life and of our relation to God in it.

While it is helpful to identify the different aspects of experience, it is important, especially in school, to keep in mind the wholeness of our encounter with the creation. For this reason unit studies are particularly valuable in the lower grades. A unit study deals with a topic in a way that includes several aspects of experience. As students move up into the middle grades, their maturing mental abilities make it possible for them to profit from a more detailed study of specific aspects. In high school it makes sense to deal with subjects like biology, history, and English, but even there we need to keep in mind the integrity of our life experience. Hence cross-cultural studies in which more than one teacher participates are important.

The realization that God is speaking to us in each of the school studies presents a danger. It is easy to turn this line of thought into a moralistic way of teaching, and to use the law-ordered nature of the universe as leverage to urge children to try harder to be "good" children. But this is a dangerous, legalistic way of dealing with education. What we and our students need is not an expanded set of rules to follow. We need simply to recognize the depth of our attempted independence and come to the Lord with our hands dirty and our shirt tails hanging out. What we need is grace. Our weakness, not our strength, is our point of contact with Him. "Just as I am, without one plea, but that thy blood was shed for me, and that thou bids't me come to thee, O Lamb of God, I come, I come." If we will take our students by the hand and come with them in this repentant spirit, the Holy Spirit will do what needs to be done in their hearts and ours to enable us to reach new levels of God-honoring, God-loving life and activity.

The analysis of the aspects offered here is, at best, tentative. It is hoped that it will provide teachers with starting points toward finding their work irradiated more and more by the Word of God and thus effective in leading their students into a deepening touch with the Lord through the creation.

The Spatial Aspect

The spatial aspect of experience relates most directly to the study of geometry, though, as we shall see, there is a spatial side to everything, and space enters into all the other subjects. The key idea of this aspect is continuous extension. Two points define a line but not a space. The addition of another point can define a two-dimensional space, with length and breadth, and a fourth point in another plane can give us a three-dimensional space, with height.

The important beginning point for Christian teaching of geometry is the awareness that space exists because God spoke it into being and continues, instant by instant, to hold it there. Space is not a value-free natural law. "Nature," in this context, is a subterfuge to avoid facing the possibility that there might be a living God to whom we are all accountable. Space, whether physical or nonphysical, is a wonderful gift of God's love. To be reminded of the blessings it provides for us in the physical realm, one has only to experience a broken leg or to watch a paraplegic in action. Room to move, and the ability to do so, is a wonderful blessing from the Lord. By the same token, room to think is an inestimable gift!

As suggested above, the spatial aspect appears in the other aspects of experience as well. Plants and animals have life space. They can thrive only in certain environments and at certain elevations. People have life space as well, both materially and immaterially. We have certain emotional limits within which we are able to operate. These define our emotional life space. There are limits to logical space as well. Cultural space is no different, for cultures are not worldwide. They usually stop at the border of a tribe or nation. Languages, too, are limited in their extent, and social classes outline the boundaries that separate groups within a given culture. The gulf between rich and poor is a sign of the boundaries of economic space. Since the 1960s there are those who insist that there are no limits to artistic space, that artists must be free to express themselves no matter how offensive their work may be to some people. This is an example of the postmodern emphasis on rights to the exclusion of responsibilities. Some things, however, are so widely regarded as offensive that they are not usually offered for public view. So artistic space is not entirely unbounded. Legal space is clearly limited, although there are lawyers who spend their lives finding ways around the regulations. Ethical space, or room for love, is severely limited by our sinful selfishness. Confessional or faith space is recognized by many people and denied by those who fear the implications of admitting that they believe something. That something they believe is religious, even though they do not call it that. So the spatial aspect reappears in all the others.

Perhaps the simplest way to outline a Christian approach to space is to remember that space did not just happen and that it does not finally belong to us. We didn't invent it; we were born into a world that has space. We were born with a being that occupies a certain amount of space; we can be weighed and measured. We also have the blessed privilege of moving about in space. Space was God's idea, and it belongs to Him. We use it properly only as His guests or His servants. "The earth is the Lord's and the fulness thereof; the world and they that dwell therein" (Psalm 24:1). If we are enabled to inculcate this concept in our students' minds, we will see them growing in their awe and respect for the Lord. The Holy Spirit will bless them with a biblical perception of space.

THE KINEMATIC OR MOVEMENT ASPECT

The next aspect is the kinematic. The word comes from the Greek word for motion, and that is what this aspect deals with. Motion is usually considered under the science of physics, but physics deals with matter and energy as well, so the correspondence between subjects and aspects is not exact. Nevertheless, motion is an important aspect of our experience and is worthy of separate consideration.

By this time it will be evident that the order of the aspects is not arbitrary. To have movement, it is essential to have space. Space is defined for us by lines, but lines are impossible without points, which means that the quantitative aspect is foundational to the spatial. The same dependency will be seen to hold as we move up the list of aspects.

Movement is so fundamental a part of our experience from babyhood that we automatically think of it as something that belongs to us, something we have a right to. We object strenuously when anyone deprives us of our freedom to move. What is distinctive about a Christian approach to the topic is simply the realization that movement is something invented, created, and sustained by God. It occurs according to His laws, in keeping with His covenant with creation. Enlightenment thought imagines that if we have identified the physical cause of a certain movement, we understand the movement. But this is not so. Something lies behind the physical causes we identify. The wind blows, the waves move, even the mountains move only at the Word of the Lord. Just as pleasures are shafts of God's glory touching our sensibilities, so movement is a sign of the presence and power of the living God. We are never far from Him. "In Him we live and move and have our being" (Acts 17:28). Because of sin, we resist this awareness fiercely, but when, under the gentle and powerful influence of the Holy Spirit, we begin to sense it, praise and thankfulness rise spontaneously from our hearts. The facts of motion are the same for us as for the non-Christian; the meaning is entirely different. Now motion regains its God-intended function of revealing God and serving as a channel through which we can respond to him. Freedom to move is a great gift from Him.

Motion can be physical, like walking through the front door, or nonphysical, like taking a particular path through life. The Bible calls us to walk in the way of the Lord. This is not a geographical way but a confessional way, a way of love for God and neighbor. Our lives are either on the straight and narrow way that has God's approval or on the broad way that leads to destruction.

Inanimate things and plants can be moved, and plants can move in their growth. Animals and humans can move on their own with a large freedom. The distinction between animate and inanimate things is not as ironclad as it seems. At the atomic and subatomic levels there is tremendous movement, even in rocks, soil, water, and air.

Motion enters into all of schooling, from preschool through graduate school. It pervades all the other aspects. But it is not "natural" in the sense of independent existence. It is part of the fabric of the created order that is upheld, and redeemed, by the Word of God. This awareness is a significant part of the alternative perspective that Christian teaching seeks to promote.

THE PHYSICAL ASPECT

The core meaning of the physical aspect is energy. The motion of physical things, of which we have just been speaking, always involves the expenditure of energy. Energy interchange takes place at all levels in the creation, from the most basic mineral to the human level. The energy, however, is not an inherent characteristic of created things. Energy is always the power of God's Word. Colossians 1:17 says that in Christ "all things hold together," and Hebrews 1:3 says that He upholds "all things by the word of His power." Thus energy or power is one more of God's ways of addressing us, of showing us something more of Himself. Someone has suggested that energy might be described as a servant God has created for His creatures.

That we, as humans, have an intricate variety of systems in our bodies, all of which involve the transmission of energy in one way or another, is an awesome reality that calls on us to acknowledge the power of God's Word and to praise Him for the physical properties we possess. The chemical, electrolytic, and other energy systems in us are not self-activated or self-sustaining. By His Word God holds us together at every moment, even while He gives us the most amazing freedom to use or misuse His gifts of energy. Kicking a soccer ball, pushing a pencil, or tapping on a computer keyboard—these all use energy. The more we realize the source of this energy, the more we will strive to respond to God in love in the use of our physical properties.

The physical side of our experience includes matter, energy, atoms, and molecules. We deal with these things in physics and chemistry and the other physical sciences. However, recent developments in science, particularly in physics, have highlighted the problem of dealing with the world's facts without regard to their meaning. Virginia Stem Owens describes the centuries-old practice whereby scientists kept the facts separate from the "fairy tales" people made up to explain why things were the way they were. Then she says:

> THE NEW PHYSICS, HOWEVER, CAN NO LONGER PROPERLY REC-OGNIZE SUCH DISTINCTIONS BETWEEN KINDS OF TRUTH. IT TELLS US THAT . . . EVERYTHING IS RELATED TO EVERYTHING ELSE. TRUTH CAN-NOT BE COMPARTMENTALIZED. THE IMPLICATIONS OF THIS ARE YET TO BE FELT BY A SOCIETY THAT INSISTS SCIENCE AND SPIRITUALITY ARE SEPARATE DISCIPLINES TO BE PURSUED IN SEPARATE FACILITIES SO THAT ONE MAY NOT CONTAMINATE THE OTHER (*GOD SPY*, P. VII).

Owens says that the physicists keep discovering new particles and giving them strange names, "but they hesitate to call them 'things.' They are more accurately described as necessary parts of a thought process." This is not the place to pursue this topic, but the idea that Christian teaching restores meaning to the facts could hardly be demonstrated more clearly. The entire creation exists in a lawful fashion, held in being by the Word of the Lord. And the whole point of this marvelous collection of "matter" (whatever that is) and energy, space, and movement is to tell us that God is God and that He has us in His view in the most particular and loving ways. Perhaps the most vivid biblical illustration of the possibilities for Christian teaching in this area occurs at the end of the book of Job, referred to above. When God had talked to Job about the physical creation, Job's response was, "I have heard about you by the hearing of the ear, but now my eye sees you, and I abhor myself and repent in dust and ashes"

(Job 42:5–6). Thus, properly considered, the physical world has power to convict us of sin and lead us to repentance.

Once again, in the world of physical things, the important goal is to help children recognize the way things really are. They need to catch glimpses of how near God is, of His desire to reveal Himself to them in His power and His love. They need to perceive afresh that ordinary things can be channels of communion with God and of service to Him.

THE BIOTIC ASPECT

The four previous aspects are logically conceivable without the aspect of life, but the latter could not occur without them. The key idea of the biotic aspect is vitality or life. Familiar as we are with life in our own experience and in our experience of the living things around us, life is very difficult to define. We usually circumvent the problem by saying that if something takes in food, grows, reproduces, and can die, then it has life. We even speak of the life of nonphysical things such as a political regime, a house, or a book. This metaphorical use illustrates again the intricate interrelationship among the aspects wherein each one appears in all the others.

But what is life? It is a gift from God, the work of His living, powerful Word (Hebrews 4:12). God spoke the first human into being when He breathed into his nostrils the breath of life and man became a living soul (Genesis 2:7). The life of all living things is in God's hands (Job 12:10). When He takes away His breath (His Word), they die (Psalm 104:29–30; 148:7 and 9). Uko Zylstra discusses this question helpfully:

HOWEVER, LIFE IS NOT A CONCRETE SOMETHING; RATHER, IT IS A WAY IN WHICH CONCRETE THINGS FUNCTION. FOR SOMETHING TO BE ALIVE IT MUST HAVE A LIFE (VITAL) FUNCTION WHICH WE EXPERIENCE AS A VITAL PHENOMENON SUCH AS GROWTH AND REPRODUCTION. WE

CAN STUDY, DESCRIBE, AND DEFINE THESE VARIOUS VITAL PHENOMENA, BUT WE CANNOT DEFINE LIFE ITSELF. LIVING BEINGS ARE NOT LIVING BECAUSE THEY POSSESS A CERTAIN SUBSTANCE CALLED LIFE; THEY ARE LIVING BEINGS BECAUSE THEY HAVE BEEN CREATED WITH A VITAL (BIOTIC) FUNCTION OR MODE OF BEING (SHAPING SCHOOL CURRICULUM: A BIBLICAL VIEW, P. 120).

Life, then, is not a "natural" or automatic thing. It is, and it is only, a gift from God. The tenacity with which we cling to it is a reflection of our long-forgotten longing for God. Our lives depend moment by moment on His Word. Hence we read that "Man does not live by bread alone, but by every word that proceeds from the mouth of God" (Matthew 4:4). If we can help our students to become conscious of their lives as gifts from God in which He is revealing Himself to them and through which they can give themselves back to Him, we will have done them a very great service.

THE SENSITIVE (PSYCHIC) ASPECT

Living things can perceive and feel. The sensory aspect covers both these sides of experience. Perception includes the received messages of the various senses: sight, sound, smell, taste, and touch. Feelings are the emotions we experience in connection with our perceptions. We pass in this aspect from the highest level at which plants can be characterized to one shared by animals and humans. There is a sensitive, or feeling, aspect to every experience we have.

Neither perceptions nor feelings are good or bad in themselves. The problem is that custom has often confused our handling of our feelings with the feelings themselves. Anger at a personal injustice is not wrong in itself. If we respond by trying to get even or by allowing ourselves to hate the person who wronged us, then we have a problem that calls for repentance and faith. Christ's redemption makes it possible for us to hear God's voice in our feelings and respond to them in a way that sets us free within the "perfect law of liberty" (James 1:25).

God speaks to us in our feelings. As noted earlier, C. S. Lewis described pleasures as shafts of God's glory touching our sensibilities. The fact that we rarely recognize this and instead think of pleasure as a product of the experience, thing, or person involved only shows how deeply sin has turned us into idolaters. When we recognize that only God makes pleasures (Psalm 16:11; James1:17), our experience of them becomes a form of prayer and lets us find one way, at least, of fulfilling Paul's injunction to "pray without ceasing" (1 Thess. 5:17).

One writer summed up all our emotional drives in terms of two: "I am of value" and "I am incomplete." Both are messages from the Lord. However, because of sin, we misinterpret and mishandle both. We forget that our value consists in bearing the image of God and that consequently a good self-image involves humility rather than arrogance. We try to make up for our incompleteness with something in the creation instead of with the Lord, and thus we fall into the bondage of idolatry. Neither pleasures, possessions, nor power can satisfy our incompleteness; only God Himself can. He can do it through something created, or He can do it directly, but He is the One who must do it.

In the feeling of pain, as in that of pleasure, the Lord is addressing us. He is warning us that there are ways to go in life that lead to dead ends and are to be avoided. Pain is to be avoided, not merely for our own sake, but in response to Him whose love calls us to avoid it. He bore it in its ultimate extremity that we might be delivered from it.

Feelings are identical neither with values nor with imagination, both of which will be discussed later. Dividing educational taxonomies into cognitive, affective (emotional), and psychomotor is a dubious procedure because it violates the integrity that God has built into our humanness. The modern concept that separates facts from values is an illustration of this error. It has left modern Western people with no consensus on the nature of truth and falsehood, or good and bad.

The Normed Subjects 17

As we deal with the aspects of experience, it is convenient to speak of laws. In His covenant with creation, God has built His laws into the world. The creation below the human level obeys those laws implicitly. The Lord has established laws for all the other aspects as well, but with them the implicit obedience disappears. Sin has made us addicts to some false god or gods, and we do not obey the will of God in these areas of our experience. Hence it is convenient to speak in these areas of norms rather than laws. The norms spell out the ways we ought to act. The power of Christ's redemption is such that when we are gripped by His Word, we learn gradually how to honor Him by obeying those norms. The aspects considered in this chapter are all normed aspects.

The Logical (Analytical) Aspect

The key idea of the logical or analytical aspect is distinction. Because we have an analytical ability that is analogous to the logical aspect, it is possible for us to abstract the various aspects from our ordinary experience and so develop the various sciences and school subjects. This is done in the lower or law aspects by means of the scientific method. The claim commonly made today that the study of the normed aspects can also utilize the scientific method is open to severe and devastating criticism. The reliability of empirical evidence is far less in those areas than in the physical side of life. However, our logical ability does enable us to analyze things, including events. We can take them apart into their components and put them back together again. We can perceive cause and effect, logical order and progression, and many other intricate relationships.

The ancient Greeks absolutized this capacity and called it "reason." They regarded it as the divine element in humans. Hence they spoke of people as rational souls in animal bodies. This deification of the analytical ability led to the fatal dualism of body/soul or Form/Matter that has stumbled thinking people ever since and has even penetrated Christian theology. It reappeared forcefully in the rationalism of the eighteenth and nineteenth centuries. But God did not give us reason as an autonomous guide capable by itself of leading us to the truth. Our reason always follows our hearts. Our hearts are always religiously committed either to the true God in Jesus Christ or to some idol. Hence Pascal said that the heart has reasons that the head knows nothing about. Human reason devoid of a relationship to Christ is never a safe guide to, or judge of, truth.

What God gives us when we are in Christ is understanding, of which the fear of the Lord is the most important and basic element (Proverbs 1:7, margin). The reason why our analytical ability is incapable of discovering the truth is that Truth is a Person, Jesus Christ, and rationality does not operate independently in sinful human beings. Sin has diverted our hearts from their intended allegiance and in doing so has rendered reason incapable of giving us reliable direction in life. This is why rationality is a normed side of our experience. It can be trustworthy or not, depending on where our heart finds its true home.

That God should give us the ability to understand things, and that He faithfully holds the world together by his Word so that it can be understood, are very precious gifts. However, reason can mislead as well as safely lead us. School children need to learn that the ability to discriminate is a gift from God and that their hearts need to be submissive to the lordship of Jesus if they are to use this ability rightly. The power of reason thus used becomes a beautiful form of service that pleases God.

THE HISTORICAL ASPECT

Once the capacity to differentiate logically is present in redeemed humans, the next step is to give specific shape to the life of the human community. This happens in the development of customs for cultural relationships such as marriage and family, in economic practices, in artistic productions, in legal matters, and in religious beliefs and practices. Culture formation is the essence of history, and the key idea of the historical aspect is formative power in human culture. History is not simply the sum total of all that has happened in the past. It is the account of the developments that have given a culture its particular cast. Thus history is an account of how humans have responded to God's command to have control over the creation in which He has placed us.

In our imagined independence, we suppose that our activities in culture forming are totally free expressions of our own creativity. In reality, culture is formed under the influence of powerful spiritual forces that grip the hearts and minds of whole societies at a given period of time (Ephesians 1:21, 6:12, and others). Rationalism, "manifest destiny," and the quest for *lebensraum* are instances. The call to form cultures is implicit in the command of Genesis 2:15 to cultivate and keep the Garden of Eden. Humans have obeyed this cultural mandate, but they have done so most frequently without regard to their obligation to the God who issued it, and the consequences have often been tragic. For example, the building of the Tower of Babel in Genesis was in direct disobedience to the command to spread out and repopulate the earth. Yet in the dispersion that followed God's judgment, the people fulfilled God's command but missed the blessing that could have come from obeying willingly.

Reception of the gospel involves Christians in the obligation to think through cultural developments and offer alternatives to a world that is involved in idolatrous and disastrous ways of living. So in our historical studies, our task is to discern the spirits (Matthew 16:1–4). We are to see what idols are shaping our times. We are to confront and expose them and offer people other ways of structuring their lives. This is an exciting and engrossing calling. Students should be helped to see it, and they should be challenged by it so that they can escape the self-centeredness that is characteristic of Western culture, particularly in this century.

THE LINGUAL ASPECT

One of the first ways in which culture is formed lies in the development of language. Since language is the most significant bearer of a culture, the prohibition of a native language is one of the most effective ways to destroy a culture. Such a policy played a disastrous part in the efforts of white Americans to "civilize" the Indians. The same thing happened during the early decades of this century when the Japanese prohibited the Taiwanese from using their language during the Japanese occupation of the island.

The key idea in the lingual aspect is symbolic meaning, which is present in every experience we have. Symbolism is one of the most misunderstood and undervalued things in human life, especially for Christians. We often stop with the symbolism of the communion table, where the bread and wine speak of the broken body and the poured-out blood of Christ. But, as Alexander Schmemann points out, the whole creation is sacramental. Everything in it reveals God. "The heavens declare the glory of God; and the firmament showeth His handiwork" (Psalm 19:1). The psalmists frequently call the entire created world to praise God. They do so because that is what God created the world for. And He created humans to be the mouthpieces of that praise. He made the world to speak to us of Himself (Romans 1:20). That is why Christ incarnate is called the Word of God.

We use words because we bear the image of God. The first thing God told Adam to do was to name the animals, and that responsibility has not ceased. We are still called and privileged to "name the animals," i.e., to see what God is saying to us in the creation and to give the creation back to Him by the way we talk about it and use it. That is what school is all about.

The problem is that sin has twisted human language so that often it no longer serves God or others. But the Bible tells us that our speech should be always with grace, seasoned with salt, so that it will build up the hearers (Colossians 4:6, Ephesians 4:29). Properly conceived, speech is an awesome thing because it reflects God's self-giving in His address to us in the creation. We need to learn to read the creation, to see what the Lord is saying to us in it, and then to communicate the nourishing, life-strengthening message of God's love and glory in our use of the gift of speech. As children become conscious of this, their awe will be used by the Holy Spirit to direct their speaking into channels that reveal their love to God and neighbor.

THE SOCIAL ASPECT

The key idea of the social aspect is social intercourse. God did not invent humans to be isolated individuals. He created them for the joy, comfort, and strength that come in relationships with others. This is why the Bible, which begins in a fairly solitary Garden, ends in the City of God, the Bride of the Lamb coming down out of heaven. Humans as social beings are sensitive to the deprivation of human contact that is involved in solitary confinement. Their loneliness stems from the fact that sin has cut them off from God and each other. In an effort to deny or escape this loneliness, we still shake hands or hug each other, eat and play and dance together. We need each other, even though the sense of need has been dulled by the grinding self-centeredness of our society. The proliferation of technology in modern times has deepened rather than relieved the need, leaving us more and more isolated from each other. That is probably why we find a recorded answer to our telephone call vaguely uncomfortable.

In each experience there is a social aspect. This is one of the ways in which we encounter God's world and its created inhabitants. The ideal of social intercourse is found in the Trinity: Father, Son, and Holy Spirit (Ephesians 3:14–15). Our need for human companionship reflects the longing for God that is part of our being created in His likeness. The brokenness of frequent divorce, single-parent families, and isolated generations that characterizes today's society is a tragic witness to the consequences of idolatrous service. For when we use human relationships for something other than the loving service of God, we serve idols. The Body of Christ is intended to be the showcase of restored relationships. It promises the satisfaction of our hearts' need and an upbuilding that can come in no other way. Studying the sociological aspect of our experiences, then, we are to plan for and work toward a redemptive way of life that will exemplify the reuniting power of Christ's salvation and invite others to enjoy it.

THE ECONOMIC ASPECT

Here we encounter the idea of care in managing scarce goods. We are people with needs, and God has put us into a world that can meet those needs. The ultimate answer to our needs is God Himself. One of His ways of coming to us is through the created world with its capacity to meet our needs. We misconstrue this created reality when we suppose that the creation itself has power to meet our needs. Only God can do that, but He often does it through the creation.

However, God has not endowed our environment with a limitless capacity to meet needs. There are boundaries.

If we do not recognize our covenant responsibility to use the world's resources with an eye to God's will and the good of our neighbor, creation itself will begin to strike back at us. We are already experiencing this in the pollution of our water and air, acid rain, the greenhouse effect, the shrinking of the ozone layer, and a host of other ways. Our economic systems—such as capitalism and socialism—are not autonomous. They have no power within themselves to bless us or provide for us. God provides for us, and He speaks to us in the economic provisions He makes for us. Our task is to be aware of this and to use those provisions responsibly, particularly with concern for the poor and underprivileged of the world.

Money is simply a convenient means of handling the resources of the creation, but it is something that easily leads to idolatry. Jesus warned that we cannot serve both God and mammon. When we respond to the Lord as Christians in the economic sphere, we have a tremendous opportunity to demonstrate a different way of dealing with money—making friends with it for eternity (Luke 16:9). In our society with its strong ethos of consumerism, children need to develop an alternative consciousness in relation to money and possessions. Christian teaching is meant to lead them in that direction.

THE AESTHETIC ASPECT

The key idea of the aesthetic aspect of experience is harmony or lack of it. (Calvin Seerveld, an expert in this area, prefers the word *allusiveness*.) We associate aesthetics with beauty or ugliness, but what do these terms mean? C. S. Lewis suggests that behind beauty lies longing (see *The Weight of Glory*), and he is probably right. The soul's restlessness is a restlessness for God, as Augustine said, and the beauty of the Lord is ravishing to the redeemed heart. The world's beauty is really God's beauty coming to us through the medium of the creation. He speaks to us also in the ugliness of the world to remind us of the wreckage that sin has wrought, particularly in human life.

Aesthetics is the area of the fine arts: music, dance, drama, poetry, literature, painting, sculpture. It is the area of creativity, imagination, and originality. Aesthetics is the domain of the "right brain," and it is much more important, even in science, than we have thought. "The eventual acceptance of the Copernican theory was based solely on aesthetics: its simplicity and economy of constructs made it superior to Ptolemy's theory." (Owens, *God Spy*, p. 25) This trend has not diminished in modern physics.

THEORETICAL PHYSICS IS BECOMING, UNDENIABLY, AN EXERCISE IN AESTHETICS. SOME HAVE EVEN CLAIMED IT AS THE ART OF THE TWENTIETH CENTURY. ITS PRACTITIONERS DEMAND CONCEPTUAL SATISFACTION FROM ITS STRUCTURES. LIKE KEATS, THEY BELIEVE THAT THERE IS AN ULTIMATE EQUATION IN WHICH TRUTH AND BEAUTY DEFINE ONE ANOTHER (IBID., P. 101).

It is noteworthy that when the school curriculum becomes crowded, the first things to be dropped are the arts. This should be particularly strange to us as Christians when we realize that two of the principal things the Bible tells us about heaven are that there will be music and silence. Do our curricula really prepare children to be at home there?

When the Westminster Catechism says that man's chief end is "to glorify God and to enjoy Him forever," it speaks about beauty, for glory and beauty are closely related concepts. We are to see the world's beauty as God's beauty coming to us through the creation. It is His beauty that satisfies our hearts, whether in a flower or a lover. As this consciousness grows in us and in our students, we will honor Him by giving Him a larger place in our hearts and lives. As He has loved us, so we love Him, in and through the beauty of His world. Thus we exercise the priesthood for which we have been bought with Jesus' blood (1 Peter 2:9; Hebrews 13:15). We receive the beauty of the creation, and we give it back to God in praise and worship.

THE JURAL, OR JURIDICAL, ASPECT

The jural, or juridical, aspect is the realm of law, civics, and government. The key idea here is one of recompense or retribution. The institution of the state is here, and the basic business of the state is to provide public justice. The idea of recompense or retribution can be either positive or negative. Good actions should be approved and encouraged; evil should be punished and, if possible, corrected.

This is a very large topic, and we can only hint here at some of its dimensions. Where does the state get its authority? All authority belongs to Christ; therefore, whatever authority the state has must be derived from Christ. Does the state have total authority over the lives of its people, as totalitarians believe, or does it have little or no authority, as libertarians hold? The biblical answer is that the state is responsible for public justice and nothing more. It has no right to dictate what a congregation should hear in church, or the arrangements inside the family except when these become issues of public justice.

Should Christians be involved in politics? If the state's authority comes from Christ, and the church is Christ's Body on the earth, it would be inconsistent for the church to have no interest in the definition of public justice. This does not mean, however, that Christians should attempt to legislate their morality by gaining control of fifty-one percent of the legislature. There is enough consensus on public morality in a pluralistic society that Christians can properly hope for God's blessing and enablement as they try to influence legislation in the direction of public justice. Their contributions to public discussions of justice can be used by God and can clear their own consciences in the matter. Chapter 13 of Roy Clouser's *The Myth of Religious Neutrality* provides an excellent treatment of this topic, but it is unusual enough in its approach that the chapter should be read only after chapters 11 and 12 have been digested.

THE MORAL ASPECT

Ethics or morality is usually studied in philosophy, where it is commonly divorced from any connection with the living, loving God so that it withers like a cut flower. For what is right is not determined by the human being involved (subjectivism) nor by the object with which she or he is involved (objectivism). It is determined by God, in whom we live and move and have our being (Acts 17:28). God has summed up the whole field in the two commands to love Him with all our heart and to love our neighbor as ourselves. When these two conditions are ultimately fulfilled in the New Jerusalem, we will see an exposition of morality such as we have hardly dreamed of here.

The moral aspect, the domain of right and wrong, is intimately connected with our ideas of freedom. Therefore it may be well to digress momentarily to distinguish two kinds of freedom, absolute and contingent. In our independence as sinners, we dream of absolute freedom to do whatever we please. This seems to us one of the most important goals in life. The reality is that no one except God can have absolute freedom. Our lust for it is a sign that we have imagined ourselves to be gods. The only kind of freedom we can actually have is contingent freedom, that is, freedom within the will or law of God. A river with no banks will spread out and become a lake. A diesel freight train can move across the country in a matter of days on a railroad track; without tracks it can go nowhere. Similarly, for humans true freedom is possible only within the law of love for God and neighbor. It is thus contingent freedom.

All our experiences include an ethical or moral aspect. None of them is exempt from the privilege and responsibility of a loving response to God, our neighbor, and the creation. The God-intended learning center for this—particularly for children—is the family. That is where they are to learn, from the example and instruction of their parents, how central to life is the business of love. "My life for yours" is the way Tom Howard defines it.

Love is central in schooling as well. We should never divorce morality from ordinary life, for the key idea of the moral aspect is love in temporal relations. There is an ethical aspect to everything we study, say, or do. This only makes studying richer and more fruitful—more meaningful in the long run. Love is an important part of the alternative consciousness that Christian teaching seeks to instill in students.

THE PISTIC OR FIDUCIARY OR CONFESSIONAL ASPECT

The key idea here is faith, or firm assurance. *Pistis* is the Greek word for faith, and faith is a side of every experience we have. All people learn by faith and live by faith, though most don't realize it. We confess our faith, the deep down allegiance of our lives, in everything we do. Each of us has a fundamental confidence in his or her view of the world, and we live out that confidence in the decisions we make and the actions we take. Thus all of life, Christian or non-Christian, is genuinely religious. The denial of this truth, which is widespread in the West today, is a covert effort to escape the burden of being responsible to God.

The important thing is to recognize what is the object of our faith. If it is not the true God in the Person of Jesus Christ, then it will be some aspect of the creation (material or nonmaterial) that we have elevated to the place in our hearts that only God can rightly occupy. We have faith either in God or in the idols. No one can live without faith. No one can learn without it either.

The pistic is the highest of the aspects because it looks out on the transcendent. It expresses the meaning and direction of our lives. The object of our faith will, in the long run, determine the way we handle any object, study any subject, make sense of any experience. If we as parents and teachers can help our students understand this, we will have taken a long step in making their education truly Christian. We will also have helped to bring in the Kingdom and to prepare God's people to give a more effective witness in today's secular, pagan society.

POSTSCRIPT

The pattern of human experience is like a fine Persian rug. It contains many threads in beautiful colors. In each aspect of experience are interwoven strands of all the other aspects. Our goal is to help parents, teachers, and children to pull it all together under the lordship of Christ and to experience the thrilling unfolding of their lives that is possible when they are gripped by the Word and Spirit of God. The approach most likely to succeed is to become conscious ourselves of the way in which the word of God expresses itself in God's law for each aspect of our experience and for our whole experience of reality. As our consciousness deepens, we can bear witness to our students and trust that the Holy Spirit will make our witness meaningful in their hearts.

Part IV

Methods
in
Christian
Schooling

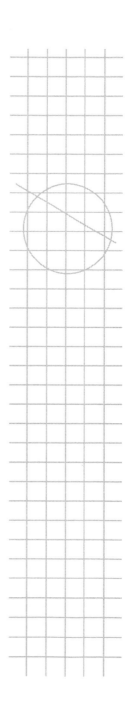

WALKING BY THE SPIRIT

"IF WE LIVE BY THE SPIRIT, LET US ALSO WALK BY THE SPIRIT."

GALATIANS 5:25

Up to this point we have been dealing mainly with the content of Christian schooling. This might be called the intellectual side of the Christian mind. It concerns the way we think and talk about the creation and about redemption. The Christian mind has another side. We could call this the walk side as contrasted with the talk side. Coming now to methods in Christian schooling, we turn to the walk side—or the life side—of the Christian mind. This discussion will not be so much about teaching techniques as about the kind of life that should underlie their use in Christian teaching. There are techniques for teaching, and they are important. But even more important is the quality of life that underlies the use of the techniques.

The emphasis on something below the level of technique needs an explanation. Techniques are often thought of as something objective that can be employed without the need for any particular quality of life on the part of the one employing them. The problem with this viewpoint is that nothing in human life exists outside the creative and sustaining power of God's Word. God's Word is more than an information source. It is God's dynamic way of revealing Himself. Since we bear His image, this means that we are both privileged and required to respond to Him in whatever we learn in His world, including teaching techniques. Teaching techniques are not merely objective skills to which the teacher can add his or her own value system. They are created, and hence they reveal God. They call on us for a particular kind of life in

213

relation to God. This chapter provides a beginning description of that relationship.

THE TWO MINDS

The book of Romans describes two minds, the mind of the flesh and the mind of the Spirit (Romans 8:1–11). Each of these minds involves a way of thinking about the world, a worldview. Each also involves a way of being in the world, a relationship to God that is of primary significance to the one whose mind it is. Romans 8:6 says that the mind of the flesh is death but the mind of the Spirit is life and peace. Obviously, what happens in the Christian school classroom will be powerfully influenced by which of these two minds dominates the teacher. No refinement of teaching techniques will make up for the absence of the mind of the Holy Spirit.

The mind of the flesh is characterized by its independence from God and hence its enmity against Him. It can be easily defined by thinking of the temptation in the Garden of Eden. To the unsuspecting eyes of the first pair, the fruit of the tree looked to be good for food. It promised pleasure. It looked delightful to the eye; it was a desirable possession. It promised wisdom, and hence power or being, to the one who ate it. All these were, of course, false promises. Schmemann points out that this was the one tree God had not blessed to His human creatures. They were attempting to get from the tree what was meant to come to them from the Lord through the other trees in the Garden. They were thus declaring independence from God.

This definition of the fleshly mind is confirmed by the fact that the temptations of Christ, the last Adam, were identical to those three in the Garden, with only a slight difference in the order. The temptation to make stones into bread was a lure to pleasure-seeking. The offer of the entire world was a temptation to possession outside the will of God. The suggestion of jumping from the temple wall was a proposed shortcut to popular favor. It belonged to the same category as the Pharisees' frequent requests in the following years for a sign of Christ's messianic status. The Apostle John reiterates the same evil threesome:

> FOR ALL THAT IS IN THE WORLD, THE LUST OF THE FLESH AND THE LUST OF THE EYES AND THE BOASTFUL PRIDE OF LIFE, IS NOT FROM THE FATHER, BUT IS FROM THE WORLD (1 JOHN 2:16).

There they are—pleasure, possessions, and power all over again.

THE MIND OF THE SPIRIT

It is not easy to find such a clear definition of the mind of the Spirit. We are told in 1 Corinthians 2:16 that we have the mind of Christ. Clearly, His mind is the mind of the Holy Spirit, for all that He did, from His birth in Bethlehem to His death on Golgotha, was done in the Spirit's power (Luke 1:35; Hebrews 9:14). One way to describe the mind of the Spirit, then, might be to contrast our Lord's mind with the threefold definition of the mind of the flesh outlined above.

First there is the quest for pleasure. One's first reaction in thinking of Jesus is to say He was not a man of pleasure but a man of grief. He wept over Jerusalem. He wept for the friends of Lazarus before raising Lazarus from the dead. Jesus was "a man of sorrows and acquainted with grief." On second thought, however, He *was* a man of pleasure—not His own pleasure but his Father's. "I delight to do Thy will, O my God; thy Law is within my heart" (Psalm 40:8.). "Jesus said to them, 'My food is to do the will of Him who sent Me, and to accomplish His work' " (John 4:34). His burning desire to do his Father's will accounts for the paradox of His being known as a man of sorrows and yet being able to promise His own deep joy to His disciples (John 15:11). The mind of the Spirit, then, seeks first of all the pleasure of God. It thus involves at the same time an attitude of grief over the wreckage of sin in our lives and in the world, and an attitude of deep joy in God.

With regard to Jesus' view of possessions, there is again a paradox. He was a poor man. He didn't own a house or a piece of land. He lived on the contributions of His followers. He was even buried in a borrowed tomb. He who was the Creator and Sustainer of all things had no place to lay His head. Yet He demonstrated that poverty can be wealth. To be penniless can mean to be immensely rich. It is not that Christians should give everything away and live on welfare. But we should reject the idolatry in which money so easily entangles us. Truly, we cannot serve both God and mammon. Jesus said:

> MAKE FRIENDS FOR YOURSELVES BY MEANS OF THE MAMMON OF UNRIGHTEOUSNESS; THAT WHEN IT FAILS, THEY MAY RECEIVE YOU INTO THE ETERNAL DWELLINGS (LUKE 16:9).

The mind of the Spirit sees money as a good servant but a bad master. From the current American ethos of consumerism, this constitutes a radical departure.

Finally, the mind of the flesh seeks being, or power. Jesus had power. He could heal the sick, raise the dead, and control the wind and the waves on the Sea of Galilee. He could have had twelve legions of angels for protection when He was arrested in the Garden of Gethsemane, yet He would not use them. He told Pilate without hesitation that He, Jesus, was a king. Then He submitted to Pilate's grossly unjust condemnation to crucifixion. So He was not one who sought to use power in a political way, even when He had it. He was vulnerable in the extreme. And in His weakness He overcame the devil and death itself. The mind of the Spirit is one of vulnerability. This is a hard lesson for us to learn. We are weak because we are finite.

We are much weaker because we are sinful. But it is hard for us to admit our weakness, addicted as we are to the deceptive attraction of power. Yet our weakness is the key to our approach to God. We do not understand God's grace until we learn to come to Him, not in our strength but in our weakness. His strength is made perfect in our weakness (2 Corinthians 12:9). Thus the mind of the Spirit is at every point the exact opposite of the mind of the flesh.

Another way to discuss the methodology of Christian school teaching is to list some major life qualities associated with walking in the Spirit and consider their importance in the Christian school classroom. These are fundamental and irreplaceable qualifications for Christian teaching. As the paragraph above suggested, the Christian teacher will, first of all, be a person of humility. Philippians 2:5–11, the most powerful New Testament passage on the humiliation and exaltation of Christ, was written as an exhortation to the Philippian Christians to cultivate humility. When, in the Beatitudes, Jesus listed the qualities characteristic of members of His kingdom, He first gave poverty of spirit, or humility. A broken-hearted awareness of our innate sinfulness is sure to result in humility.

As happiness is a by-product of obedience to the will of God, so humility is a by-product of repentance. And repentance is an ongoing quality of the Christian mind, without which one cannot expect the blessing of God on one's efforts to teach. Etymologically the word *repentance* means "a change of mind." When Romans 12:1–2 exhorts us not to be conformed to this world but to be transformed by the renewing of our minds, it is calling us to repentance. One of the old Puritan preachers said that when blinded Samson was turning the Philistine mill to grind grain, his hair began to grow again, and his repentance grew with his hair. So for us repentance is an ongoing quality of life. It is not easy, for it involves a deepening awareness of our weakness, but it is richly blessed. Without it our efforts to teach Christianly will be flawed.

Humility will deepen, however, as love for God in Christ deepens. Against the backdrop of Christ's holy humanness, our own arrogance and self-centeredness will become increasingly repugnant to us. Our task is not to be preoccupied with the level of humility we think we have achieved. While we need to be aware of the importance of humility, focusing our attention on Christ is the best way to grow in it. A Spirit-given realization of Christ's deep love and grace to us in our need will deepen our humility. Then our love for Him who accepts us just as we are is bound to grow as well. And when that happens, there will be a different atmosphere in the classroom.

That leads us to another quality of the mind of the Spirit, namely, love. In 1 Corinthians 13, Paul interrupts his discussion of spiritual gifts to stress the importance of love. He says that without it nothing—neither gifts of speech nor unusual knowledge nor even faith—is worth anything. He concludes the chapter with the observation that of the three—faith, hope and love—love is the greatest.

What does Paul mean by love? Certainly he means more than a physical relationship; more also than a warm feeling of affection given or received. Love was defined above as "my life for yours"—certainly its meaning in the instance of Christ, "who gave Himself for us, the just for the unjust, that He might bring us to God." In the classroom its importance is inescapable. Love is an essential part of learning or teaching, as will be seen in the next chapter. Without love in the mind and heart of the Christian teacher, there is little likelihood that students will experience the deepening love for God and neighbor, and the growth in their Christian life that can happen as they study.

Faith is another quality of the mind of the Spirit. What the Christian teacher hopes to do is to nurture in her students an alternative perspective on life and the world. This, however, is in the final analysis the work of the Holy Spirit.

The teacher will at times see very encouraging signs of progress. In many instances, however, fruit may be long in coming. It may be ten or fifteen years before the teacher learns, if she ever does, that her instruction and example were received by the student and have issued in a maturing Christian life and vision. So in Christian schooling there is need for faith. Without it the prayer needed to water the seed that the teacher has sown is not likely to be offered. And without that, the classroom will not become the place it could be.

Another side of the mind of the Spirit is hope. The need for hope is perhaps more apparent today than ever before. The promise of the Enlightenment has proved false. Physical convenience in lifestyle has grown immeasurably, but human relations have rarely been as demonic as those we have experienced in the twentieth century. As a result, many modern people have fallen into hopelessness. But hope is a prominent element in the gospel. Christ died in weakness, and His disciples thought their hopes had been completely dashed. Then He rose from the dead, and in the hope of that victory the gospel spread throughout the Western world. Currently, because the church has given in far too much to the declarations of the Enlightenment, even it is struggling with a loss of hope. But the basis of Christian hope has not changed, and hope must be a prominent characteristic of the Christian teacher.

What difference will all this make? To begin with, we shall learn to see our students as if they were Jesus Christ's (Matthew 18:5). Of course they aren't, but we are commanded to receive them as if they were. That will be possible only as the love of God is poured into our hearts by His Spirit. And as we experience the mind of the Holy Spirit, the fruits of the Spirit will appear in the classroom: love, joy, peace, longsuffering (patience), kindness, goodness, faithfulness, gentleness, and self-control. These qualities will change the atmosphere in any classroom.

This change does not mean permissiveness. Love must be tough as well as tender. But as the Holy Spirit increases His control in our hearts, He will also work in the hearts of our students. The goal of the instruction will then shift from the acquisition of factual information (though that will happen even more effectively than before) to the cultivation of responsible discipleship, both in our own lives and in those of our students. Perhaps one of the most remarkable differences will be the sense that we are all traveling together on the pathway to discipleship. When students realize that we teachers are still learning too, they are likely to improve remarkably in their own participation in the process. The mind of the Spirit carries with it the presence and the blessing of the Spirit. What more could we hope for in the improvement of teaching methodology?

THE PLACE OF LOVE IN LEARNING

19

Schooling that is really Christian is like a large diamond, and one of its facets is the place of love in learning. Is love an important part of learning? We have not been taught to think so. Secular schooling, which most of us have experienced, is supposed to be about facts and skills, and we do not normally associate love with facts and skills. We think of love as an emotion, and information is not something we usually become emotional about in the secular world. What link can we imagine between school learning and love?

The earlier chapters have suggested that the task of the Christian school is to encourage in our students a consciousness alternative to that of the modern world that surrounds them and us. Indeed, it does more than surround us. It permeates us so that we find its thought patterns and lifeways comfortable and attractive, and we often follow those patterns without even thinking about them. As Christians, we sometimes make strenuous efforts to combine those patterns with what we read in the Bible about the Christian way of life. The result is that we live life on two planes. The ordinary level of our lives looks very much like that of the world around us except for some moral standards we feel obligated to uphold. It is on the spiritual level that we really have touch with God—in our Bible reading, praying, involvement in church, and perhaps our active witnessing. The difficulty with this approach is that it puts our ordinary life under the government of something other than Christ. The prevailing thought patterns of our age tend to dominate us as much here as they do non-Christians. Thus we live a dualistic life. As noted earlier, this involves us in idolatry, which is no more pleasing to God today than in Old Testament times. The fact that it isn't thought of as idolatry doesn't make it any less so.

To underline the need for a renewed consciousness, let's look briefly at what drives modern people to live the way they do. Since human hearts don't really change over the centuries, we can do this by looking again at what happened to Adam and Eve in the Garden of Eden (Genesis 3:6). They were next to the tree which, as Schmemann puts it, God had not blessed to them. They thought the fruit looked good for food. That is, it promised pleasure. It was a delight to the eyes. In window-shopping terms, it was a possession that would be good to have. And further-more, it was to be desired to make one wise, and it promised independent power. Pleasure, possessions, and power—is there anything sinful about these things? Not necessarily. They are gifts from God to be received through the creation. But, while they come from God through the creation, they cannot be derived directly from the creation without idola-try. To suppose that they can come from something *in* the creation rather than from God *through* the creation is to put a piece of the creation in the place of God. That is idola-try, and idolatry always crushes those who indulge in it. Like alcohol or drugs, it is addictive.

When our first parents took the step of picking and eating the fruit, their consciousness changed. They be-came estranged from God and from each other. Even the created world was now a problem for them. Love was re-placed by mistrust of each other, hatred for God, and enmity with the soil and the animals.

How different is the consciousness of people today from that of Adam and Eve after the fall? Pleasure is still a primary goal. Think of the prominence in the media of advertisements for vacations. Possessions are prized; we have become a consumer society. Power is attractive to us; we seek power over things, and we manipulate people to our own advantage. However, because we seek these things from the creation and not from God through the creation, the pleasure, possessions, and power we desire get away from us. We spend our lives pursuing them, only to have them slip through our fingers when our time comes to leave this world.

What would a biblical consciousness look like? The life of Jesus demonstrates one. Instead of seeking His own pleasure, He sought that of His Father. He was not burdened with the ball and chain of possessions. What few things He possessed, such as a seamless gown, did not possess Him. And, although the power of twelve legions of angels was available to protect Him from a painful death, He would not call on them. He gave up His life in weakness, to take it again in everlasting power and majesty at the resurrection.

If this is the alternative consciousness that Christian schools seek to develop in their students, what possible connection can it have with reading, writing, and arithmetic? Aren't matters of morality separate from the secular world's value-free facts? The Bible denies it. The "facts" are all created by God as a means of revealing Himself to us, and the God they reveal is a God of love. If that is so, then perhaps love has something to do with school learning after all.

WHAT IS LOVE?

Today the word *love* is like someone who has been tarred and feathered. It has picked up so much extraneous matter that it doesn't look like itself any more. How shall we define it then? After discussing our liking for subhuman things, C. S. Lewis in *The Four Loves* describes four categories of human love: affection, friendship, eros (sexual love), and charity (love for God). The modern Western world has so confused love with sexual attraction that its most common identification is with eroticism. Curiously (to minds immersed in modernity), the word *eros* does not even appear in the Greek New Testament.

Wherever it has not been twisted by our sinfulness, the word *love* seems to mean a willingness to sacrifice for someone or something. It conveys the idea of treasuring or valuing something or someone even more than life itself. Thus Jesus said that if we do not hate father, mother, wife, and even life itself, we cannot be His disciples (Luke 14:26). He did not mean hatred in the form of bitter or vengeful feelings; He meant that we value the saving lordship of Christ more than anything else in the world.

The New Testament supports this definition. The two words used almost exclusively there for love are *phileo* and *agapao*. The former has the idea of friendship, as in the proper name *Philadelphia*, which means "city of brotherly love." The latter occurs most commonly and has the idea of self-sacrifice. While its Old Testament parallel is rooted in sexual attraction, the New Testament no longer defines the word in that way. It is used of both God and humans, and in each instance it involves sacrifice. "For God so loved the world that He gave" (John 3:16). "Greater love has no one than this, that one lay down his life for his friends" (John 15:13). Again we think of Tom Howard's definition for love, "my life for yours." Howard calls attention to the way this principle runs through the whole of life.

LOVE'S PLACE IN LIFE

In a society in which license plate holders say, "I'd Rather Be Shopping at Nordstrom's" or "My Other Car Is a BMW" or "He Who Dies With the Most Toys Wins," it is difficult not to believe that the ultimate goal in life is possessions. Yet even a cursory review of the Bible demonstrates that this is not true. For example, "The Great Shema" ("The Great *Listen* or *Hear*") reads as follows:

HEAR, O ISRAEL! THE LORD IS OUR GOD, THE LORD IS ONE! AND YOU SHALL LOVE THE LORD YOUR GOD WITH ALL YOUR HEART AND WITH ALL YOUR SOUL AND WITH ALL YOUR MIGHT. AND THESE WORDS, WHICH I AM COMMANDING YOU TODAY, SHALL BE ON YOUR HEART; AND YOU SHALL TEACH THEM DILIGENTLY TO YOUR SONS AND SHALL TALK OF THEM WHEN YOU SIT IN YOUR HOUSE AND WHEN YOU WALK BY THE WAY AND WHEN YOU LIE DOWN AND WHEN YOU RISE UP. AND YOU SHALL BIND THEM AS A SIGN ON YOUR HAND AND THEY SHALL BE AS FRONTALS ON YOUR FOREHEAD. AND YOU SHALL WRITE THEM ON THE DOORPOSTS OF YOUR HOUSE AND ON YOUR GATES (DEUTERONOMY 6:4-9).

Clearly, the central issue in life for the godly Israelite was not entertainment, or financial success, or a luxurious lifestyle. It was love for God, to be lived out in daily and family life. The New Testament message is no different. When an expert in the Mosaic law asked Jesus what was the greatest commandment, Jesus responded:

YOU SHALL LOVE THE LORD YOUR GOD WITH ALL YOUR HEART, AND WITH ALL YOUR SOUL, AND WITH ALL YOUR MIND." THIS IS THE GREAT AND FOREMOST COMMANDMENT. THE SECOND IS LIKE IT, "YOU SHALL LOVE YOUR NEIGHBOR AS YOURSELF." ON THESE TWO COMMANDMENTS DEPEND THE WHOLE LAW AND THE PROPHETS (MATTHEW 22:37-40).

A NEW COMMANDMENT I GIVE TO YOU, THAT YOU LOVE ONE ANOTHER, EVEN AS I HAVE LOVED YOU, THAT YOU ALSO LOVE ONE ANOTHER. BY THIS ALL MEN WILL KNOW THAT YOU ARE MY DISCIPLES, IF YOU HAVE LOVE FOR ONE ANOTHER (JOHN 13:34-35).

1 Corinthians 13 underlines the importance of love in living. Between two chapters on spiritual gifts, Paul pauses to rhapsodize over the importance of love. He says it is more important than any of the other gifts, it is superior to the greatest wisdom, and it is greater than philanthropy or martyrdom. Of the three paramount virtues—faith, hope and love—"the greatest of these is love." It sounds as if the English poet was right when he said that "God leaves us here

for a little while to learn to love." If we as professing Christians were to learn and practice what it means to put love first in all our relations, our activities, and our understanding of life, we might well be amazed at the impact we would have on today's self-centered society.

THE SOURCE AND PATTERN OF LOVE

The source and pattern of love is undoubtedly the love within the Holy Trinity: Father, Son, and Holy Spirit. While the nature of the Trinity and the relationships of the members to one another are shrouded in impenetrable mystery for us, we do know something about it. We know, for instance, that each of the members loves the others without the slightest reservation. Each gives Himself to the others totally. There is none of the mask or reserve behind which we hide ourselves from each other. Since we declared independence and broke the relationship God had created between us and Him and between each other, we have tried to protect ourselves for fear of being vulnerable. Within the Trinity there is nothing like this. Love flows back and forth there, and mutual self-giving exists there, in infinite measure. We are so used to our efforts at self-protection that this sort of total vulnerability to each other is neither comprehensible nor attractive to us. In our holiest moments of fellowship with God, we catch only a brief and partial glimpse of it.

However, the Scriptures promise that God by grace imparts His love to us. It is the glorious richness of this kind of love that Paul speaks of when he says, "The love of God has been poured out within our hearts through the Holy Spirit who was given to us" (Romans 5:5). Since the fall into sin, love is not natural to us. It is a gift from God. "We love because He first loved us" (1 John 4:19).

LOVE AND LEARNING

Perhaps now we are ready to consider the intimate relationship between love and learning. There are at least three ideas involved here. The first is that creation is only real because God loves it. The second is that true human knowledge is impossible without love. The third is that love has formative power in learning.

Creation is only real because God loves it. When Genesis 1 says repeatedly that God saw that His creation was good, it means that God loved it into being. God liked what He had made. "When the morning stars sang together, and all the sons of God shouted for joy" (Job 38:7), it was a happy occasion! This concept runs more deeply through the Bible than is often recognized. God feeds the wild animals. He clothes the lilies. He waters the soil so that it produces food. These things He does because He loves His creation. Creation is the expression of His loving, creative Word. It is not merely a work of disinterested power; it is a work of love. C. S. Lewis says, for example, "God, who needs nothing, loves into existence wholly superfluous creatures in order that He may love and perfect them" (*The Four Loves*, p. 176).

In the passage referred to earlier, in which Robert Capon outlines the way an onion's beauty reveals the glory of God, he adds:

PERHAPS NOW YOU HAVE SEEN AT LEAST DIMLY THAT THE UNIQUENESSES OF CREATION ARE THE RESULT OF CONTINUOUS CREATIVE SUPPORT, OF EFFECTIVE REGARD, BY NO MEAN LOVER. HE *LIKES* ONIONS, THEREFORE THEY ARE. THE FIT, THE COLORS, THE SMELL, THE TENSIONS, THE TASTES, THE TEXTURES, THE LINES, THE SHAPES ARE A RESPONSE NOT TO SOME FORGOTTEN DECREE THAT THERE MAY AS WELL BE ONIONS AS TURNIPS, BUT TO HIS PRESENT DELIGHT—HIS INTIMATE AND IMMEDIATE JOY IN ALL YOU HAVE SEEN, AND IN A THOUSAND OTHER WONDERS YOU DO NOT EVEN SUSPECT. WITH PETER, THE ONION SAYS, "LORD, IT IS GOOD FOR US TO *BE* HERE.' YES, SAYS GOD. *TOV*, VERY GOOD (*THE SUPPER OF THE LAMB*, PP. 15-16).

The world around us is real because God loves it. His love is not something He felt long ago at the first creation and has allowed to lapse since. He loves the creation to-day, at every second of its existence. This is what is involved when we say that He "upholds all things by the Word of His power" (Hebrews 1:3). His love for His creation keeps it going and makes it real. If this is so, and if the creation reveals God, then we, as His image bearers have a responsibility. We must not only receive the world from His hand, but we must return it to Him as we handle it in loving service to Him and our neighbor. This means that we cannot truly know the creation unless we love it.

The second idea involved in the relationship between love and learning is that true human knowledge is impossible without love. For example, Paul says:

AND THIS I PRAY, THAT YOUR LOVE MAY ABOUND STILL MORE AND MORE IN REAL KNOWLEDGE AND ALL DISCERNMENT, SO THAT YOU MAY APPROVE THE THINGS THAT ARE EXCELLENT, IN ORDER TO BE SINCERE AND BLAMELESS UNTIL THE DAY OF CHRIST; HAVING BEEN FILLED WITH THE FRUIT OF RIGHTEOUSNESS WHICH COMES THROUGH JESUS CHRIST, TO THE GLORY AND PRAISE OF GOD (PHILIPPIANS 1:9-11).

Paul speaks of his prayer

... THAT CHRIST MAY DWELL IN YOUR HEARTS THROUGH FAITH; AND THAT YOU, BEING ROOTED AND GROUNDED IN LOVE, MAY BE ABLE TO COMPREHEND WITH ALL THE SAINTS WHAT IS THE BREADTH AND LENGTH AND HEIGHT AND DEPTH, AND TO KNOW THE LOVE OF CHRIST, WHICH SURPASSES KNOWLEDGE, THAT YOU MAY BE FILLED UP TO ALL THE FULNESS OF GOD (EPHESIANS 3:17-19).

Again, Colossians 2:3 speaks of the full assurance of understanding that comes from a true knowledge of Christ, "in whom are hidden all the treasures of wisdom and knowledge." Under the influence of Enlightenment thinking, the modern church has, in a dualistic and idolatrous interpretation, concluded that these verses refer only to "spiritual" or theological knowledge and not to ordinary knowledge. Nothing could be further from the truth or more dangerous, for such an understanding imprisons us in a false and empty way of knowing ordinary things.

The answer to the question What has love to do with schooling? is just this: true knowledge is impossible apart from love. To grasp this concept, we may need to revise our definition of knowledge. The Bible says that truth is a Person, the Son of God, who holds all things in being moment by moment by the power of His Word (John 14:6 and Hebrews 1:3). Genuine human knowledge is not a mere arbitrary collection of value-free facts. All the things we know are created and upheld by Christ, and since they are made to reveal God, it follows that any true knowledge involves a response to Him. The first great commandment tells us that this response should be one of love. Learning and love are meant to be yoked together. Only the chaos of sin has torn them apart and brought us into a desert where it is natural to think that learning has nothing to do with love.

At the end of 1 Corinthians 12 and in preparation for his remarkable thirteenth chapter, Paul speaks of love as "a more excellent way." Commenting on this, A. A. Van Ruler writes:

> IT IS THE WAY PAR EXCELLENCE, THE WAY FOR LIFE IN TIME, THE WAY THROUGH THE TEMPORAL, CREATED REALITY. IT IS POSSIBLE REALLY TO LIVE, TO LIVE IN REALITY, ONLY ALONG THE WAY OF LOVE. FOR A MAN CAN TRULY EXPERIENCE REALITY ONLY IF HE LOVES IT (*THE GREATEST OF THESE IS LOVE,* P. 7).

This is a radical idea. Let me try to justify it more carefully. The greatest commandment is that we are to love God. Deuteronomy 6:5 says that we are to do so with all our heart, soul, and might. Matthew 22:37 specifies all our heart, soul, and mind. Now knowledge is the outcome of learning. True knowledge, in whatever area, is meant to be responsive because creation reveals God, and our response to Him must be wholehearted love. If He loves what He has created, can we possibly understand His creation without loving it too, and loving Him through it? We are so accustomed to thinking of the creation as mere atoms and molecules governed by "natural law," and useful for our selfish purposes, that the concept of love in learning is difficult to grasp. But the encouragement of love in learning is one of the basic foundation stones of Christian schooling.

What this means is that we cannot understand reality unless we relate it to God. We do this by cultivating awe, love, and praise to Him and by rendering loving service through the creation to Him and our neighbor. Knowing value-free facts is not true knowledge! Van Ruler says again:

> THE POSSESSION OF LOVE DETERMINES EVERYTHING ELSE THAT A MAN CAN BE OR DO. LOVE IS A REALITY THAT PERMEATES AND FULFILLS HUMAN EXISTENCE. WHERE LOVE IS LACKING, ALL EXISTENCE IS EMPTY. IT IS A VACUUM, THOUGH IT BE PACKED WITH THINGS" (*THE GREATEST OF THESE IS LOVE,* P.9).

And once more,

> "LOVE GIVES LIFE TO ALL THINGS. IT GIVES MORE THAN LIFE; IT GIVES REALITY. LOVE CREATES. THINGS RECEIVE REALITY AND WORTH ONLY WHEN MEN LOVE THEM. THE WORLD IS CREATED, AS IT WERE, ONLY WHEN IT IS LOVED. IT IS SAID OF GOD THAT HE CREATED THE WORLD. THIS IS SO BECAUSE HE LOVED THE WORLD. IN AND THROUGH LOVE, THE WORLD FIRST BECAME REAL. MAN IS NOW CALLED TO SHARE IN THIS CREATIVE ACTIVITY OF GOD. MAN, TOO, MUST BEGIN TO LOVE THE THINGS GOD CREATED. ONLY THEN DO THEY BECOME REAL TO HIM. AND THEN HE, TOO, BECOMES MORE THAN AN EMPTY SOUND" (IBID., P. 11).

Statements like these don't make much sense to us, because we have learned so well to think of created things in terms of their monetary value. We are consummate consumers. But we are in desperate danger, with this mind-set, of gaining the whole world in the objective, factual sense and losing our own souls.

Through assertions like Van Ruler's, the indissoluble relation between love and learning begins to take shape in our minds. The creation is meant to bring us into touch with God. We can know the scientific facts about creation in their value-free sense and yet have no true touch with God. But then we don't really know the creation at all. Our understanding of it is empty and valueless, however well it may fit into the modern concept of knowledge. Knowing in that way, we have saved the husk and thrown away the kernel. Love is basic to learning. Without love it is impossible genuinely to learn and know anything. What might happen to Christian schooling if this awareness were to grip us and find expression in our teaching?

A third idea in the relation of love to learning involves the formative power of love. Love, and only love, changes us in a positive direction. Our thinking, our understanding, our character—these are shaped by love. If we are Christians, with our sins forgiven and our hearts drawn in some measure to God, this is due entirely to the love God has for us. Jesus loved Lazarus out of his tomb. He does the same thing for us. We are what we are as Christians because God's love has formed us.

AND WE HAVE COME TO KNOW AND HAVE BELIEVED THE LOVE WHICH GOD HAS FOR US. GOD IS LOVE, AND ONE WHO ABIDES IN LOVE ABIDES IN GOD, AND GOD ABIDES IN HIM. . . . WE LOVE, BECAUSE HE FIRST LOVED US" (1 JOHN 4:16, 19).

There is a corollary to this thesis that applies to the Christian school as well as to the Christian home and church. Children are formed through the love of their parents and teachers. God's love works, not only directly, but through the medium of human teachers. Our love can be the channel God uses to shape another human being. "And this commandment we have from Him, that the one who loves God should love his brother also" (1 John 4:21). "The love of God has been poured out within our hearts through the Holy Spirit who was given to us" (Romans 5:5). Neither true teaching nor true learning is possible apart from love. The formative function of human love should take place in the classroom as well as in the home. It is the primary channel through which children are taught to know and to give love. So love is inseparable from both teaching and learning. Van Ruler deals further with the topic in this way:

> I NOT ONLY LIVE IN LOVE; LOVE OVERSHADOWS ME. IT NOT ONLY OVERSHADOWS ME, IT OVERSHADOWS MY NEIGHBOR; AND NOT ONLY MY NEIGHBOR BUT ALL THINGS. IT IS IN THE LOVE OF GOD THAT I DISCOVER MY FELLOW MAN; IT IS IN THE LOVE OF GOD THAT I DISCOVER THE WHOLE OF CREATED REALITY (*THE GREATEST OF THESE IS LOVE*, P. 10).

Others have also borne witness to this intimate relationship between love and learning. In his book *To Know As We Are Known: A Spirituality of Education*, Parker J. Palmer unfolds the thesis that just as God knows us in love, so it is imperative that we know Him and His creation, including each other, in love. We cannot learn to know truly or teach effectively in any other way. All knowledge that is not infused with love will turn out in the end to be mere gravel in our mouths.

In commenting on the videotape describing the making of the first atomic bomb, Palmer points out that knowledge today is driven by two motives, curiosity and control. Curiosity gives us pure science, and control gives us technology. Then he asserts that there is a third component that is regularly disregarded but essential to true knowledge—compassion, or love. To achieve this element we need to cultivate an alternative way of thinking about reality. We must enter into the significance of God's covenant with His creation, which unfailingly obeys God's laws for it. It obeys because God loves it, and His love has the power to produce unwavering obedience. In a world shaped and upheld by the love of God, is it conceivable that we could know it or teach others to know it without loving it and loving God through it?

Thus love, learning, and teaching all belong together. Teachers can learn to teach effectively only when they learn to love the created studies as well as to love their students. Students can truly learn their studies only when they learn to love God through them and each other in working with them. Both teachers and students have before them the exhilarating possibility of coming to know God by way of their love relation to each other and to the created studies that form the curriculum. This does not mean that teaching and learning will be soft and easy. Love can be tough, and it needs to be. But love is essential.

CONCLUSION

That love is essential to learning is one more aspect of the alternative perspective essential for Christians today. We live in a violent world. In professional (and often in amateur) sports, in business, in education, in virtually every phase of modern life, competition is keen, and the struggle is ruthless. Schools are usually conducted with the intention of preparing young people to stand up and win in such a milieu.

But there is a different battle and another armor for Christians. These are described in Ephesians 6. The section comes as the summary and conclusion to the exhortation that began with the previous chapter:

THEREFORE BE IMITATORS OF GOD, AS BELOVED CHILDREN; AND WALK IN LOVE, JUST AS CHRIST ALSO LOVED US AND GAVE HIMSELF UP FOR US, AN OFFERING AND A SACRIFICE TO GOD AS A FRAGRANT AROMA (EPHESIANS 5:1-2).

The Christian warfare, Paul says, "is not against flesh and blood, but against the world forces of this darkness, against the spiritual forces of wickedness in the heavenly places" (verse 12). That is, we are not to be engaged in fighting with individual people, but with the cultural forces that shape our society and world. However, our warfare is waged on an entirely different basis than that of today's violent, competitive world. It is different because it issues from a different way of seeing things. It involves seeking first the pleasure of our Father, being freed from the power of our possessions, and learning that God's strength is perfected in our weakness. The formation of that awareness in the minds of the children of Christians is accomplished through love. Love and learning must go together.

Hospitality is a Christian grace that the Scriptures urge upon us. "In love of the brethren be tenderly affectioned one to another . . . given to hospitality" (Romans 12:10–13). "For the bishop must be blameless, as God's steward . . . given to hospitality" (Titus 1:7–8).

> BUT THE END OF ALL THINGS IS AT HAND: BE YE THEREFORE OF SOUND MIND, AND BE SOBER UNTO PRAYER: ABOVE ALL THINGS BEING FERVENT IN YOUR LOVE AMONG YOURSELVES; FOR LOVE COVERETH A MULTITUDE OF SINS: USING HOSPITALITY ONE TO ANOTHER WITHOUT MURMURING: ACCORDING AS EACH HATH RECEIVED A GIFT, MINISTERING IT AMONG YOURSELVES, AS GOOD STEWARDS OF THE MANIFOLD GRACE OF GOD" (1 PETER 4:7-10).

When there were no Motel 6's or fast-food outlets like McDonald's or Kentucky Fried Chicken, the need for hospitality had a high priority. But, in a world in which technology and violence have isolated us more and more in the hoped-for security of our privacy, the need has not diminished but increased.

The word *hospitality* has to do with guests. The German word for it means friendship for the guest, and the Dutch word means freedom for the guest. Clearly, we are dealing here with a host-guest relationship. But what has hospitality to do with teaching?

A penetrating and richly suggestive answer is found in Henri Nouwen's book, *Reaching Out*. The book deals with what Nouwen calls the three aspects of the spiritual life: from loneliness to solitude, from hostility to hospitality, and from illusion to prayer. He suggests that in relation to ourselves, when we become Christians we begin to move from loneliness to solitude. In relation to other people, we move from hostility to hospitality. And in relation to God, we move from illusion to prayer. It is the move from hostility to hospitality that concerns us here. We are all fearful of being exposed to others for fear they will not like what they see. Our consumption-driven, competitive, and often violent culture magnifies our fears. The twentieth century has been unparalleled in its destruction of some 187 million people through wars, holocausts, and national genocides. In America violence is moving increasingly out of the ghettos into the other parts of the cities and to the suburbs. We no longer walk abroad at night, or even in the daytime, without fear. Children face fears at school. They fear their teachers, and they fear their peers. They do not think of themselves as welcome guests who bring gifts for the benefit of others.

Nouwen's point is that genuine hospitality reduces fear. He develops this thought in relation to parents and children, and to teachers and students. As to parents, he suggests that they must think of their children not as possessions but as guests. Children will not stay at home very long. In fifteen or twenty years they will leave the nest. Parents do not have the right to impose on their children their own goals or directions for their children's lives. They should, of course, teach the children what it means to love, and demonstrate before them a life of trust in Christ and devotion to God. But children come with their own gifts from God, which may lead them to choices in vocation or life that differ from those of their parents. The parents' task is not to imprison children in parental decisions but to elicit, within the framework of the love of God, the gifts children bring with them. This is probably the real thrust of Proverbs 22:6: "Train up a child in the way he should go, even when he is old he will not depart from it." The "way he should go" is not some standardized educational program that fits all children but the peculiar individual way to which each child's God-given gifts summon.

In discussing education, Nouwen sees the goal of the teacher as the provision "of a free and fearless space where mental and emotional development can take place" (*Reaching Out*, p. 60). If, as Calvin suggests, knowledge of ourselves is one of the two most important kinds of knowledge in all of life, then the school should encourage it. Tragically, it usually isn't a primary item in school objectives. Children are so afraid of failure or ridicule that they hardly ever become disentangled from the rush of the classroom program enough to look seriously at what is happening in their hearts. Even Christian schools too commonly overlook this sort of growth. As teachers we deceive ourselves into thinking that if we can just get the students to act in the ways we think are ideal, their inner growth will take place. Students are good at reading our minds, and they can often fabricate the responses they think we want. But their inner growth may well be something else altogether.

The suggestion of hospitality in the classroom raises a problem. Nouwen captures it in the following words:

BUT IS IT POSSIBLE TO BECOME HOSPITABLE TO EACH OTHER IN A CLASSROOM? IT IS FAR FROM EASY SINCE BOTH TEACHERS AND STUDENTS ARE PART OF A VERY DEMANDING, PUSHING AND OFTEN EXPLOITATIVE SOCIETY IN WHICH PERSONAL GROWTH AND DEVELOPMENT HAVE BECOME SECONDARY TO THE ABILITY TO PRODUCE AND EARN NOT ONLY CREDITS BUT A LIVING. IN SUCH A PRODUCTION-ORIENTED SOCIETY EVEN SCHOOLS NO LONGER HAVE THE TIME OR SPACE WHERE THE QUESTIONS ABOUT WHY WE LIVE AND LOVE, WORK AND DIE CAN BE RAISED WITHOUT FEAR OF COMPETITION, RIVALRY OR CONCERNS ABOUT PUNISHMENT OR REWARDS. . . . WHEN WE LOOK AT TEACHING IN TERMS OF HOSPITALITY, WE CAN SAY THAT THE TEACHER IS CALLED UPON TO CREATE FOR HIS STUDENTS A FREE AND FEARLESS SPACE WHERE MENTAL AND EMOTIONAL DEVELOPMENT CAN TAKE PLACE (*REACHING OUT* , P. 60).

Nouwen then goes on to discuss two ways in which the teacher can provide this sort of space, by revealing and by affirming. As schools have developed in the modern West, students are much more accustomed to receiving than to giving. Yet each one comes to school with gifts given by God. It is up to the Christian teacher to help students realize they have something to give and then to draw out those gifts. Nouwen continues:

> WE WILL NEVER BELIEVE THAT WE HAVE ANYTHING TO GIVE UNLESS THERE IS SOMEONE WHO IS ABLE TO RECEIVE. INDEED, WE DISCOVER OUR GIFTS IN THE EYES OF THE RECEIVER. TEACHERS WHO CAN DETACH THEMSELVES FROM THEIR NEED TO IMPRESS AND CONTROL, AND WHO CAN ALLOW THEMSELVES TO BECOME RECEPTIVE FOR THE NEWS THAT THEIR STUDENTS CARRY WITH THEM, WILL FIND THAT IT IS IN RECEPTIVITY THAT GIFTS BECOME VISIBLE (IBID., P. 61).

As Christians we believe God gives gifts to each one. In the Christian home or school it is our task to recognize and draw out those gifts. This is why *A Vision with a Task* cites unwrapping student gifts as the first step in leading students to responsive discipleship.

There is one more step in dealing with gifts. Once gifts are revealed, they need to be affirmed. We tend as humans to be very much afraid of being exposed to the view of others. This is one of the effects of our sinful independence from God. For students who have been encouraged to believe they have gifts, it is important to have someone affirm those gifts in the presence of others. This must not be done in a manipulative way. If it is done in genuine, loving interest, it can be very supportive to the giver.

A question may well arise at this point: What has all this to do with teaching content areas like arithmetic, grammar, history, and science? The answer depends on one's concept of the creation as curriculum. If the studies are composed of value-free facts, then the connection is difficult to make. If, on the other hand, creation does indeed reveal God, if He is giving Himself to us in it, then the connection is immediate and powerful. It is possible for the facts and skills we teach to become channels through which both we and the students become increasingly aware of the awesomeness and love of God and through which we respond in loving service to Him. This is, however, a development that depends on the Holy Spirit. Students' gifts differ, and with the differences come different ways of exploring and understanding God in His creation. Not all students will explore best by the logical-linguistic method. The teacher's effort to elicit their gifts must be approached slowly and prayerfully, with a deepening recognition of differences in student giftedness. As we ourselves experience communion with God through the creation, we will be guided into ways of helping our students to express their own giftedness.

When we think of giving children room to grow through their schooling, it is useful to remember the parable of the sower in Matthew 13:3–9. Some of the seeds were eaten by the birds. Others fell on rocky places and germinated quickly, but, because of the thinness of the soil, the plants withered in the hot sunshine. Other seeds fell among the thorns, "and the worry of the world, and the deceitfulness of riches" choked the plants so that they bore no grain (Matthew 13:22). There is a great deal in present-day American culture that tends to choke out the seed of spiritual life in ourselves and our students. Ours is a rich country, and deceitfulness is, if anything, more characteristic of riches than ever. We will need to be busy and use our God-given wisdom to try to keep the cultural thorns out of the classroom.

The freedom to teach in a way that gives students room to learn to know themselves and to know God through the school studies depends on learning to listen and to love. Students do not easily reveal their inner fears and hesitations. Listening means more than hearing words; it means becoming sensitive to the feelings and constraints that are beneath the surface of the student's life, that lie beneath the words. To listen in this way requires love. It involves a willingness to lay down our lives for theirs.

However, our attachments get in the way of our loving God or our neighbor. An attachment, in psychological terms, is an affinity for, or a choice of, something that I imagine will satisfy my longing and make me secure. Each of us has a deep longing for God, though we usually fail to identify it as that. Augustine spoke of the heart's being restless until it rests in God. However, an attachment to any created thing is really an idolatry, an attempt to use something in the creation as a substitute for God. Paul speaks of this in Romans 1:25 when he says, "They exchanged the truth of God for a lie, and worshiped and served the creature rather than the Creator, who is blessed for ever. Amen." We have only so much capacity to love, and our attachments absorb this capacity so that there is no room left to love God and our neighbor. This means that addiction manifests itself in more ways than simply in alcoholism and substance abuse. As mentioned earlier, according to Gerald G. May,

"ALL OF US SUFFER FROM ADDICTION. . . .THE PSYCHOLOGICAL, NEUROLOGICAL, AND SPIRITUAL DYNAMICS OF FULL-FLEDGED ADDICTION ARE ACTIVELY AT WORK WITHIN EVERY HUMAN BEING." (ADDICTION AND GRACE, PP. 3-4).

Even religious orthodoxy can become an addiction. It did that for the Pharisees, to whom Jesus spoke with such devastating candor: "You search the scriptures, because you think that in them you have eternal life; and it is these that bear witness of me; and you are unwilling to come to me, that ye may have life" (John 5:39–40). The essence of sin lies in our addictive idolatries that we pursue in the attempt to get from the creation what can come only from God Himself through the creation.

What May has given us in modern medical terms is a definition of the biblical doctrine of sin or total depravity.

Our attachments to the creation rob us of the freedom to learn. Those attachments, whether to some habit-forming physical substance, or to any of a multitude of other created things—ourselves, our goals, our gifts, our possessions, our treasured relations with others, even our spirituality—keep us from having room to love God and our neighbor. And since only love can cast out fear, they leave us subject to fears, named or nameless, from which we are powerless to free ourselves. Our children experience this too. They are subject to fears and to the oppression of their idolatries. They are born with the tendency to be independent of God, and they learn from our lives to practice that independence. They come to school with fears, and the pressure of the competitive classroom and their critical peers tends only to deepen those fears. What can we do to provide them with a fearless environment where they are free to grow educationally?

The answer, in one word, is grace. God's grace is the most powerful force in all reality. It alone is strong enough to break our servitude to idols. His free gift of forgiveness and of living union with Jesus Christ by the Holy Spirit is the only avenue of escape from our prison of fear and failure. That His grace is offered to us freely, without any kind of bargain on our part, is the good news of the gospel.

The difficulty is that there is no technique that enables us to bring grace under our control. This is what we deeply desire and can never achieve. Grace is not something that can be stored up, managed, or manipulated. Sin has made our lives very much like a wilderness. May points out that as we travel through it, grace comes like the manna to the children of Israel in their desert wanderings. But, like the manna, grace cannot be stored up. If kept overnight the manna bred worms and stank. Grace must be received day by day and moment by moment.

How do we receive grace? By coming, against all that seems reasonable and with a deepening sense of our unworthiness, and asking for it. Our approach to God must be from the standpoint of our weakness, not our strength. Because we want so much to be independent, this is very hard for us. The change of mind involved is the repentance without which we cannot see the Lord (Hebrews 12:14). It is meant to deepen as we go on in life, and with its deepening comes the miracle of the spreading abroad of God's love in our hearts (Romans 5:5). Paul had to learn this lesson in connection with his thorn in the flesh (2 Corinthians 12:9). He prayed three times to be delivered from it. God's answer was that His strength was perfected in Paul's weakness. So Paul learned to rejoice in his weakness. This did not mean indulging his sinfulness. It meant believing that God was greater than his weakness and would use him in spite of his undeservingness.

But what has this to do with hospitality in the classroom? The way to make room for children to learn without fear is to become experienced as teachers through our own reception of grace in our weakness and waywardness. Can this be done in dealing with the ordinary studies? It can if we realize that the creation is sacramental. The cleansing that occurs as we partake of the bread and wine in the Lord's supper is the iceberg's tip of the holiness of ordinary things. God intends to speak to us and to listen to us in and through the creation. As we learn to hear Him and respond to Him in the meaning-laden information of the school studies, we will be guided into ways to help our students do so as well. There is no mechanical technique for teaching this way, although some techniques are more expressive of hospitality than others. But there are the sure promises that if we ask we shall receive, if we seek we shall find, and if we knock the door will be opened to us.

FREEDOM TO TEACH THROUGH SELF-KNOWLEDGE 21

John Calvin begins his *Institutes of the Christian Religion* by saying that the two most important kinds of knowledge in the world are the knowledge of God and the knowledge of ourselves, and that the two are so closely related it is difficult to tell which comes first. What he means is that we cannot really know ourselves unless we know God, and that the better we know God, the better we shall know ourselves. In the search for the most effective methodology for teaching Christianly, a proper self-knowledge, flowing out of a knowledge of God, is a prime requisite.

Jesus said, "If you abide in My word, then you are truly disciples of Mine; and you shall know the truth, and the truth shall make you free" (John 8:31–32). Freedom to teach effectively, then, is dependent on knowing the truth about God and about ourselves. Knowledge is used here in the biblical and not the secular sense. It is not mere factual information stored in our mental computers. It is responsible knowledge that involves answering God from our hearts in loving worship and service in all of life.

In *The Greatest of These Is Love* (now out of print), A. A. Van Ruler pinpoints the difficulty we find ourselves involved in here. We not only *are*, but we *know* that we are; we have both being and consciousness. The curse of sinfulness lies heavily in the false consciousness it inflicts on us. Animals, and the creation below them, have being, but they do not have self-awareness in the way we do.

The problem is that our consciousness has become perverted through our declaration of independence from God. Using the metaphors we used earlier regarding human beings, when the first pair were still in fellowship with God, they were original IMAGES and were conscious of themselves as God's friends and His servants. There was no conflict in their awareness of themselves because God upheld them by His Spirit as His children. Being and consciousness were in perfect harmony. The first man and woman were experiencing genuine freedom.

When they turned from God to seek from the unblessed tree the pleasure, possession, and power that God meant them to receive from Himself through the other parts of the creation, their consciousness changed drastically and, as far as their strength to change it was concerned, irremediably. They thought of themselves now as ULTIMATE ORIGINALS. This consciousness was a curse, not a gift from God, who could not and would not defend or support it. In their being they still were potential image bearers of God, but in their consciousness they were cut off from Him. This consciousness they had to defend for themselves. As a result they saw God as their enemy and thought of each other in the same way. We have been perpetuating this broken condition in ourselves and in the human race ever since. There isn't room in the world for more than one ULTIMATE ORIGINAL. Adam and Eve did not achieve the freedom they sought but found themselves entangled in servitude to idols: first, their own imagined independence and, more deeply, the Evil One himself. Humans are not made to be independent. They are creatures who will inevitably serve either the true God or the idols (Romans 1:21–25).

There was no way for our first parents to undo what they had done. They could not restore the harmony between their being and their new false consciousness. They had to defend that on their own. God would not do it for them, but they were powerless to repair the damage. The solution came from God Himself, promised in the Garden and accomplished many years later through the incarnation, life, death, and resurrection of Jesus Christ. He came as the representative Man to live the life we ought to live and to die, in our place, the death we deserve to die. His was a true human consciousness. There was in Him none of the conflict we experience. We are always trying to project before others a consciousness of being worthy. The efforts we make to maintain this sad charade would be humorous if they were not so tragic. We spend our strength in the effort to defend it. The only solution for us is to become identified with Christ in such a way that His consciousness becomes ours. This is why the New Testament speaks of Him as the true vine, the Bridegroom of His church, and the head of the Body. Freedom, including the freedom to teach, depends on our mystical union with Him, which can afford us an alternative consciousness. Thomas Merton's view of education coincides with what was has been said above:

> MERTON'S MESSAGE IS CLEAR: AN EDUCATION WHICH WOULD SAFEGUARD THE PERSONAL CAPACITY FOR FREE, CREATIVE, AND GENUINE RELATIONSHIP WITH OTHERS IN THE WORLD MUST ULTIMATELY PROVIDE FOR SELF-DISCOVERY. (THOMAS DEL PRETE, IN CHAPTER 3, "SELF-DISCOVERY AS THE PURPOSE OF EDUCATION," OF *THOMAS MERTON AND THE EDUCATION OF THE WHOLE PERSON*).

For Merton the product of genuine education is not a "what" defined by credits and degrees but a "who." This "who" is not some ideal version of the "true self"; that is, it is not an object for self-reflection, an image, or an abstract conceptual realization. Rather, it is the existential "who," the whole person in existential reality, "the radical self in its uninhibited freedom" (Ibid., pp. 31–32). This "who" is, however, never only an individual, but it is always a person in relationship—to God, others, and God's creation. This wholeness of the person and its attendant freedom is possible only when, in union with Christ and in the consciousness of our own brokenness, our being and consciousness are brought together again in dependence on Christ through the Holy Spirit.

Merton contrasts the false self with the true self. The false self believes its reality depends on fulfilling its needs and wants. "It therefore mistakes the 'individual and empirical ego' for the true self." This false self is afraid of death and is constantly trying to affirm itself, to demonstrate its significance.

The false self thus acts as its own source of being and fulfillment; in terms of interaction, it is challenging and defying . . . seeking either to dominate or to placate all that it confronts.

. . . the 'hidden drive to self-assertion' which characterizes the false self is mirrored and magnified in the collective realm of society (Ibid., pp. 35-36).

The true self, by contrast, doesn't have to defend its being by putting up a front. It is different from the false self because it is motivated by love:

Therefore, in contrast to the illusory life that the meaning-making false self is devoted to creating, the life of the true self is free. At the same time, recognizing the source of its being outside itself, it is conscious of its fundamental connectedness to all living beings. Therefore, the true self does not assert itself over and against the world as object, nor does it seek to possess the world . . . it apprehends the world more as a living expression of being, of love, of God (Ibid., p. 40).

Merton's conception of education is evident in the following:

True self-realization is a creative, life-affirming event in which the self and its life-giving source meet. . . . If it is to nurture the growth of the true self, education clearly will have to nourish a subjective experience of knowing. Education driven solely by a view of knowledge as a matter of discrete and objective, if not manipulable, entity will provide

LITTLE SUPPORT FOR TRUE SELF-DISCOVERY. SUCH EDUCATION HA-
BITUALLY REMOVES KNOWLEDGE FROM THE REALM OF PERSONAL
EXPERIENCE AND CONNECTEDNESS TO THE WORLD. IT FAILS TO EN-
HANCE ONE'S SENSE OF REALITY AND IS THUS LIFELESS (IBID., PP. 41, 44).

To become free to teach, Christian teachers must themselves be gripped by the knowledge that enables them to
discover their true selves in Jesus Christ. Otherwise, they
will not be able to lead their students to that goal.

Objective knowledge is the pride and delight of modern
education. Merton's views raise the question of whether this
sort of knowledge is really valid in Christian schooling. The
answer has to be negative. Parker Palmer raises the same
question. He suggests that it was the *kind* of knowledge
Adam and Eve sought that was wrong, for they wanted

... A KNOWLEDGE THAT DISTRUSTED AND EXCLUDED GOD. THEIR
DRIVE TO KNOW AROSE NOT FROM LOVE BUT FROM CURIOSITY AND CON-
TROL, FROM THE DESIRE TO POSSESS POWERS BELONGING TO GOD ALONE.
THEY FAILED TO HONOR THE FACT THAT GOD KNEW THEM FIRST, KNEW
THEM IN THEIR LIMITS AS WELL AS THEIR POTENTIALS.
IN THEIR REFUSAL TO KNOW AS THEY WERE KNOWN, THEY REACHED FOR
A KIND OF KNOWLEDGE THAT ALWAYS LEADS TO DEATH (*TO KNOW AS WE
ARE KNOWN: A SPIRITUALITY OF EDUCATION*, P. 25).

Objective knowledge is concerned with value-free facts
that impose no demands on the knower but are useful for
whatever purposes the knower conceives. This kind of knowledge belongs to the false self. It can never nurture the true
self. It cannot set one free to know or to teach. It centers on
the self as ultimate.

By contrast, the Christian school should deal with
the creation (which is the material for the curriculum
in any school) not in an objective relationship but in a
responsive one. We are to know God through His creation but to know Him in love as we are known by Him
in love. Palmer's concept is expressed in these lines:

THE TEACHER IS A MEDIATOR BETWEEN THE KNOWER AND THE KNOWN, BETWEEN THE LEARNER AND THE SUBJECT TO BE LEARNED. A TEACHER, NOT SOME THEORY, IS THE LIVING LINK IN THE EPISTEMOLOGICAL CHAIN. THE WAY THE TEACHER PLAYS THE MEDIATOR ROLE CONVEYS BOTH AN EPISTEMOLOGY AND AN ETHIC TO THE STUDENT, BOTH AN APPROACH TO KNOWING AND AN AP- PROACH TO LIVING. I MAY TEACH THE RHETORIC OF FREEDOM, BUT IF I TEACH IT *EX CATHEDRA*, ASKING MY STUDENTS TO RELY SOLELY ON THE AUTHORITY OF "THE FACTS" AND DEMANDING THAT THEY IMITATE AUTHORITY ON THEIR PAPERS AND EXAMS, I AM TEACHING A SLAVE ETHIC. I AM FORMING STUDENTS WHO KNOW NEITHER HOW TO LEARN IN FREEDOM NOR HOW TO LIVE FREELY, GUIDED BY AN INNER SENSE OF TRUTH. . . . I TEACH . . . A WAY OF BEING IN THE WORLD. THAT WAY, REINFORCED IN COURSE AFTER COURSE, WILL REMAIN WITH MY STUDENTS LONG AFTER THE FACTS HAVE FADED FROM THEIR MINDS (IBID., PP. 29-30).

Intimately related to this quest for true self-knowl- edge is the biblical emphasis on longing for God. It is expressed, for example, in Psalm 63:

OH GOD, THOU ART MY GOD; I SHALL SEEK THEE EARNESTLY;
MY SOUL THIRSTS FOR THEE, MY FLESH YEARNS FOR THEE,
IN A DRY AND WEARY LAND WHERE THERE IS NO WATER.

Or in Isaiah 55:1–2:

HO! EVERY ONE WHO THIRSTS, COME TO THE WATERS;
AND YOU WHO HAVE NO MONEY COME, BUY AND EAT.
COME, BUY WINE AND MILK WITHOUT MONEY AND WITHOUT COST.
WHY DO YOU SPEND MONEY FOR WHAT IS NOT BREAD,
AND YOUR WAGES FOR WHAT DOES NOT SATISFY?
LISTEN CAREFULLY TO ME, AND EAT WHAT IS GOOD,
AND DELIGHT YOURSELF IN ABUNDANCE.

This theme is repeated and climaxed in Jesus' words at the feast:

IF ANY MAN IS THIRSTY, LET HIM COME TO ME AND DRINK. HE WHO BELIEVES IN ME, AS THE SCRIPTURE SAID, "FROM HIS INNERMOST BEING SHALL FLOW RIVERS OF LIVING WATER." BUT THIS HE SPOKE OF THE SPIRIT, WHOM THOSE WHO BELIEVED IN HIM WERE TO RECEIVE; FOR THE SPIRIT WAS NOT YET GIVEN, BECAUSE JESUS WAS NOT YET GLORIFIED (JOHN 7:37-39).

To long for God is, paradoxically, the way to know oneself. For when we long for God, we love Him. And when we love Him, we learn to love our neighbor (in this instance, our students). Thus self-discovery comes with self-forgetfulness. We gradually acquire an alternative consciousness in which we are satisfied with what Christ is and can forget our efforts to promote a worthy facade in our self-centeredness. Our consciousness can shift increasingly from our effort to be something in our own eyes to our satisfaction with what Christ is as He indwells us by His Spirit. With this will come increasing freedom to teach. We will be able to use the creation as curriculum in such a way as to increase the freedom of students to be what they can be in Christ. In forgetting ourselves while we love God and our students, we will achieve new levels of self-knowledge otherwise impossible to us.

As has been mentioned above, this does not mean constantly repeating these concepts to students. There is no mechanical way to promote self-knowledge in ourselves or in our students. It means a steady, plodding practice of looking to Jesus, who is the Author and Finisher of our faith, and of offering the students enough hints so that those who are ready to hear can hear and grow. The possibility that the teacher can achieve freedom to teach through the self-knowledge acquired from God in connection with the school studies is an exciting one indeed. The excitement deepens when we realize that, if we can achieve self-knowledge through the knowledge of God in His creation, then it will be possible for us to lead students into this kind of self-knowledge also. When that happens, the Christian school becomes school as God intends it to be.

Meaningful Teaching 22

Moses and Daniel were two brilliant men, highly educated in the universities of their day, who held their extensive learning in an entirely different framework from that of their contemporaries. Moses attended the University of Egypt, and Daniel that of Babylon. We do not know who their teachers were outside those universities, but whoever they were, they were eminently successful in guiding their students to meaningful learning. That is, both men put the teaching of their pagan teachers into a framework in which the living God provided the meaning of their knowledge. They understood the biblical worldview of creation, fall, and redemption. They understood that God had made and continued to uphold the creation with the specific purpose of revealing Himself and that the creation was the channel through which they were to worship and serve God.

It would be fascinating to know what believing agents God used to guide Moses' and Daniel's young minds. That information is inaccessible to us, but the parallel of their earthly situation and ours speaks to the task of the Christian school teacher. We teach the same information as the secular school, but we endeavor to do so in a way that shapes the students' minds in a consciousness different from that of the world around them. We endeavor to lead them to see the true meaning of the ideas presented.

In considering the topic of meaningful Christian teaching, we do well to review the nature of the school. Stuart Fowler defines it thus:

THE DISTINCTIVE NATURE OF THE SCHOOL IS THAT IT IS AN ORGANIZATION OF PEDAGOGICAL POWER IN A COMMUNAL BOND OF LOVE OF LEARNING.

To put that more simply, the school is an organization of human resources for the sake of learning. . . . The school is the living community of teachers and students in which the teachers lead students in learning ("Schools Are for Learning," in No Icing on the Cake, Jack Mechielsen, ed., pp. 34-35).

Fowler goes on to say that both the authority of the teacher and the discipline of the classroom are limited by the nature of the school. The teacher is limited to the authority "to lead students in learning; to guide them so that they learn by their experience of the creation in believing response to the Word of God." Likewise, school discipline is valid only when it promotes learning. Discipline is not an end in itself; it is a means to promote meaningful learning.

Another way to look at the definition of the Christian school is to compare it with other kinds of schools, which can be Christian or non-Christian. A barbers' college trains people to be barbers as a chefs' school prepares its students to be cooks, and a mechanics' school trains its attendees to be mechanics. What does the ordinary school prepare children and young people for? It gets them ready to be mature adults who can live acceptably in their society and contribute to it. A Christian school aims to prepare Christians with a viewpoint and attitudes that will make them responsive disciples of Jesus Christ. Our difficulty here is that we are not accustomed to thinking of the school subjects, or content areas, as having any integral relation to the Christian life. The reason is that we have torn the creation, which provides the materials for the curriculum, away from God. We have become accustomed to thinking of subjects like science, mathematics, geography, and history as secular, and of the Bible and theology as spiritual. We have seen that this view is a modern form of the ancient heresy of gnosticism. The Bible states clearly that God made the world the way He did for the express purpose of revealing Himself and promoting our worship and service to Him. This is the meaning that the Christian teacher endeavors to provide for students.

The importance of meaning in education is recognized by non-Christian educators. Philip Phenix defines humans as creatures who can experience meanings, and says that "general education is the process of engendering essential meanings." William Glasser insists that if the material offered in the classroom is not meaningful to the students, it should not be taught. For Christians it is obvious that meaning is important and that the meaning of the creation is ultimately God's self-revelation or self-giving.

But how can we communicate this sort of meaning to children? The answer raises a disturbing question for us as Christian adults. How well have we understood the kingdom of God? Jesus said that one must become like a little child to enter the kingdom. This does not mean that a small child can explain complicated theological doctrines. Rather, it says that the quality of trust and dependence characteristic of childhood is necessary if we are to enter the kingdom. Children can understand the kingdom at their own level because they know what it means to lean on a trusted adult. It is possible to present the school subjects in ways that, for the child who is ready, promote reliance on and love for Jesus. Psalm 29, for example, teaches about a thunderstorm, in a way that is calculated to increase our awe of and trust in the living God. Our usual approach to teaching about thunderstorms in school, however, deals with electrical potential built up in a cloud mass and discharged with a flash of lightning and a roar of thunder. The Christian teacher intent on promoting meaning will give the modern scientific explanation of a thunderstorm in a framework that accords with Psalm 29. Meaningful understanding is important, particularly in the Christian school.

What does this mean for the practice of Christian teaching? Perhaps we need to look again at the example of Jesus Himself:

"COME TO ME, ALL WHO ARE WEARY AND HEAVY-LADEN, AND I WILL GIVE YOU REST. TAKE MY YOKE UPON YOU, AND LEARN FROM ME, FOR I AM GENTLE AND HUMBLE IN HEART; AND YOU SHALL FIND REST FOR YOUR SOULS. FOR MY YOKE IS EASY, AND MY LOAD IS LIGHT" (MATTHEW 11:28-30).

The Christian teacher is gentle and humble in heart. He or she stands in the place of Christ for the student and takes the student into the learning yoke. Teacher and student learn together of the God who reveals Himself in the creation, only the teacher leads because he or she is farther along this path than the student. Or, again, we might think of the foot-washing incident at the Last Supper. When that was finished, Jesus said,

"DO YOU KNOW WHAT I HAVE DONE TO YOU? YOU CALL ME TEACHER AND LORD; AND YOU ARE RIGHT, FOR SO I AM. IF I THEN, THE LORD AND THE TEACHER, WASHED YOUR FEET, YOU ALSO OUGHT TO WASH ONE ANOTHER'S FEET. FOR I GAVE YOU AN EXAMPLE THAT YOU ALSO SHOULD DO AS I DID TO YOU" (JOHN 13:12-15).

The Christian teacher who desires to teach meaningfully must become a servant leader who is so gripped by the meaningfulness of the subject matter that she cannot help leading her students in that direction.

There are certain qualities that will enable teachers to communicate meaningful learning. In general they need to have love, vision, and wholeness: love in the way Tom Howard defines it, "my life for yours"; vision in the sense of a Christian worldview of creation, fall, and redemption; and wholeness in the sense of refusing to split life into sacred and secular, or natural and supernatural. More specifically, teachers need to understand, by way of personal experience, the distinctive nature of the Christian life. They need a Christian mind in both its understanding and its character sides. They need a vision of the goal of teaching—insight directed to service. They ought to have some historical and cultural awareness of the way life and culture have been formed and deformed through the ages. Such awareness will provide them with a basis for discerning the spirits of the world today and of the secular textbooks that they may need to use. They need an integrated view of the created order, including humans and their place in it. In practical terms, the Christian teacher needs the ability to transmit serviceable insight. This will involve a lot of listening in love, for the teacher needs to meet students where they are. This involves a respect for the students as image bearers of God, and an ability to deal with them in terms of their learning styles and their understanding and skill levels. The teacher needs to be a model of discipleship, a sensitive learner who enjoys learning. And he needs to have and cultivate the ability to nurture radical discipleship.

The promotion of meaningful learning involves a number of topics that can only be suggested here. There is the need, for instance, to become aware of, and adapt to, the students' varied learning styles. A number of authorities are available on this topic. They generally agree that there are four distinct learning styles, though their definitions and their nomenclature vary. Adapting the teaching process to the students' learning styles is simply part of receiving them as if they were Jesus. Again, there is the whole field of group learning, or mutually assisted learning, which is receiving increasing attention today. There is the topic of thematic unit studies and their power to tie the various subjects together in a meaningful learning experience. Geraldine Steensma suggests that the development of a conceptual framework promotes meaningful learning. Students can be helped to realize that a conceptual framework has faith roots and that the allegiance of the heart determines our interpretation of the "facts." Students need help to realize that the framework they adopt will give direction and meaning to their lives. One way to do this, Steensma suggests, is to state concepts so that they reflect a Christian framework. Other important factors she mentions are the distinction between rote learning and discovery learning, the adjustment of the levels of abstraction in a discipline to the student's ability level, and the appropriate intermixing of inductive and deductive learning. Each of these could occupy a chapter by itself.

One of the items in the above paragraph needs renewed emphasis here, although it is too large for a detailed discussion. This is the issue of curriculum integration. James A. Beane sums up a 1995 article he wrote on curriculum integration in the following paragraph:

CURRICULUM INTEGRATION CENTERS THE CURRICULUM ON LIFE ITSELF RATHER THAN ON THE MASTERY OF FRAGMENTED INFORMATION WITHIN THE BOUNDARIES OF SUBJECT AREAS. IT IS ROOTED IN A VIEW OF LEARNING AS THE CONTINUOUS INTEGRATION OF NEW KNOWLEDGE AND EXPERIENCE SO AS TO DEEPEN AND BROADEN OUR UNDERSTANDING OF OURSELVES AND OUR WORLD. ITS FOCUS IS ON LIFE AS IT IS LIVED NOW RATHER THAN ON PREPARATION FOR SOME LATER LIFE OR LATER LEVEL OF SCHOOLING. IT SERVES THE YOUNG PEOPLE FOR WHOM THE CURRICULUM IS INTENDED RATHER THAN THE SPECIALIZED INTERESTS OF ADULTS. IT CONCERNS THE ACTIVE CONSTRUCTION OF MEANINGS RATHER THAN THE PASSIVE ASSIMILATION OF OTHERS' MEANINGS (*PHI DELTA KAPPAN*, APRIL 1995, P. 622).

As Beane defines it, curriculum integration means something much more radical than a multidisciplinary approach to schooling. It centers teaching around themes that have immediate relationship to the students' personal lives and themes that involve issues or problems in the larger world. At the same time, he insists that the subject areas are not in opposition to an integrated curriculum but are actually supportive of it.

As noted above, this topic is too big for thorough discussion here, but there are at least two reasons why Christian school people should think much more seriously about curriculim integration than we have so far. First, the Christian worldview stresses the wholeness of human life and knowledge. The fundamental importance of the Word of God, which provides the underlying laws for each aspect of human experience, inevitably stands in opposition to a curriculum that fragments knowledge into subject areas. Second, Jesus' admonition to seek the kingdom of God first underlines the importance of our relationship to God and neighbor in a way that raises serious questions about a fragmented approach to school studies. Probably developing our curriculum around the standard content areas is one more way in which we have allowed ourselves to conform to this world rather than striking out in a far more radical way. We need to look more carefully at where we want to go and where we are actually going.

To return to the theme of this chapter, meaningful teaching involves the teacher in managing the curriculum rather than simply teaching a textbook. Steensma and Van Brummelen suggest the following ideas for curriculum management ("Directives for a Biblically Grounded Curriculum," *Shaping School Curriculum*, p. 24):

1. THE GOAL OF EDUCATION IS TO STRUCTURE THE CURRICULUM SO THAT HEARTS ARE PREPARED FOR THE "STILL, SMALL VOICE." IT SHOULD BE STRUCTURED TO DEMONSTRATE THAT ALL CREATION PROCLAIMS ITS CREATOR AND SO THAT STUDENTS ARE CALLED TO RESPOND WITH THEIR WHOLE LIVES.

2. CURRICULUM CONTENT AND EXPERIENCES SHOULD BE CHOSEN AND ORDERED WITH THE FOLLOWING PRINCIPLES IN MIND:
    A. THE RELATION OF THE BIBLE TO THE DISCIPLINE
    B. THE MEANING INVOLVED IN THE ASPECT OF LIFE INVESTIGATED BY THAT DISCIPLINE
    C. THE METHOD OF INQUIRY USED IN THAT DISCIPLINE
    D. THE INTERRELATION OF OTHER ACADEMIC DISCIPLINES WITH THIS ONE
    E. THE IMPLICATIONS OF THE ABOVE FOUR TOPICS FOR THE ELEMENTARY AND SECONDARY CURRICULUM

One final topic that calls for some comment is the matter of evaluation. In general, at least the following important principles should be kept in mind. Evaluation of a student should be done for the individual student and not to establish competitive levels in the classroom. It should be done in terms of each student's gifts and with a view to the best goals each student can be helped to adopt. It should be done with the cooperation, in some form, of the student.

Shaping School Curriculum offers a list of helpful ideas about evaluation. Since the book is out of print and may be difficult to find, a slightly edited copy of those is presented here:

1. USE FREQUENT POSITIVE, HELPFUL FEEDBACK.
2. REVISE PLANNED ACTIVITIES ON THE BASIS OF DAILY OBSERVATION OF THE STUDENT.
3. LET STUDENTS EVALUATE THEIR OWN WORK IN ORAL REPORTS TO YOU.
4. LET THEM HELP EACH OTHER IN IMPROVING THEIR WORK (NOT IN EVALUATING IT, ED.).
5. GIVE ORAL OR WRITTEN COMMENTS ON WORK TURNED IN, AND GIVE THE GRADE (IF A GRADE IS NECESSARY) WITHIN TWO OR THREE DAYS.
6. DON'T OVEREMPHASIZE TESTS; EVALUATE DAILY WORK.
7. MAKE TESTS MEANINGFUL, NOT MERELY TESTS OF MEMORY.
8. USE TESTS TO FIND AND CORRECT WEAKNESSES, NOT JUST TO RANK STUDENTS.
9. AVOID PEER COMPETITION SITUATIONS.
10. KEEP A RECORD OF OBSERVATIONS DURING EVALUATION AND IMPROVE TEACHING NEXT TIME.
11. GIVE ANECDOTAL REPORTS INSTEAD OF GRADES IF YOU CAN, AND TELL THE CHILD BEFORE YOU TELL THE PARENTS.

A more recent and also very valuable discussion of

evaluation is found in *A Vision With a Task*, edited by Stronks and Blomberg. The authors suggest five ways in which present methods of evaluation can be improved: authentic tests, portfolios, self-evaluation, projects, and exhibitions. Another recent and valuable source is *Walking With God in the Classroom* by Harro Van Brummelen. The author identifies both a formative and a summative goal in evaluation. The former evaluates in order to help the student grow. The latter summarizes student growth over a period of time or in a particular project. He also mentions the following evaluation guidelines. First, evaluation is limited in its function. We must judge students' "behavior and products, not their personhood." Second, any evaluation should be respectful of the student and should seek to upbuild the student lovingly. Third, ranking should not be the main objective of our evaluation. Children's gifts differ, and our evaluation should recognize that fact. Van Brummelen's extended treatment of evaluation is eminently worth reading.

In summary, Christian teaching should, above all, be meaningful. This means that the learning should come to be associated in the student's mind with the knowledge of God—not knowledge *about* God in the form of theological propositions but personal touch with God via the created subjects. For this to happen, the teacher should be experiencing the grip of the Word of God in this way. We cannot lead our apprentices into experiences to which we are strangers.

NOTES

COMMUNITY IN THE CHRISTIAN SCHOOL 23

The Calvin Study Center topic for the 1992–1993 academic year was Christian schooling in the twenty-first century. The vision that the assembled scholars developed was that the goal of Christian schools should be responsive discipleship. This was unfolded in three particular objectives: eliciting student gifts, sharing joys and sorrows, and seeking shalom (justice through Christ's redemption). At first glance, these do not look very much like academic goals. Where is the mastery of the 3 R's? The development of skills? The ability to solve higher level thought problems? On second glance, however, the picture changes. If education is simply the acquisition of value-free facts that will enable the student to rise to the top in a competitive society oriented toward self-fulfillment, the relational objectives listed above do seem out of place. However, if the subjects reveal the living God and have the potential of becoming channels for communion with and service to God, then relationships take precedence over profits or power, and a genuine understanding of the curriculum will lead to those objectives as right ones for true education.

The validity of this assertion lies in the importance of community and in the model for communal relationships found in the Holy Trinity. The Trinity is the model for all rich and valid human relationships, whether in marriage, family, social groups, society, or citizenry. "For this reason, I bow my knees before the Father, from whom every family in heaven and on earth derives its name" (Ephesians 3:14–15). Within the Trinity there is a totally unrestricted giving of each member to the others, an unparalleled mutual love with no reservations whatsoever. This awesome mutuality of infinite love is the model for all covenant-keeping human communities. Proper Christian education will not skimp on the development of knowledge and skills, but it will demonstrate its best characteristic in the encouragement of human relationships such as those involved in the three objectives above.

The staggering richness of the promises that Jesus made to His disciples and makes to us eludes us because we have read the verses frequently and assume we have exhausted their meaning. Actually we have barely caught a glimpse of their awesome possibilities.

"AND I WILL ASK THE FATHER, AND HE WILL GIVE YOU ANOTHER HELPER, THAT HE MAY BE WITH YOU FOREVER; THAT IS THE SPIRIT OF TRUTH, WHOM THE WORLD CANNOT RECEIVE, BECAUSE IT DOES NOT BEHOLD HIM OR KNOW HIM, BUT YOU KNOW HIM BECAUSE HE ABIDES WITH YOU, AND WILL BE IN YOU. I WILL NOT LEAVE YOU AS ORPHANS; I WILL COME TO YOU" (JOHN 14:16-18).

"IF ANYONE LOVES ME, HE WILL KEEP MY WORD; AND MY FATHER WILL LOVE HIM, AND WE WILL COME TO HIM, AND MAKE OUR ABODE WITH HIM" (VERSE 23).

"BUT THE HELPER, THE HOLY SPIRIT, WHOM THE FATHER WILL SEND IN MY NAME, HE WILL TEACH YOU ALL THINGS, AND BRING TO YOUR REMEMBRANCE ALL THAT I SAID TO YOU" (VERSE 26).

"IF YOU KEEP MY COMMANDMENTS, YOU WILL ABIDE IN MY LOVE; JUST AS I HAVE KEPT MY FATHER'S COMMANDMENTS, AND ABIDE IN HIS LOVE" (JOHN 15:10).

"WHEN THE HELPER COMES, WHOM I WILL SEND TO YOU FROM THE FATHER, THAT IS THE SPIRIT OF TRUTH, WHO PROCEEDS FROM THE FATHER, HE WILL BEAR WITNESS OF ME, AND YOU WILL BEAR WITNESS ALSO, BECAUSE YOU HAVE BEEN WITH ME FROM THE BEGINNING" (VERSE 26).

The thrust of these verses is that Christ's intent is to reproduce among His people on Earth a fellowship or communion that is like the oneness within the Trinity. In the

Trinity there is a total vulnerability of each Person to the others. There is no holding back whatsoever. What one does, all do. The circulation of love among the Three Persons is so bright it blinds us, who know very little of true openness. But the message is unmistakable. Jesus intends to see this level of loving self-giving in the community of His people on Earth, because that is the way they should bear the image of God and witness to a world that is so severely fractured by the lack of love.

The problem that troubles us at this point is that our sinful declaration of independence in the persons of the first human pair cut the race off from trust in and experience of the love of God, who then became our enemy. But God is the source of all true love. With their fellowship with Him broken, Adam and Eve had nowhere to go to find another source of love. So the whole weary business of putting on a mask of false love to hide our poverty began. It continues to this day. The flip side of our selfishness is a barely disguised hatred for others. As long as there is no shortage of the things we want, we can put on a front of amiability and friendship, but when real shortages develop, tempers flare and people get hurt.

All this says that the development of true community is an extremely important part of a Christian school program. It should take place on several levels, beginning with the classroom. Here we must try to reverse the qualities of competitiveness, unilateral exchange in learning, and alienation that Nouwen sees as characteristic of teaching as a violent process. Children, both in the family and in the Christian classroom, need to feel that they are gifted and needed. They have a contribution to make, a part to play, and the production will be incomplete without their participation. This effort will demand some fairly severe rethinking on the teacher's part. We have grown so accustomed to honors that go to the intellectually or athletically gifted that we have trouble imagining any other way to structure a school environment. What else could we do? Music, for example, is an important gift from God. One of the few things we know about heaven is that there is music there. We are not told whether SAT scores will be posted in heaven. Artistic ability is a gift that contributes to the community. Yet when the budget tightens, music and art are the first casualties. But there is much more. A love that is able to empathize with another's problem or pain, a compassion that recoils from the temptation to make cutting or belittling remarks, a willingness to be helpful to those in need—these are just the beginning of the qualities that make up true community. They need to be recognized as well.

Community in the classroom does not mean cutting everyone down to a least common denominator level so no one can feel above anyone else. It entails an honest recognition of giftedness. But this should be done in such a way that the value of the person is seen in relation to the group. Does this raise competition from the individual to the group level? No, the group carries the self-giving character of Christ. It is committed to loving service, not to competitive boasting. Love is always giving. True humility does not deny one's own God-given gifts, but it endeavors to enjoy those of others as much as its own. Love for the community also helps one to remember that to whom much is given, of him shall much be required. Those with outstanding gifts are meant to help and guide others, not to bask in the light of their own glory.

Community in the classroom will not grow with any luxuriance if it is not characteristic as well of the faculty room. It is no good telling children to love one another if they cannot see that their teachers love each other. Teachers can easily slip into a mode of exaggerated independence. Once the classroom door is closed, each teacher feels secure in his or her little castle. Only the principal can freely cross the moat over the drawbridge. Even then, there may be a fair amount of tension in the ensuing visit. So teachers need to learn to love each other just as mothers and fathers in the family need to display a genuine solidarity of mutual love before their children. The tendency for a teacher to be critical of others is deeply ingrained. We resist the voice that suggests that we should ask for help. We do not want to become accountable to each other. We prefer to keep walls between us and others. The only resolution of our problem is the cultivation of the love that 1 Corinthians says is a more excellent way—patient, kind, not jealous or bragging or arrogant. It does not act in an unbecoming manner, seek its own, or become easily provoked. It does not keep lists of wrongs, or rejoice in another's failure. It bears, believes, hopes, and endures all things. Love never has a flat tire. Such love is quite impossible for us on our own, but we have the promise that God will, by His Spirit, pour His love for each other into our hearts. Faculty meetings need to keep this kind of love before the group as a primary goal. It is a goal that is often more easily achieved at the elementary than at the secondary level. Isolation tends to increase rather than decrease among the high school faculty. The important thing is to set the goal and keep working toward it. Then it will be much easier to promote community in the classroom.

The relation of administrators to teachers is another level where community is indispensable. Teachers lead their students, and administrators lead their teachers. The quality of this leadership is critical for the development of community within the faculty and in the classrooms. The only safe example of it is the Lord Jesus Himself. The patience with which He nurtured His twelve apostles and His other disciples during those tumultuous three years of ministry is breathtaking. There was never any question as to who was in charge. He could speak very bluntly at times, as He did to Peter when Peter rejected the idea of His going to Jerusalem to die. But He was, first and last, a servant leader. He washed the apostles' feet when not one of them would do the task that a slave usually performed for guests. In His last days the apostles added to His already overwhelming sorrow the further irritation of demonstrating callous competition for first place in the kingdom. Yet He loved them, and loved them right to the end. The principal who can do room visits or annual evaluations in such a way as to enable the teacher to disclose her own sense of success and failure and her own goals for improvement will demonstrate a practical kind of love that contributes perceptibly to the development of community. The teacher who can humble himself enough to listen to gentle criticism and be helped by it will do the same thing.

The school's support staff is another rung in the community ladder. Poet John Milton lamented and yet validated his own blindness when he wrote, "They also serve who only stand and wait." The second most important contributor to the miracle of the feeding of the five thousand was not an apostle but the little boy who was willing to risk his sack lunch of five biscuits and two small fish. Administrators and teachers wear more epaulets than do other staff people, but the school could not get along without its support staff. Here again, the importance of each member of the community needs to be prayerfully and thoughtfully remembered, developed, and expressed. Love has to be cultivated. Community doesn't grow unless we weed, fertilize, and water the garden.

Another relationship in which community is essential is that between the school board and the staff. Board members are busy people who are responsible for policy formation for the school. They own the school. In a real sense, they *are* the school. It is easy for them to treat their responsibility as they would a board position in the business world, but to do so would cast a shadow over the development of community at all the levels below them. Community in the board will not grow automatically. Grace, love, and forbearance are as necessary here as anywhere. Most important is the awareness that community is essential if the board is to function with God's blessing. So building community needs to be one of the first priorities of the board officers.

Finally, community must develop within the constituency, and between the constituency and the school personnel. If a school's vision is truly Christian, parents may be somewhat puzzled by it. Churches are not always supportive or even sympathetic to the cause of Christian schooling, so there is need to cultivate an awareness among the parents of what the school is trying to do. Schools should provide at least an entry-level seminar for parents before their children are admitted. At this seminar every effort should be made to clarify the school's educational philosophy and mission, and to encourage parents to think about how their influence in the home will support rather than hinder the school's pursuit of its objectives. Since genuine Christian thinking is not widespread today, even in the church, a required annual seminar for parents would be desirable. There the mission of the school could be reinforced and explained in a way that would help them catch the vision. That is an idea which, as far as this writer knows, has not caught on yet with any Christian school.

Community, then, is important. Someone has expressed it as based on responsible freedom at all levels. Students need help to respond freely to their teachers. Teachers need this freedom toward their administrators and boards. Parents need encouragement and freedom to approach teachers and administrators. The faculty and other staff need unity in vision, understanding, and love. Only in community will a true vision of Christian schooling take root and grow. And without that vision, it would be better not to waste the money and energy it takes to establish and maintain a Christian school. Mutual love is the key ingredient in true community.

NOTES

Conclusion

What Are We Really Trying to Do?

"God was in Christ, reconciling the world to Himself
... and He has committed to us the word of reconciliation."
(2 Corinthians 5:19)

As we come to the end of these essays on Christian schooling, we look again at the question we seek to answer: What is the Christian school attempting to do? We've seen that the goal is not merely to acquire the skills needed to live in today's world. The Christian school teacher is concerned primarily with helping students become true disciples of Jesus Christ. To do this, they must not only understand the gospel but must learn to see the created world in a way different from that of the culture around them.

The only basis for curriculum available to any school is the creation. Everything we study in school has been created and is upheld by the Word of God, though often it is deeply corrupted by human sin. What the Christian teacher attempts to do with the student's discovery of the creation, however, is distinctively different from what the non-Christian teacher aims at.

This difference hinges on a truth revealed in the Bible. Human experience is limited, with one exception, to the created world. The exception lies in the ability of the human heart to have touch with God, an ability that transcends the creation and is beyond investigation by human scientific analysis. There is a mystery involved here that we cannot fully penetrate. However, what makes Christian teaching different is the biblical revelation that the study of the creation can be a means of learning to know and serve God better. This realization gives the school studies tremendous potential value. It defines the particular goal of the Christian school curriculum. We can consider that goal from both a negative and a positive standpoint.

Negatively, the Christian school does not have, nor does it seek, a new set of discoverable information about created reality. God has made only one world, so far as we know, and He has gifted non-Christians as well as Christians with the ability to unlock some of its secrets. For this reason Christian schools should not look down on the discoveries of non-Christian research scientists.

It is important, however, to distinguish genuine scientific discoveries from metaphysical opinions. When a scientist talks about evolution as the true explanation of the origin of the cosmos, he has departed from the field of science and entered that of philosophy and religion. His scientific credentials carry no special authority in these areas, nor is the Christian student obliged to believe him. The situation is further complicated by the realization that science does not mean the same thing in the human areas such as psychology, sociology, and ethics as it does in the physical sciences. The success of scientific investigation in the early period of the scientific revolution made academics in other areas eager for the kind of respect that the physical scientists had achieved. But investigations in those human areas often do not offer the same kind of repeatable experiments as they do in the physical sciences. Therefore, one needs to look carefully at claims of scientific credibility and to remember that there have been radical paradigm changes even in the physical sciences.

In the above discussion of the information available to the Christian school, the word *facts* was deliberately avoided. The concept of facts as neutral, value-free entities is so deeply imbedded in the modern Western consciousness that Christians have trouble recognizing its falsity. To be value-free, facts would have to be meaningless, but all created realities are full of meaning. Neutral facts simply do not exist. God makes and maintains the creation to reveal Himself to us. The idea that there are realities that exist independently of God is a dangerous delusion. It is part of the idolatry that makes modern people think of themselves as independent, or autonomous. It is part of the modern delusion that facts are public and values are private. Religion, of course, is relegated to the private area—hence the current U.S. insistence that religious concepts have no place in public discussions. But if facts are actually meaning-laden, then it is unreasonable to exclude religious convictions from the discussion of public truth.

However, if Christians accept the position that facts are value-free, they can easily look to the secular school to teach their children what is real in the world and then expect the home and church to teach them how they ought to live there. This separation of ethics from the sciences is even characteristic of some Christian universities—but it is an unbiblical separation. Realities thought of as neutral are thus made independent of God. At the same time, they are always considered dependent on some aspect of the creation that is thought of as independent. These independent aspects may be things like numbers, sensory perception, logic, or even biology. They are believed to be independent of God and, at the same time, to be the basic reality on which everything else depends. For example, the number-world theory maintains that numerals stand for real entities in another world or dimension of reality and that these are what make observable things possible for us. Clouser says that this view was not only held by some ancient Greek philosophers, but some version of it is still held by mathematicians today (*The Myth of Religious Neutrality*, pp. 112–113). But nothing in the world is independent. To suppose something is independent of God is to make it into an idol. Romans 1:25 strictly forbids our doing this.

When we say that Christian schools do not seek new information about the creation, we must note exceptions. The Christian school may legitimately seek improved versions of theological propositions. Some of our standard evangelical theological doctrines still carry admixtures of pagan Greek thinking that were picked up centuries ago. Christian schools may properly investigate these and advocate changes. They may also engage in research that leads to new scientific discoveries. Such activities, of course, happen more on the university level than in the primary or secondary schools. The point to remember is that the Christian school deals with the same realities as the secular school, but it has the biblical key to the meaning of experienced reality.

Not only does the Christian school lay no claim to alternative information about the world, although it interprets the information differently; its goal is not a new set of moral standards either. God's standards for our conduct are contained in the Bible. We have the needed moral direction for our lives in the Ten Commandments, summed up in the two great commands of love to God and neighbor, and enlarged on in many parts of the Bible. The moral or ethical side of human life ought not to be separated from the other aspects of our experience. Since all we experience is created by God, and all of it reveals Him, each thing we learn carries within it an obligation to respond to God in awe, love, and service. Thus it carries a moral aspect. For example, language has an ethical side. It can be morally uplifting or degrading. Hence the Bible says that our speech should be with grace, seasoned with salt, to build up those who hear us (Colossians 4:6). So the Christian school curriculum offers neither new information about the world nor a new code of morals. It simply reveals the meaning of our knowledge of the creation, and the privileges and obligations that knowledge carries in our relation to God.

On the positive side, there are at least three goals for the Christian school curriculum. The first is reconciling, or reuniting, creation and redemption. The second is encouraging reconciled lives that give visibility to the Christian worldview of creation, fall, and redemption. The third is nurturing students in such a way that through the school studies their awe, love, praise, and service to God are deepened.

As to the first goal, is it really true that the modern Christian church has found ways to separate creation from redemption? Yes, for redemption is regularly thought of as something spiritual, related primarily to the forgiveness of our sins and our acceptance into the family of God. The created world, on the other hand, is often regarded even by Christians as related to God distantly at best, and related mainly by His original creation of it. It is not usually considered "spiritual." Even Christians are likely to think of it as secular. That's strange when most Christians would insist that we humans bear the image of God, and yet they see us as part of this so-called secular creation. The disconnection between creation and redemption is a major reason for the view that such matters as politics, business, and education really have little or nothing to do with religion. Hence there is little discomfort for Christians who allow the secular public school to educate their children.

How did this polarization happen? It was clearly not present in Old Testament Israel, where all of life was recognized as within the covenant with Jehovah. Nor was it present in the early church. The most common reason for the persecution of first-century Christians was a political one. They would not bow to the image of Caesar and acknowledge him as divine. Hence they were called "atheists." For early Christians life was not divided between the spiritual and the secular.

Historically, the change that separated the sacred

from the secular took place in two principal steps. During the early centuries of our era, Christian theology was considerably influenced by Greek philosophy. Augustine, for example, was touched by neo-Platonism. Gradually the view of Christian thinkers, commonly known as scholasticism, came to carry a good many ideas derived from the pagan Greeks rather than from the Bible. The development of scholasticism came to a head in the thirteenth century, when the writings of Aristotle first found their way into the newly established universities of western Europe. Aristotle was much more concerned with the physical world than Plato had been. The question now was, Can Christian thinkers accept the teachings of Aristotle? The answer given by Thomas Aquinas at the University of Paris was that this was permissible as long as it was remembered that Aristotle was dealing with ordinary things, whereas the Bible dealt with spiritual things. This led to the dualistic perspective called Nature/Grace, with nature including ordinary things and grace, spiritual ones. In the spiritual area Christ was the Lord, and the Bible was needed. In ordinary things, human reason was all that was necessary. This concept, growing out of the Roman Catholic view that the fall of man hurt his will but not his reason, resulted in a form of idolatry. In spiritual things, Christ is Lord; in ordinary things, reason is. This view puts reason, something created, in the place of God. Thus it is idolatrous.

The separation between creation and redemption is not a biblical one. It has been perpetuated in Christian thinking by the terms "general revelation" and "special revelation." General revelation is found in the creation and has little to say about redemption. Special revelation is found in the Bible and deals with salvation. Gordon Spykman suggested the alternative terms "fundamental revelation" and "redemptive revelation." These offer a better choice. The modern evangelical church's emphasis on the message of salvation has driven creation and redemption apart in the minds of Christians.

The reality is that everything God created reveals Him, as Psalm 19, Romans 1:20, and other passages attest. Any genuine perception of God's revealing Himself in the creation shows faith and is bound to be redemptive. In the closing chapters of Job, when God talks to Job, He speaks exclusively of created reality. Job's response is, "I have heard of Thee by the hearing of the ear, but now my eye sees Thee; therefore I retract, and I repent in dust and ashes" (Job 42:5–6). This is a redemptive response to God's self-revelation in the creation. It is true, of course, that when the race fell into sin, it lost the capacity to read the creation aright. So God provided the Scriptures and then the incarnation, death, and resurrection of Christ to open the way for a return to Him in redemption and for a renewed understanding of the created world. Redemption includes the whole of reality as well as our individual souls. The Bible explains it as embracing the restoration of the creation to what God originally intended it to be. Thus one important goal of the Christian school curriculum is leading students to see that the creation does reveal God and that, once we know God through Christ, we can come more and more closely into touch with Him through our understanding of His world.

A second goal of the Christian school curriculum is to encourage students to live lives that incarnate the Christian worldview of creation, fall, and redemption. When we love God with our whole hearts and our neighbors as ourselves, we clothe the biblical worldview with visible lives. We seek first God's kingdom and His righteousness. This can take place in all aspects of life, including home, school, business, and government, as well as church. When parents in the home treat each other and their children with self-sacrificing love, they practice the gospel. They illustrate the Christian worldview.

This should happen in the Christian school as well. An excellent recent book on Christian schools, *A Vision with a Task*, suggests three steps that lead students to responsive discipleship: unwrapping students' gifts, sharing each other's joys and burdens, and seeking Christ's *shalom*, the biblical peace and justice that heals brokenness and restores creation. When students are helped to do these things, they flesh out the Christian worldview. When a Christian businessman feels responsible for overcoming the pollution from his factory that has fouled a river and killed its marine life, he is doing the same thing. When a Christian government official finds ways to move the government toward its biblical objective of promoting public justice, he also makes the Christian worldview visible. In spite of the grip of sin on the world and on our lives, opportunities for positive kingdom activity abound in every phase of life. One of the goals of the Christian school curriculum is to help students learn how to do this. It means helping students to function as reconcilers (2 Corinthians 5:17–21).

A third goal, growing out of the first two, is to nurture students in such a way that they can experience a new relationship to God through their school studies. This goal is really an elaboration of Jesus' definition of eternal life: "And this is eternal life, that they may know Thee, the only true God, and Jesus Christ whom Thou has sent" (John 17:3). That this possibility is so little recognized in the church today is both surprising and saddening.

Yet there can be no question that the Bible asserts that the creation reveals God. The passage from Job referred to above is an illustration. What a strange outcome for a lesson on natural science! Many Bible passages refute the modern misconception that facts are value-free or meaningless. It is the compassionate and loving purpose of God that His creation should reveal Him. Hence a life-changing knowledge of God in and through the creation is both an outstanding feature and a special goal of the Christian school curriculum. There are several sides to the knowledge of God involved here.

The first side is that a deepening realization of God's immediate and intimate involvement in the creation will lead to a growing reverential awe for Him. This is what the Bible speaks of as the fear of God, which it further calls "the beginning (or chief part) of knowledge" (Proverbs 1:7). God has put us in an environment marvelously adapted to our life needs. He maintains that environment and us moment by moment by the power of His Word (Hebrews 1:3). This speaks loudly of His loving wisdom, care, and grace. As students begin to sense His nearness in ordinary experiences, the Holy Spirit can work in their hearts to deepen their awe for Him and hence their knowledge of God in Jesus Christ.

This is not, however, something that the Christian school teacher can convey to her students by preaching at them. While she will surely speak of it at appropriate moments, it is much more likely to find its way into their hearts to the extent that it has become a reality to the teacher herself and an integral part of the curriculum. As her own reverential awe for God deepens in her consideration of the studies she is trying to lead her students to appreciate, she will find imaginative ways, guided by God's Spirit, to suggest the same possibility to her students. To fear God in this biblical sense is part of what it means to know God. It is one of the important goals of the Christian school curriculum.

This does not diminish the academic content of the curriculum. The information contained in the school studies is what it is, in whatever school it is considered. Christian school students need to get to know the creation as well as they can within the parameters of their varying gifts. Students gifted with logical and linguistic ability, for example, should be helped to achieve the high-excellence they are capable of. Whatever approach a student's gifts indicate, the new element added by the Christian school's approach is the meaning of the information. And that meaning is not merely new cognitive information; it is an altered life growing in the fear of God as He is seen in the creation. Reality calls for a response to God.

A second side to knowing God through school studies is a deepening love for Him. For example, the wonders of the human body, as studied in physiology, are capable of moving us almost to tears and certainly to love when we realize how wisely God has invented them and how tenderly and faithfully He sustains them. Again, the study of geography and astronomy has the potential to move us to love when we realize how delicately the planetary system has been adapted to our comfortable living within a very narrow environmental band on the surface of the earth at just the right distance from the sun, and how amazingly God has arranged our protection from certain harmful rays of the sun. The whole field of the arts is loaded with reasons for loving God. The beauty we enjoy so much in the sunset or a waterfall or a beloved friend is not finally in these things but comes through them. As C. S. Lewis said, pleasure is "a shaft of the glory touching our sensibilities." When this becomes real to a student, the consequence is bound to be a deepening love for God.

Growing love will manifest itself in a third form of knowing God: namely, a deepening level of praise to Him. As suggested in an earlier chapter, we do not usually think of praise as work, but the angels do. Had Isaiah asked the seraphim why they didn't do something worthwhile, he might well have been knocked into the next county by an angel's wing (Isaiah 6:1–4). We measure everything in terms of money and imagine that the value of a human depends on how much he or she earns. However, praise is really the most important as well as the most enjoyable work that humans can do. We simply need an altered consciousness to begin to appreciate that. Hence Romans 12:1–2 calls us not to be conformed to this world, but to be transformed by the renewing of our minds that we may prove what is the good and acceptable and perfect will of God. Praise is one more facet of the knowledge of God that is meant to arise from our study of the creation.

A final form of knowing God is the deepening desire to serve Him. As students and teachers develop their awareness that this is God's world, held in being moment by moment by His Word for our good, the sense of happy obligation to serve Him in it will be inescapable. The forms that service can take are innumerable, but they will always be a fulfillment of the two great commands to love God and neighbor. (And that includes taking care of the world for the neighbor's well-being.) The modern world's goal of success in life can be summarized as the pursuit of pleasure, possessions, and power—the three elements in the temptation in the Garden and in Christ's temptation in the wilderness. They have found their way into our lives as evangelical Christians more deeply than we like to recognize. The alternative vocation of serving God and neighbor in love in all that we do is the Christian's calling. As students come to know the Lord in and through His creation, that vocation will more and more become their goal.

In conclusion, the distinctive goal of the Christian school is to use the curriculum as a means to help students grow in the reconciliation of creation and redemption, in their expression in life of a Christian worldview, and in their knowledge of God. That knowledge will be demonstrated in their reverential awe of Him, their love for Him, and their increasing praise and service to Him. They need to know the academic information commonly taught in school, but they need to know it in the context of its true meaning, which is that it reveals God and calls for a response to Him.

NOTES

BIBLIOGRAPHY

Beane, James A. "Curriculum Integration and the Disciplines of Knowledge." *Phi Delta Kappan*, April, 1995.

Berger, Peter L. *A Rumor of Angels*. New York: Anchor Books, 1970, 1990.

Berkouwer, G. C. *Man, the Image of God*. Grand Rapids, Michigan: Eerdmans, 1972.

Blomberg, Doug. *No Icing on the Cake*. Melbourne: Brooks-Hall Publishing Foundation, 1980.

Brand, Paul and Philip Yancey. *Fearfully and Wonderfully Made*. Grand Rapids, Michigan: Zondervan, 1987.

Brueggemann, Walter. *The Prophetic Imagination*. Minneapolis: Fortress Press, 1978, 1989.

Capon, Robert. *The Supper of the Lamb*. New York: Pocket Books, 1970.

_____. *Bed and Board*. New York: Pocket Books, 1970.

_____. *An Offering of Uncles*. New York: Crossroad, 1982.

Clouser, Roy. *The Myth of Religious Neutrality*. University of Notre Dame Press, 1991.

del Prete, Thomas. *Thomas Merton and the Education of the Whole Person*. Birmingham, Alabama: Religious Education, 1990.

Edman, Irwin. "Arts and Experience," in *Arts and the Man*. New York, 1928, 1939.

Ellul, Jacques. *The Presence of the Kingdom*. New York: Seabury Press, 1967.

Fowler, Stuart. "Schools Are for Learning." In Doug Blomberg. *No Icing on the Cake*, Melbourne: Brooks-Hall Publishing Foundation, 1980.

Gardner, Howard. *The Unschooled Mind*. New York: Basic Books, 1991.

_____. *Frames of Mind*. New York: Basic Books, 1993.

Goudzwaard, B. *Aid for the Overdeveloped West*. Toronto: Wedge Publishing Foundation, 1975.

Howard, Thomas. *Hallowed Be This House*. Seattle: Alta Vista College Press, 1983.

Knight, George R. *Philosophy and Education*, 2nd Edition. Berrien Springs, Michigan: Andrews University Press, 1989.

Lewis, C. S. *Letters to Malcolm, Chiefly on Prayer*. London: London and Glasgow. *Letters* 1974.

_____. *The Abolition of Man*. New York: McMillan, 1947.

_____. *The Weight of Glory*. Grand Rapids, Michigan: Eerdmans, 1949.

_____. *The Four Loves*. San Diego: Harcourt Brace and Company, 1991.

Loder, James. *The Transforming Moment*, 2nd edition. Colorado Springs: Helmers and Howard, 1989.

Martin, James E. "Toward an Epistemology of Revelation." In *The Reality of Christian Learning*, edited by Harold Heie and David L. Wolfe. Grand Rapids, Michigan: Eerdmans,1987.

May, Gerald G. *Addiction and Grace: Love and Spirituality in the Healing of Addictions*. Harper San Francisco, 1991.

Newbigin, Lesslie. *The Other Side of 1984*. New York: World Council of Churches, 1983.

Nord, Warren A. *Religion and American Education: Rethinking an American Dilemma*. Chapel Hill, North Carolina: University of North Carolina Press, 1995.

Nouwen, Henri. *Reaching Out*. New York: Doubleday, 1975.

Owens, Virginia Stem. *God Spy: Faith, Perception, and the New Physics*. Seattle: Alta Vista College Press, 1988.

Palmer, Parker. *To Know As We Are Known*. Evanston, Illinois: Harper and Row, 1983.

Peterson, Eugene. *Working the Angles*. Grand Rapids, Michigan: Eerdmans Medina, Washington:, 1994.

_____. *Answering God*. Harper San Francisco, 1989.

Phenix, Philip H. *Realms of Meaning*. New York: McGraw-Hill, 1964.

Postman, Neil. *The End of Education.* New York: Alfred A. Knopf, 1996.

Sayers, Dorothy. *The Whimsical Christian*. New York: Collier Books, 1987.

Schmemann, Alexander. *For the Life of the World*. Crestwood, New York: St. Vladimir's Seminary Press, 1988.

Seerveld, C. *Rainbows for the Fallen World*. Toronto: Tuppence Press, 1980.

Sibley, George. "The Desert Empire," *Harper's Magazine*, October, 1977.

Steensma, Geraldine. *To Those Who Teach*. Terre Haute, Indiana: Signal Publishing Corporation, 1971.

Steensma, Geraldine and Harro Van Brummelen. "Directives for a Biblically Grounded Curriculum," in *Shaping School Curriculum*, Terra Haute, 1977.

Stronks, Gloria Goris and Doug Blomberg. *A Vision with a Task*. Baker, 1993.

Taylor, Paul W. "Realms of Value." In *Theories of Value and Problems in Education*, edited by Philip G. Smith. Urbana-Champaign, Illinois: University of Illinois Press, 1970.

Van Brummelen, Harro. *Walking with God in the Classroom*. Medina, Washington: Alta Vista College Press, 1992.

Van Ruler, A. A. *The Greatest of These Is Love*. Grand Rapids, Michigan: Eerdmans, 1958.

Veith, Gene E. Jr. *Postmodern Times: A Christian Guide to Contemporary Thought and Culture*. Wheaton, Illinois: Crossway Books, 1994.

Walsh, Brian and Richard Middleton. *The Transforming Vision*. Downer's Grove, Illinois: InterVarsity Press, 1984.

Wells, Ronald A. *History Through the Eyes of Faith*. Harper San Francisco, 1989.

Zylstra, Uko. "Biology." In *Shaping School Curriculum*. Edited by Geraldine Steensma and Harro Van Brummelen. Terre Haute, 1977.

Index

L

LANGUAGE 19
LAWS 131, 162, 182-183
LEARNING 39-49, 221-234
LEARNING STYLES 255
LEWIS, C. S. 57-58,
    96, 125, 137, 168-169,
    172, 197, 205, 223
LINGUAL ASPECT 202-203
LOCKE, JOHN 6
LODER, JAMES 119-120
LOGICAL (ANALYTICAL) ASPECT
    199-200
LOVE 118, 122, 218, 221-234,
    254, 255, 263-267, 278
LUTHER, MARTIN 5, 139
LYOTARD, JEAN-FRANCOIS 17

M

MARTIN, JAMES E. 94, 117-119
MARX, KARL 186
MARXISM 101
MAY, GERALD 140-141,
    240-242
MELANCTHON 69
MERTON, THOMAS 55-57,
    245-246
METAPHYSICS 16, 75
MIDDLETON, RICHARD 30-31,
    87, 143-145
MIND OF THE SPIRIT 215-216
MOORE, G. E. 128-130
MORAL ASPECT 208-209
MORALITY 12, 17, 24, 35, 207
MOVEMENT ASPECT 191-193
MYSTICAL UNION 245

N

NATURAL LAW 79, 156
NATURE/FREEDOM 69-70, 116
NATURE/GRACE 68-71
NATURE/REASON 6
NEO-THOMISM 71

NEWBIGIN, LESSLIE 7, 20, 28,
    74, 142
NEWTON, ISSAC 6, 125
NIETZSCHE 17, 19
NORD, WARREN A. 17, 27
NORMS 131, 162, 182-184,
    199-210
NOUWEN, HENRI 57,
    235-242, 263

O

ONTOLOGY 75
ORIGINAL IMAGE 106, 243
ORIGINAL SIN 9
OWENS, VIRGINIA STEM 80,
    87-88, 93, 125, 153, 176,
    194, 206

P

PALMER, PARKER J. 122, 232,
    247
PASCAL 123
PETERSON, EUGENE 47, 89, 92,
    176
PHENIX, PHILIP 99, 253
PHILEO 224
PHILOSOPHY XIII, 6, 31, 65-78
PHYSICAL ASPECT 193-195
PISTIC ASPECT 209-210
PLATO 68, 274
PLEASURE 52, 109, 168, 215,
    222-223
POLANYI, MICHAEL 121
POLITICAL CORRECTNESS 24
POSSESSIONS
    53, 109, 216, 222-223
POSTMAN, NEIL 35
POSTMODERNISM 15-25, 70
POWER 53, 109, 216, 222-223
PRAGMATISM 16-17
PRAISE 52-61, 278-279
PRAISE AS WORK 52-61
PRAYER 57
PROGRESS 9, 19

NOTES